INSIGHT GUIDES

FINLAND

APA HOUGHTON MIFFLIN

D0123540

Created and Directed by Hans Höfer

INSIGHT GUIDES

FINLAND

Edited by Doreen Taylor-Wilkie
Principal photography by Lyle Lawson

Editorial Director: Brian Bell

HOUGHTON MIFFLIN COMPANY

APA PUBLICATIONS

FINLAND

First Edition (2nd Reprint)
© **1994 APA PUBLICATIONS (HK) LTD**
All Rights Reserved
Printed in Singapore by Höfer Press Pte Ltd

Distributed in the United States by:	Distributed in Canada by:	Distributed in the UK & Ireland by:	Worldwide distribution enquiries:
Houghton Mifflin Company	**Thomas Allen & Son**	**GeoCenter International UK Ltd**	**Höfer Communications Pte Ltd**
222 Berkeley Street	390 Steelcase Road East	The Viables Center, Harrow Way	38 Joo Koon Road
Boston, Massachusetts 02116-3764	Markham, Ontario L3R 1G2	Basingstoke, Hampshire RG22 4BJ	Singapore 2262
ISBN: 0-395-66793-3	ISBN: 0-395-66793-3	ISBN: 9-62421-177-9	ISBN: 9-62421-177-9

ABOUT THIS BOOK

That great traveller Karl Baedeker, writing in 1914, advised his readers: "It is important to remember that in Finland the lavatory is called *Miehille*, and for women *Naiselle*. For a gentleman to say *Viekää minut Naiselle* ('Guide me to the women') is to court disaster; and in any case the beds are very lumpy."

Today we can report that, although the beds are somewhat less lumpy, the language retains its pitfalls. What most impresses visitors to Finland, however, is how much the natural world seems to be part of everyday Finnish life. Even in the capital, Helsinki, one is never far from lake and forest.

It was this aspect of the country which first attracted the editor of *Insight Guide: Finland*, Scottish journalist **Doreen Taylor-Wilkie**, in the early 1980s and has kept her going back ever since. But it is not the only side of Finland she emphasises in her chapters on the classic "triangle" route from Helsinki, to the old "capital" of Turku, north to Tampere, and back to Helsinki. One other side is the astonishing diversity of the cultural and artistic life of this small country of only 5 million people, and another is Finland's interesting political position.

"It's a Nordic country, close to Scandinavia but not part of it," she says. "In a changing Europe, Finland could be an important ingredient of a new grouping of countries around the Baltic."

An expert team

Taylor-Wilkie, who has also edited Insight Guides to Norway, Sweden and Denmark, had little difficulty in assembling an expert team of writers and photographers who shared her fascination for the country.

Like all Insight Guides, this book owes much to its superb photography. The images here are mostly the work of inveterate world traveller **Lyle Lawson**. An American who lives in England, she edited and photographed Insight's *Inland Waterways of Europe*, and has contributed to many books in the 150-strong series. Dashing round this vast country in two marathon journeys, she captured the beauty of its scenery, the colourful costumes and festivals of the Sami people in Lapland, and Helsinki's great architectural heritage.

James Lewis, who wrote the history section and the chapters on Eastern Finland and the wilderness way north, also loves Finland's wide skies and open land. Having started with a full-scale elk hunt in the early 1980s, he has concentrated on the wilderness areas and, in particular, cross-country skiing. In 1990, he joined a Finnish/German TV expedition to the Russian border.

Anita Peltonen is in a good position to write, among other things, about modern Finland's politics and economy: she works in Helsinki as a broadcaster with Finnish Radio, writes for several international papers, and is married to a Finn. Born in New York City, she has a good international perspective after working spells in Montreal and London as well as the Nordic countries. She has also contributed to *Insight Guide: Norway* and other Insight guides.

Another American-born Insight veteran, **Anne Roston**, editor of *Insight Guide: France* and *Insight Guide: Provence*, first came to Finland in 1989 for a Christmas visit but soon returned for an indefinite stay. For a writer, Roston says, Finland is a fount of plenty,

Taylor-Wilkie   *Lawson*   *Lewis*   *Peltonen*   *Roston*

much of it as yet untapped. Roston contributed the chapters on Helsinki, where she lives, and on music, in which she specialises.

The short chapter on Finland's best-known film makers comes from Scottish film critic **Allan Hunter**, who has been following the careers of the Kaurismäki brothers.

Sylvie Nickels has long given up counting the times she has travelled in Finland since her first visit in 1956 – but it must be "well over 30". Her visits include a 10-month stay teaching English to hotel staff and "having a go at Finnish, with some quaint results." She has also written for British papers such as the *Financial Times* and has been responsible for several guidebooks. For this book, she has written on Intrepid Travel and The Great Lakes, and on the Sami people and their country, Lapland. She is herself an intrepid traveller: in her late forties, she took up long-distance canoeing with her husband, lecturer and explorer George Spenceley, and they have canoed the length of Finland.

Although **Robert Spark**, an expert on Scandinavian countries, was familiar with much of Finland, he welcomed the chance to write the chapters on the west coast because it was one area that he had previously overlooked. He found it a fascinating coastline, linked closely with Finland's maritime past and with strong links to Sweden. "Like many of life's best things, Finland is probably an acquired taste," Spark says. "But, the more you discover about the country, the more it compels you to return."

Kristina Woolnough has been in Finland every summer for more than 20 years – which is not surprising as, taught by her Swedish-Finnish mother, Woolnough could speak Swedish before she knew English. With relatives in Borgå, including a Swedish-speaking cousin who married a Finnish-speaking Peruvian, she is an ideal person to sort out the complexities of cultural cross-currents in the chapter Finns Who Speak Swedish, and to cover art, architecture and design. Regular summer berry-picking expeditions gave her a sense of the crucial importance of the environment, which she covers in the chapter In Defence of Greenness.

Louis Borgia, another American, is correspondent for *Travel Trade Gazette (TTG) Europe*. He is based in Stockholm but, married to a Finn, sails regularly across the Baltic and so is just the person to write about ferries. He is also an addict of (and contributes the short chapter on) that peculiarly Finnish pastime, the sauna.

Valuable assistance

The editor is grateful for the valuable help given by **Marjatta Haapio**, Finnish Tourist Board deputy director in London, and her colleagues in England and Finland. **Jill Anderson** was responsible for the book's production in Insight Guides' London editorial office, **Mary Morton** proofread and indexed the book, and **Maija McKinnon** cast an expert eye over the complicated Finnish spellings.

Nickels   *Spark*   *Borgia*

History

Features

Places

Maps

TRAVEL TIPS

Compiled by Anita Peltonen

**For detailed information
see page 273**

THE FINNISH CHARACTER

To what extent can a land be judged by its ancient heroes? In the case of many countries, only an enemy would wish to invoke the memory of certain inglorious characters. With Finland, however, the idea is quite appealing. The main characters in the Finnish epic the *Kalevala* are patriotic, and the heroes are noble warriors. Yet these strong men are troubled hair-tearers in private, and have great difficulty in waxing poetic when they set out to woo and win the girl. The women are strongheaded, matriarchal, and very family-orientated.

The land itself is full of nature and wood-spirits. No one in the *Kalevala* would deny that the woods have sanctity, and that the lakes and rivers are their little bit of heaven on earth. When one of the female heroes wants to escape her fate, she turns into a nimble, stream-swimming fish... and so on.

One can only take the analogy so far, of course, but it's far better to start with a nation's self-made heroes than the stereotypes others have created for them.

There are so many paradoxes in the Finnish character that it would be hard to convince the sceptical foreigner that there isn't more than a dash of schizophrenia in the national character. For every ranting drunk, there's a raving teetotaller. For every patriotic Finn who is as attached to Finland as to his own soul, there's one who leaves as soon as he can afford the fare, never to return. For every shrinking violet, there's an arrogant, cigar-smoking bombast who's never happier than when he's showing off his possessions and singing his own praises.

The Finnish character is in great part moulded by the fact that Finland is small – not in area (it's Europe's fifth largest country in size) but in inhabitants. Its population, at just over 5 million, is homogeneous by the standards of many larger countries that have both old and new ethnic mixes as part of their genetic make-up.

Preceding pages: detail from the roof of Virrat Church; shop front for eager fishers; haystacks under an autumn sun; skiing at Saariselka, in Lapland. <u>Left</u>, typical Karelian dress wear. <u>Right</u>, watching the ski races.

Nordic links: The typical Finn is the result of a genetic combination that is 75 percent identical to that of Swedes or other Scandinavians, but 25 percent derived from tribes that wandered to Finland from east of the Ural Mountains, though some experts now dispute this (*see page 28*). This more oriental strain accounts for certain physical traits that set Finns apart from their Nordic neighbours – finely pronounced cheekbones and quite small eyes, which are slatey-grey or blue.

Karelians (Finns from the very east of the

country) are stockier and also have more sallow complexions than other Finns. They are slightly smaller in stature than people from the west coast, whose ancestors merged with the gargantuan Vikings. Until the end of World War II, the Karelians' diet was extremely poor and they had one of the highest incidences of heart disease in the west, which may in part account for their slightly less healthy looks.

The rest of the Finns are taller, usually fair-haired (though, overall, Finns are the "darkest" of the Nords) and, much like any other nationality, vary greatly in most other ways.

Some of the most famous Finns are sportsmen and women. As a nation, Finns are great lovers of the outdoors and of sport, and some young Finns seem to live for little else but their athletic activities.

Prejudices confirmed: The Finnish personality is hard to pin down but if you go to Finland with pre-formed stereotypes at the ready, you will no doubt be able to satisfy any or all of them.

You cannot help but notice the drunks, but there will seem to be disproportionately many if that's what you are expecting to see, and the infamous Nordic reserve probably applies as much to Finns as to the others. Certainly it is characteristic of Finns to speak quietly, even in stage whispers when a cou-

While being demonstrative is not a typical Finnish characteristic, it does exist. Young women in particular have adopted the trait – in Helsinki anyway. They greet each other with hugs and kisses and big smiles, and sometimes hold hands as they cruise down the boulevards.

Older Finns: One of the oldest groups who are not ethnic Finns are the Romany gypsies, whose womenfolk are instantly recognisable by their elaborate, embroidered lace blouses and voluminous skirts. Although today most speak only Finnish, they have not intermarried to any degree, so that their dark flamboyant good looks and wilder ways of dressing stand out in startling contrast to the

ple are conversing in a public place. If you converse loudly, you will draw stares. (Perhaps many who drink heavily do so in order to gain licence to shout.) Finns put great value on privacy. Speaking quietly may be a manifestation of this, or else a kind of remnant of old-world courtesy that regards loud speech as vulgar.

The summer cabin (*kesämökki*) also tells you something of Finnish privacy. These are usually set back from the lakeshore among the trees, and as far from other dwellings as possible. The idea of time spent here is to revel in your own plot, confronting no one but Mother Nature.

fairer, calmly-dressed Finns. Some gypsy men still tuck knives into their boots.

Although most gypsies are no longer nomadic and live in regular houses and flats, some families still tend to wander, especially in autumn, from one harvest festival to another. Little horse-trading is done these days, and the gypsies' appearance at these fairs is more a vestige of a racial memory.

There is a small Turkish community, whose forefathers came to Finland in the early 19th century to trap and trade fur. (The word in Finnish for Turkey and fur coat are exactly the same: *turkki*.) Finnish and Turkish are remotely related languages, though not in any way that would help a Turk learn Finnish, or a Finn Turkish.

In the early 1990s, about 25,000 foreigners were living in Finland, a large number of them members of the diplomatic community. Few were refugees, and equally few were guestworkers. Finland has succeeded in taking in mainly "desirable" (i.e. educated, non-needy) foreigners who filled jobs that could not normally be filled by Finns.

Finland has not been ungenerous toward refugees, quite the contrary. But that help has gone mainly to refugees far from the borders of Finland. It's different when the foreigners arrive on the doorstep. The Red Cross has over the years sponsored small groups of

discourage the establishment of a policy designed to ease the situation.

Most of the Finns who did not want the Somalis to stay were not racist or prejudiced, in the opinion of popular philosophy lecturer and author Esa Saarinen. The problem, he claims, is that Finns are wary of sharing the fruits of their labour. It is psychologically difficult for them to make room for people who did not fight in the war nor help build up the economy from nothing into prosperity. Saarinen maintains that even Finns who left to go to America or Australia would be suspect, because they deserted the ship just when they were most needed by those who stayed at home.

refugees – Vietnamese and Kurdish, for example – and for the most part they were well received and well cared for. But the picture changed when refugee Somalis began showing up at the Soviet-Finnish border in 1990, uninvited, unsponsored, and unexpected.

Finland was the first Western country the Somalis could reach. Although the slow, case-by-case processing of their asylum applications was more due to bureaucratic ineptitude than anything else, there were many surprisingly xenophobic arguments set up to

Left, out of the sauna and into the ice pool.
Above, volleyball tournament.

Moving in: This goes a good way towards explaining the way in which the Finns view outsiders. To date, the society has been extremely well-protected. Work permits are rarely given to foreigners, the cost of living is prohibitive, and the location of Finland doesn't appeal to many.

Add to Saarinen's viewpoint that of Lasse Lehtinen, the author and one-time Parliamentarian, who points out that Finns have simply forgotten what it was like to have foreigners around. Before independence and during Hanseatic League days, Finland saw a brisk Baltic trade in its port towns. Foreign sailors, traders, and especially businessmen were commonplace; many started firms that still function today, like Sinebrychoff brewers (Russian) or Finlayson textiles (Scottish), though others used Finland as a kind of colonial trading post.

Fear of competition: When Finland ceased to be an autonomous Grand Duchy of Russia, these windows to the outside world were shuttered and barred. When the Somalis came, the fact that Finnish economists were predicting that Finland would need at least 10,000 imported labourers a year to keep the economy afloat (a prediction which has now been sharply revised) did nothing to help.

"The underlying, ultimate fear," says Lehtinen, "is fear of competition." Apart

from the Somalis, there was the potential of new floods of immigrants as the redefinition of Europe continued to blur borders. Finland was wary of economic integration European Community-style, which would mean free movement of labour and foreigners being able to get their hands on Finnish forestland. Also, says Lehtinen, certain circles feared "that foreign languages, habits, and ideas would spoil something very national and sacred." The Nordic region has been the last to have to cope with a postwar invasion of foreigners and, for Finland, much of the coping lies ahead.

Consider, for example, the experience of

Umayya al-Hannah, a naturalised Palestinian-Finn who is an active member of the Green Party and the Helsinki City Council. In a 1991 interview, she commented on the Finns' attitude toward foreigners: "They either treat you with suspicion or subservience." The subservience is the flip side of the coin; if you are not an object of suspicion, you are an object of wonder – foreigners still have a curious rarity value in Finland.

Conformity and consensus: How Finns act toward foreigners tells an awful lot about Finns themselves. Finland is still a mightily provincial place, where conformity rules. This is not so unusual for a small country but in Finland conformity seems to be taken to extremes. The decor in homes, the way people dress, the month in which they take their main holiday, what magazines they subscribe to, who they'll vote for in the next election – all these things you can guess blind and hit the nail on the head even if you have spent just a short time in the country.

To escape from this conformity, artists have frequently travelled away from Finland to make their mark in Europe and America, both in times past and present. But the Finns are hugely proud of their world-renowned artists, who include composers, conductors, architects, and many industrial and textile designers, and just as proud of those whose fame is not so widespread.

Many younger Finns have shed their parents' unease with the world and gone on to study, work, and travel abroad, as well as welcome things foreign to Finland as they trickle in. While some older Finns still have not abandoned the dreary, grey outfits that used to dominate the clothing racks, their grandchildren have gone improbably far in the other direction, sporting sunbursts of fluorescent clothing and embracing fads from Britain and the United States with near-fanatical fervour.

The ideas of those who would totally subjugate Finnish culture are no more appealing than those of the super-patriot who would have nothing change. Finns are on a pendulum swinging out toward the rest of the world, but they are far better equipped than they think they are to meet the challenges with equanimity.

Left, coffee break on the hiking trail. **Right**, dressed up for Easter.

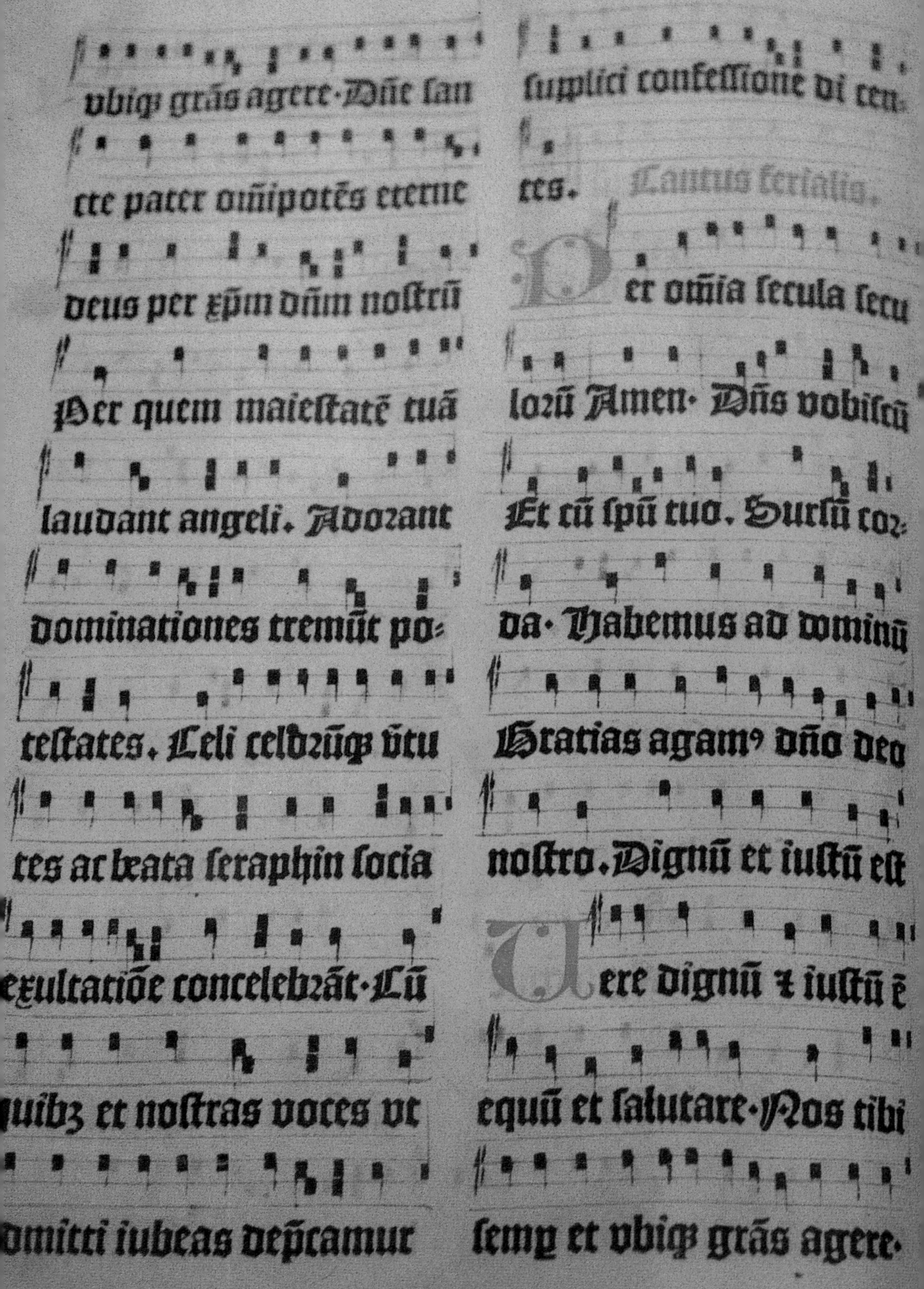

ubiqz grás agere · Dííe san

supplici confessione di cen

cte pater omnipotés eterne

tes. Cantus ferialis.

deus per xpm díím nostrũ

er omnia secula secu

Per quem maiestaté tuã

lozũ Amen · Díís vobíscũ

laudant angeli · Adozant

Et cũ spũ tuo · Surlũ coz

dominationes tremũt po

da · Tabemus ad dominũ

testates · Celi celozũqz ũtu

Gratias agam⁹ díío deo

tes ac beata seraphin socia

nostro · Dignũ et iustũ est

exultatiõe concelebzãt · Cũ

ere dignũ ⁊ iustũ é

quibz et nostras voces ut

equũ et salutare · Nos tibi

omitti iubeas depcamur

semp et ubiqz grás agere ·

TE igitur clementissime pater per ihesum xpm filiū tuū dūm nostrū supplices rogamus ac petimus vti accepta habeas ⁊ benedicas ✠ Hec dona ✠ Hec munera ✠ Hec sācta sacrificia illibata · In primis que tibi offerimus pro ecclesia tua sancta catholica quā pacificare · custodire · adunare et regere digneris toto orbe terrarū vna cū famulo tuo papa nro · N · et antistite nostro · N · et rege nostro · et omnibz orthodoxis · atqz catholice et apostolice fidei cultoribus ·

Memento dūe famulorū famularūqz tuarū · N · Memoria vivorum · et omniū circūstantiū quorz tibi fices cognita est ⁊ nota devotio pro quibz

Race study was an infant science in 1844 when M.A. Castren pronounced: "I have decided to prove to the people of Finland that we are not a… nation isolated from the world and world history, but that we are related to at least one-seventh of the people of the globe." Castren had persuaded himself that language equalled race and had concluded that the Finns were kith and kin with every single tribe which had originated in the Altai mountains of Siberia and Outer Mongolia.

That the Finnish tongue is a branch of the

M. A. Castren

Finno-Ugric language tree is undeniable and, to those who maintain, like Castren, that language kinship equals racial relationships the matter ends there. "The Finns speak a Mongoloid tongue. *Ipso facto* they are a Mongoloid people." To a scientist-patriot such as Castren, his Siberian-Outer Mongolian theory had the added attraction of establishing a relationship between his own people and a large part of the global population.

Castren's and similar fanciful conjectures came about because of the exceptional isolation of Finnish. Hungarian was, and is, often mentioned as a language akin to Finnish. But the connection is remote. Finnish and Hun-

garian bear about as much relationship to one another as English and Persian, and only Estonian is close enough to perceive some common linguistic base with Finnish.

Castren's followers, and millions who may never have heard his name, swallowed his theory which led to the long-held belief that the Finns were a race apart from the mainstream of Europe, their language firmly classifying them as being of Asiatic extraction. No other evidence was adduced and even their own scholars and nationalists did not dispute the issue.

Theory rejected: This rather neat little slot in the huge and ever complex question of the origins of peoples and nations is still accepted by the world at large. The Finns themselves, however, those that think and those that research, have for some time totally rejected the theory.

As one leading scholar in the field of philology has written: "No valid reasons for this classification have yet been produced". Research carried out in this century, based on archaeology, points to a Baltic people moving gradually into Finland from around 1500 BC to about AD 400. There are no signs of a migration from further east. All cultural contacts point to Western Europe and Scandinavia, even from the earliest times.

The anthropological verdict now accepted by all but Castrenite primitives is that the Finns and their racial forebears are "purely European". Tallness, blondness, long-headedness: Finns have these characteristics in common with Swedes and Norwegians, who are slightly taller on average – and with Germans and Danes, who are slightly shorter, although there is a variant type amongst them known as the East Baltic.

Nevertheless, the migrants from the Baltic who took up residence in the land of lakes and forests to the north were destined to live an age-long existence isolated from the mainstream of Europe. A virile and questing people driven to sea and sea-borne exploits by inhospitable climate and country would appear to be a tailor-made fate for early Finland. But the Finns made no such moves. The longships left from the lands just over the Gulf of Bothnia or the other side of the

Danish sounds and the trading, raiding and general sea roving of the Vikings seem to have lacked any Finnish participation.

Secret past: Cut off in their sub-arctic homeland from these early days, little light has been shed on the life and times of the Finns. No chronicler emerges from the forest mists to give later generations a glimpse of primeval life. There may have been an oral tradition of poetry, song and story, a collection of folk memories passed down from generation to generation. The *Kalevala*, Fin-

priests who led them in the worship of nature and natural forces.

Just as Finnish scholars had established a theory of race and language, a parallel movement in academic circles was growing up on the subject of the arrival of Christianity. According to prevailing wisdom, the Finns were raiding the Christian people of southern Sweden and had become a nuisance and a danger. Furthermore, they were pagans. In 1157, King Erik of Sweden lost patience and set off on a "crusade" to Finland.

land's national epic, points in this direction, but the *Kalevala* was compiled and published in the 18th and 19th centuries and cannot itself claim immemorial antiquity.

When Finland emerges through the flickering candles of Roman Catholic crusading, around the year AD 1157, we find the Finns living in clans. They had apparently never developed statehood. The clans were descendants of common ancestors, often warring with one another and submitting to

Once subdued, the Finns were submitted to baptism by an English-born bishop, Henry of Uppsala. Swedish secular dominion and, in tandem with it, Roman Catholicism were both thereby introduced into Finland. Once again this theory, like the language theory, has now all but gone out of the window.

Rome has no record of these events. Available church documents make no reference to either Erik or Henry. Again, the archaeologists have come to the aid of Finnish integrity with an assertion that the Finns practised primitive Christianity years before 1157. The Swedes brought Romanism, but not a new faith.

Preceding pages: pages from Finland's first Bible in Turku Castle. Left, M.A. Castren. Above, boatbuilding in the 7th century.

ANNO 1615.

Entw. von A. Kreling.   Ausgeführt W. v. Swertschkoff in Schleissheim bei München.   Carton von W. Dietz

The Finns were part and parcel of Sweden for seven centuries (*circa* 1200–1800), but there was never a Swedish "conquest" of Finland. Instead, a race had developed between Sweden and Russia – in those days known as Novgorod – to fill the power vacuum in the land of the Finns. Sweden won the race – and did so without resorting to conquest or dynastic union or treaty. Remarkably, the future relationship was free for the most part of stresses and strains, and completely free of the vicissitudes of war.

It is quite likely that Swedes had hunted, traded and settled in Finnish lands for centuries. On both sides of the Gulf of Bothnia the land had sparse resources and gave little cause for friction. In effect, Sweden and Finland merged as constituent parts of a larger whole. No distinctions in law or property were made, and the history of these two people under one crown has been described as "a seamless garment".

Finns took part in the election of the king, though not in the choice of candidates. In areas of mixed population language was the only real difference. Castles functioned as administrative centres, not as garrisons to subdue the people. The influences of the one people on the other were neutral because the cultures were identical. In one respect only did Sweden bring a dominating influence and that was in the sphere of religion.

Various monastic orders began a slow but steady penetration of Finland during the 14th and 15th centuries. Dominicans, Franciscans and the Order of St Bridget took their place alongside the clergy and greatly strengthened the power and influence of the Roman Catholic Church. This activity gave impetus to church building and church adornment. Life became more settled in the relatively densely populated areas of Western Finland. Further east, it was more mobile, less settled, and depended on hunting

across the sub-arctic tundra, a region rich in animals and game birds, but not suitable for cultivation.

The most import centres from which the new influences spread were Turku (Åbo in Swedish), with a bishop's seat and cathedral, and Vyborg (now Viipuri). Both towns had close links with Tallin, Danzig and Lübeck as well as with Stockholm. Here artisans and professions flourished alongside the clergy and an urban culture came into being, in contrast to the ruder ways of life further east.

At the end of the 14th century there was an attempt to unite Denmark, Norway, Sweden and, by implication, Finland as a result of the ill-starred Kalmar Union of 1397. All the devices of rivalries, dynasties and treaties which had not been employed between Sweden and Finland were invoked in this ill-starred union, the great dream of the ambitious Danish Queen, Margrethe I.

In 1509 Finland, which had little say in the matter, became violently involved when the Danes burnt and sacked Turku (Åbo), the "capital" of the country. It was just one more incident in more than 100 years of conflict over the treaty, which was finally broken in

Preceding pages: Czar Peter the Great's triumph over Karl XII at Poltava ended Swedish domination of the Baltic. **Left,** Gustav II Adolf of Sweden attends the deathbed of his great general Gustaf Horn (Turku Cathedral). **Right,** Bishop Henrik in Hollola Church.

1523 in a rebellion by Gustav Vasa who became King of Sweden.

Stirrings of nationhood: Sweden was now powerful and independent. The Middle Ages were over. The Reformation challenged Rome. Here was a cocktail of influences, almost modern in their impact. Sweden and Finland were both slipping away from the old moorings. Slowly, imperceptibly, the relationship was changing. The first stirrings of nationhood date from this time. They were small and they arose from the translation of religious text into the vernacular.

"You are instructing your charges in a manner that is both nasty and lazy," wrote the Bishop of Turku to his clergy in 1548.

The split took place in May 1527. All over Sweden and Finland the church suddenly lost property, authority, ceremonies and rites. Holy water, customary baptism, and extreme unction were banned, so were colourful processions and the worship of relics. But transforming Finns from a Catholic to a Protestant people was not painless. The early Lutheran pastors were a motley rabble – drunk, debauched and "violators of the laws of man and God." Yet Finns took a leading part in the transformation and Pietari Särkilahti, Mikael Agricola and Paavali Juusten aided their Swedish brethren in severing the links with Rome.

Peasant soldiers: During the three centuries

Bishop Mikael Agricola sent out this admonition with a translation of the New Testament in Finnish, a work he had undertaken to make sure, as he put it, "that not a single preacher or teacher could cover up his laziness by claiming that he did not know Latin or Swedish."

Many more Swedes and Finns fell under the influence of Martin Luther in Wittenberg. The Reformation also attracted Gustav Vasa, because the Crown needed more revenue and the church could provide it. In fact, the Reformation was so irresistible that Sweden was the first state in western Christendom to break with Rome.

before 1809, when Finland finally broke with Sweden, the Swedish crown was at war for more than 80 years. Involvement in the Thirty Years' War and wars with both Poland and Russia raised taxes and took Finnish men away from the land – the burden of providing levies always fell most heavily on the farmers. Finns were a vital part of the Swedish army, comprising about a third of the foot soldiers and cavalry. In the wars with Russia, Finland suffered first and worst.

The farmers and the peasants took the full brunt of war. City development became sluggish and, in any case, Finnish cities frequently went up in smoke. Turku (Åbo) suffered 15 major fires between 1524 and 1624; the worst reduced the city to ashes. Pori and Viipuri also suffered a similar fate several time, though fires were not the only dangers that beset the cities.

In Turku, Helsinki, Porvoo and Viipuri, as well as in the other Baltic trading cities, many of the leading merchants, who controlled much of the foreign trade, were of German or Dutch descent. "The general area of our economic history during the 17th century and part of the 18th centuries bears a marked Dutch stamp," remarks V. Voionmaa, a prominent Finnish historian.

The Dutch and others were well established, and foreign goods and ways of doing service was compulsory except for the cavalry, in which volunteers enlisted in order to escape the harder life of an infantryman.

Carrot and stick: The Swedish crown demonstrated an inability to hold Finland against Russian assault. It lost Finland on two occasions (1721 and 1743). In 1808, Great Britain became a Swedish ally. The Russians saw a dire threat to St Petersburg and to Russian naval access to the Baltic. Yet again Russia and Sweden fought. This time Russia held on to Finland and offered the country generous terms as part of a strategy of carrot and stick. The Swedish centuries had finally come to an end.

Sweden formally ceded Finland to Russia

business gained ground in Finland. Foreign as well as Finnish capital fuelled industry and trade.

Sweden no longer dominated. Conflicts with the Russians kept recurring. The wars were destructive to Finland and read like a litany: 1554–57; a 25-year war (interrupted by truces) which started in 1570; two wars in the 17th century and the great Northern War from 1700 to 1721; war again 20 years later; and yet again from 1788 to 1790. Military

Left, Bishop Mikael Agricola's 16th-century Bible in Finnish (Turku Cathedral). Above, building Häme Castle from an old print.

by treaty on 17 September 1809. Along with Finland went the Åland Islands, halfway across the Gulf of Bothnia between Sweden and Finland, which had long been an administrative part of the Finnish half of the kingdom. Finland became a separate state whose head, the Czar-Grand Duke, was an absolute ruler; Czar of all the Russias. Yet in Finland he agreed to rule in partnership with the Finnish Diet.

This made the Czar a constitutional monarch in the newly acquired territory. It was an experiment in kingship, a whole new departure for an absolute ruler. The experiment was an unqualified success for 60 years.

A WINTER JOURNEY

At the end of the 18th century, Joseph Acerbi embarked on what was then the only practical way of crossing from Sweden to Finland in winter, and that was by sledge across the frozen Gulf of Bothnia. The distance was 43 miles (about 70 km) but, using the Åland Islands as stepping stones, that left 30 miles (50 km), "which you travel on the ice without touching on land".

He was advised that his party of three, plus two servants, would have to double their number of horses and hire no fewer than eight sledges for the crossing. He suspected that he was being swindled by the Swedish peasants who said as much but, as things turned out, it was a sensible precaution.

"I expected to travel 43 miles without sight of land over a vast and uniform plain, and that every successive mile would be in exact unison and monotonous correspondence with those I had already travelled; but my astonishment was greatly increased in proportion as we advanced from our starting-post.

"At length we met with masses of ice heaped one upon the other, and some of them seeming as if they were suspended in the air, while others were raised in the form of pyramids. On the whole they exhibited a picture of the wildest and most savage confusion, that surprised the eye by the novelty of its appearance. It was an immense chaos of icy ruins, presented to view under every possible form, and embellished by superb stalactites of a blue green colour.

"Amidst this chaos, it was not without difficulty and trouble that our horses and sledges were able to find and pursue their way. It was necessary to make frequent windings, and sometimes to return in a contrary direction, following that of a frozen wave, in order to avoid a collection of icy mountains that lay before us.

"The inconvenience and the danger of our journey were still farther encreased (*sic*) by the following circumstance. Our horses were made wild and furious, both by the sight and the smell of our great pelices, manufactured of the skins of Russian wolves or bears. When any of the sledges was overturned, the horses belonging to it, or to that next to it, frighted at the sight of what they supposed to be a wolf or bear rolling on the ice, would set off at full gallop, to the great terror of both passengers and driver.

"The peasant, apprehensive of losing his horse in the midst of this desert, kept firm hold of the bridle, and suffered the horse to drag his body through masses of ice, of which some sharp points threatened to cut him in pieces. The animal, at last wearied out by the constancy of the man, and disheartened by the obstacles continually opposed to his flight, would stop; then we were enabled to get again into our sledges, but not till the driver had blindfolded the animal's eyes: but one time, one of the wildest and most spirited of all the horses in our train, having taken fright, completely made his escape.

"The peasant who conducted him, unable any longer to endure the fatigue and pain of being dragged through the ice, let go his hold of the bridle. The horse, relieved from this weight, and feeling himself at perfect liberty, redoubled his speed, and surmounted every impediment. The sledge, which he made to dance in the air, by alarming his fears, added new wings to his flight. When he had fled to a considerable distance from us, he appeared from time to time as a dark spot which continued to diminish in the air, and at last totally vanished from our sight.

"During the whole of this journey we did not meet with, on the ice, so much as one man, beast, bird, or any living creature. Those vast solitudes present a desert abandoned as it were by nature. The dead silence that reigns is interrupted only by the whistling of the winds against the prominent points of ice, and sometimes by the loud crackings occasioned by their being irresistibly torn from this frozen expanse; pieces thus forcibly broken off are frequently blown to a considerable distance.

"Through the rents produced by these ruptures, you may see below the watery abyss; and it is sometimes necessary to lay planks across them, by way of bridges, for the sledges to pass over."

[Joseph Acerbi: *Travels Through Sweden, Finland and Lapland to the North Cape*. 1802.]

Left, Per Brahe, a famous Turku governor.

LIVING WITH RUSSIA

Annexation by Russia defied all gloomy prophecies, at least at the outset. Czar Alexander I seemed open to suggestions from the Finnish camp, and a group of leading Finns suggested that Finland should hold elections. Alexander agreed and the first Finnish Diet met at Porvoo in 1809. The Czar had styled himself "the Emperor and Autocrat of all the Russias and the Grand Duke of Finland." Invested with this new title, the prototype of future constitutional monarchs, Alexander formally opened the Diet. In return, he promised to respect and maintain the laws, religion and constitution of Finland.

The Constitution's main pillar was a unique device in the statecraft of those days. Finland was to be in personal union with the Czar. This meant that the Finns dealt direct with their head of state, bypassing the Russian government. Ultimately it became the cause of much jealousy, but the arrangement lasted for 90 years and was the basis of the relationship between Russia and Finland. When Nicholas I succeeded Alexander in 1825 a strong bond of mutual trust had developed. The change of overlord had brought advantages. The fear of attack from the east had gone; Finns could conduct their own internal affairs but, if they felt cramped in their small state, opportunities existed in the armed forces and civil service of Russia.

The Finnish army was disbanded, though its officers received generous pensions. Russian troops garrisoned Finland but never in large numbers. Taxation was raised for domestic needs only. Behind all this liberality lay firm policy: to pacify Finland and to woo it away from Sweden. To keep Sweden from harbouring revanchist sentiments, Czar Alexander concluded an agreement with it in 1812, in support of moves to unite Norway with the Swedish throne. This had become the new Swedish ambition.

New capital: The Grand Duchy needed a capital and a small rocky fishing port was chosen. Helsinki became a city of major importance on the Baltic within two generations. A visitor in 1830 remarked that the Finns were "converting a heap of rocks into a beautiful city." The urban centre was conceived and planned on an imperial scale, with neoclassical buildings designed by the German architect C.L. Engel. The university of Turku moved to grand premises on Helsinki's great square in 1828. The year before, Turku had suffered yet another disastrous fire, after which its eclipse was inevitable.

The university became the focus of a tug of

war between languages. There was no discrimination against Finns as a separate linguistic group within the Russian Empire. The idea of introducing Russian as a subject in schools was canvassed by a few bureaucrats, but not much was done. Finns wishing to serve the Czar outside Finland had to learn Russian, but to serve the Grand Duke of Finland the requirement, up until 1870, was to speak and write Swedish.

Here was the rub. Bold ideas of Finnish independence had been nurtured by educated Finns ever since the days when Sweden had started to lose its grip. Such people took a long view, perhaps the longest any

Preceding pages: Czar Alexander I opens the first Finnish Diet at Porvoo in 1809. Left, Russia's Imperial throne in Finland. Right, Czar Nicholas II by Albert Edelfelt (both National Museum).

nationalists have ever taken. Henrik Porthan (1739–1804), known as the "father of Finnish history", awakened a generation of intellectual leaders. "We must pray," he said "that Russia will succeed in situating its capital in Constantinople… But now that its capital city (St Petersburg) is located so near, I am afraid that Finland will sooner or later fall under the power of Russia."

Nevertheless, the Finnish people, he advocated, should use this as an opportunity, and not be despondent. They must think of themselves as Finns – this above all. History, language and folklore (according to Porthan) all pointed to a Finland ultimately free. But Russia – barbarous, Byzantine, eastern

the forests. But the people of the countryside – farmers and peasants – were slow to awaken to the power they possessed. In part, the peasants distrusted notions of independence. The rural poor, workers, smallholders and the landless were on the periphery of political life and thought. In contrast to the élite, they were indifferent to ideas of liberty and national independence, which were not hot topics among the masses. There was even some class-based hostility to such notions. When autonomy was in jeopardy under a changed Russian attitude at the end of the 19th century, some pamphleteers got to work to raise national consciousness. Grumpy peasants tossed back at them re-

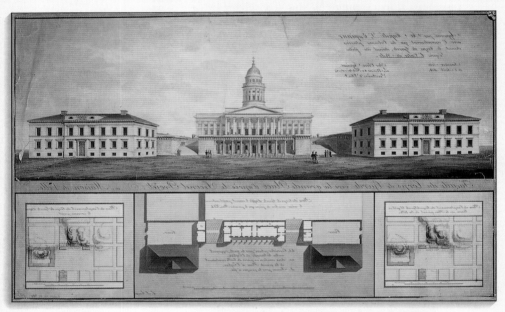

Russia – and not western, democratic Sweden, was the stepping stone to this end.

Nationalist stirrings: Porthan was ahead of his time, but his philosophy took hold and became the prevailing wisdom of his own and succeeding generations of nationalists, right up to the time when, within living memory, the goal of nationhood was achieved. His disciples realised very quickly that, if the Finnish language could replace Swedish, the battle for independence, at least in the hearts and minds of Finns themselves, was three-quarters won.

This all important vernacular already resided in the countryside, on the farms and in

marks such as "Now the gentry are in a sweat" and "These new laws don't concern us peasants, they're only taking the power off the gentry."

Yet, all the time, opportunities in higher education were increasing among such people. Into secondary education, university and the new polytechnics they brought their language – Finnish. Russian was still not an issue, but Swedish was, and Swedish was being supplanted. The peasants were growing richer. The demand for timber increased and the price rose. Freehold peasant farmers with timber land grew rich. Their wives could afford tables, sideboards and chairs in place of benches and chests. Life for some was becoming genteel and not rough-hewn. Since 1864 peasants had been able to buy land on the open market. Now their sons must have higher education, more Finnish language fodder.

Ruthless governor: Czar Alexander III, who freed the Russian serfs, knew his Grand Duchy. His son, the ill-starred Nicholas II (1894–1917) did not. The conception of a docile and contented satellite country acting as a buffer on Russia's northwest flank, the cornerstone of policy for 90 years, was cast aside. A new Governor, General Bobrikov, fresh from a ruthless administration in the Baltic provinces, was installed in Helsinki.

moted by Bobrikov. It was too much for the Finns. Winter lay across the country but, in the teeth of snow and ice, not to mention Bobrikov's agents, 522,931 signatures on a petition were collected in two weeks, many by university students who skied from remote farm to distant cottage throughout the scattered countryside.

Abroad, another petition was launched in support of the Finns. Many eminent people signed (including Florence Nightingale). They addressed Czar Nicholas: "Having read and being deeply moved by the petition of the 5th March of over half a million Finnish men and women in which they made a solemn appeal to your Majesty in support

Finland lost its autonomy. Laws, soldiering and taxation, those pivotal issues which previous grand dukes had treated so delicately, were henceforth to be Russian concerns. "While leaving in operation the existing regulations for legislation on matters of local interest which bear only on the needs of Finland, we have considered it necessary to reserve to ourselves the final determination of matters of legislation which concern the whole Empire." Thus ran a manifesto pro-

Left, C.L. Engel's original drawing for Senate Square, Helsinki. **Above**, statue of Alexander II below Helsinki's cathedral.

of the maintenance of their full Rights and Privileges first confirmed by… Alexander I in 1809… and subsequently re-affirmed in the most solemn manner by all his illustrious successors, we venture to express our hope that your Imperial Majesty will take into due consideration the prayer of the said Petition of your Majesty's Finnish subjects. It would be a matter of great regret if recent events in the Grand Duchy of Finland should retard the cause of amity among the nations of the civilised world which has in your Majesty so Illustrious an Advocate."

The "Illustrious Advocate" was unmoved. *The Times* thundered a declaration that "the

Finnish Diet can, legally, only be modified or restricted with its own consent." This too fell on deaf Russian ears. They imposed strict censorship on the Finnish press. Conscription into the Russian army was the final straw. Resistance started to stiffen. Pamphleteers got to work. Half the conscripts ordered to report for military service in the spring of 1902 did not turn up. In 1904 the Governor General was assassinated by a patriotic student, Eugen Schauman, who immediately committed suicide by turning his gun on himself. Schauman became a national hero and is buried at Porvoo.

The Russian Revolution of 1905 and the Russo-Japanese war brought a respite. The

will not become Russians, so let us be Finns," had been the cry for some decades. Now, the moment was drawing nearer and the country was united as never before in a determination to be free Finnish. The moment came during World War I, when the Russian army collapsed and Lenin seized power. Finland was allowed to go free, compliments of the Bolsheviks. Independence had come at last, but the event was to be marred by a bitter civil war which broke out contemporaneously between the "Whites" and the "Reds".

The cause, in short, was the overspilling of the Russian October Revolution into Finland, upon whose soil remained contingents

Finns took the opportunity to put forward a bold measure. The franchise was by now outmoded. Industrial workers had no representation; women no vote. This was par for the times in Europe, although New Zealand had just given women the vote. Finland proposed no less than a universal franchise and a unicameral parliament. The Czar, doubtless distracted by the first stirrings of revolt in Russia – a chain of events that would eventually bring him down – agreed. The Finns got their modern parliament. The electoral role was increased tenfold. The Social Democrats won the subsequent election.

Civil war: "We are no longer Swedes, we

of Russian soldiers. They sided with the Soviets. Thus Finland had a Red Army in its very midst. Luckily the Soviet government did not officially participate in the civil war in Finland, but Russian aid played a significant part in the Red revolt. Finnish Red Guards were supplied with arms by the Russians. Russian officers and NCOs provided leadership; in the case of the artillery, they provided the entire command.

The civil war's major contributory cause had been labour unrest. After the Bolsheviks had seized power in Russia, radical groups among Finnish socialists became determined to overcome their minority position in parliament with extra-parliamentary activity. A strike was the first step. This was accompanied by lawlessness on a considerable scale, including murder. Many parts of the country were affected. After a week the strike was called off, but only as a tactic. Events escalated. A Central Revolutionary Council formed Red Guards. They struck at the end of January 1918, in the expectation that Russian aid would be enough to secure a quick victory.

The legal government had no adequate forces at its disposal to meet this alarming situation. It did, however, appoint a commander-in-chief to a non-existent army. This was a stroke of genius. General Carl Gustaf for his brutal suppression of a peaceful demonstration. At New Year 1917, Svinhufvud travelled to St Petersburg to gain the recognition of the Council of People's Commissars for Finland's independence.

Military genius: Mannerheim had been persuaded by Premier Svinhufvud to accept the task of organising a government force to uphold law and order. On 18 January, he went to Vaasa on the west coast of Finland, to plan for and organise a "White" army. Vaasa became the seat of government when war broke out. Four cabinet members managed to escape there from Helsinki only hours before the Reds seized control of the capital on 28 January. Premier Svinhufvud

Emil Mannerheim was an inspired military leader on a par with the likes of Kemal Ataturk and "Monty" (the British general Bernard Montgomery, in World War II). Although different in character from Mannerheim, the civilian leader, Pehr Evind Svinhufvud, was his equal and counterpart. He was long a political leader and had been a member of the Turku Court of Appeal which was dismissed early in the century for indicting the Russian governor of Helsinki

Left, Eugen Schauman shoots the hated Russian Governor, General N.I. Bobrikov in 1904. Above, White troops execute Reds in Civil War of 1918.

himself had to hide in Helsinki, but eventually escaped and reached Vaasa, via wartime Germany and many adventures.

The Reds, without full Russian support and up against the strategic ability of General Mannerheim, found their hopes short-lived. First Mannerheim moved against Russian garrisons in central and northern Finland and disarmed them. These garrisons then became the bases from which government forces waged war against the enemy in the south. Tampere, Helsinki and Viipuri were liberated by the spring. After making a last stand on the Karelian Isthmus, the Red forces capitulated on 15 May. The following day Mannerheim's "people's army" held a victory parade in Helsinki.

After a brief flirtation with the idea of a monarch (from Germany), during which time both Svinhufvud and Mannerheim acted as regent, the Finns elected K.J. Ståhlberg, a professor of law and the main author of the Form of Government for the new republic, as its first president.

In 1920 the conflicts between Finland and the Soviet Union were dealt with by the Treaty of Tartu, which recognised Finland as an independent republic and ceded to it the Arctic port of Petsamo. Some small adjustments were made to the border and Finland neutralised its islands close to Leningrad.

One matter that had needed no adjustment in the constitutional arrangements of independence was the Parliament Act of 1906, far ahead of its time in granting votes to men and women without qualification. But social and economic disparities were not greatly mitigated by legalities. (Even the fact of independence could not prevent the country falling apart somewhat.) Two symptoms were manifest. One had been the sudden and violent upsurge of Red rebellion, which was ably put down but which undoubtedly caused a severe shock to the body politic. The second problem was emigration.

Land hunger: Once Russian overlordship had taken a nasty turn, the resulting insecu-

However, the Soviets seemed unable to forgive the Finns for their bourgeois defeat of revolution; in turn, there arose an almost fanatical distrust of the Soviet Union in Finland. Fear of Russia (not limited to recent events), civil war, and the political polarisation that had caused it ran deep and affected the national psyche. Sandwiched between Communist Russia and neutral Sweden, and with a militaristic Germany to the south, independent Finland was born, one historian has noted: "not with a silver spoon, but with a dagger, in its mouth". Finland survived because (to continue the analogy) it learnt the trick of sword swallowing.

rity had already started a trend towards emigration. But there were other causes, and land hunger was the foremost. "No land, no fatherland," was the cry. There was a landless proletariat of 200,000 in the 19th century, plus a host of country dwellers with meagre plots and an obligation to perform "horse days" or "foot days" for their masters. All these people looked to find wider opportunities, and the New World beckoned.

Both before and after the civil war there had been near famine in the countryside. "Nature seems to cry out to our people 'Emigrate or die'," one university lecturer told his students in 1867. "The heart pleaded no, but

46

the stomach commanded yes," ran a line in the novel *Amerikkaan*. Hunger too was behind the slide to Red revolution in 1918. By the 1920s, 380,000 Finns had left home for other lands. The majority went to the United States. The Depression hit Finland in 1929 as badly as anywhere else, and by 1930 the figure for emigration had reached 400,000.

In the 1920s the two branches of the labour movement (the bulk of the "Reds") grew further apart. For public and election purposes, the outlawed Communist Party metamorphosed into the Socialist Workers' and Small Holders' Election Organisation, while the Social Democrats began to co-operate with the bourgeois parties, culminating in a

peasants' march to Helsinki, and led to armed rebellion in 1932.

The formidable duo of the Liberation period, Svinhufvud and Mannerheim, returned and, when the Lapua movement continued even after anti-communist laws were passed, it was left to Svinhufvud to persuade the rebels to disband peacefully. Despite these strains, Finland kept its parliamentary democracy and grew closer to the Scandinavian countries, where Social Democracy was advancing politically, with a long period of co-operation between the Agrarian Party and the Social Democrats, the aptly named "red-green" coalition.

Though the infant nation's priority had to

Social Democrat government in 1926, led by their moderate leader, Väinö Tanner.

Anti-communist feeling continued, nevertheless, and led to the Lapua movement which resorted to violent methods, such as capturing and driving suspected Communist leaders to the Soviet border and forcing them to walk over. Even the respected former President Ståhlberg did not escape one attempt and was driven close to the border. In 1930, the Lapua movement inspired a great

Left, crowds riot in Turku in 1905 in support of Russian uprisings. Above, civil war bomb damage in Red stronghold of Tampere (1918).

be to survive and to strengthen its democracy, life was not all gloom. In the 1920s, sports, travel and the cinema all came into their own, the cinema and bus travel in particular having a profound effect on social habits. It was also a time of strong cultural expression, particularly in architecture and design, and a time of optimism to an extent that, despite the growing threats in Europe (particularly from Germany, so close to Finland) and Mannerheim's warnings, little was done to build up the country's armaments.

When parliament eventually approved 3,000 million marks for military procurement in 1938, it was already too late.

THE TWO WARS

By the spring of 1938 Moscow was making demands on the Finnish Government to give guarantees that, in the event of hostile acts by Germany, Finland would accept Soviet military aid. The railway line between Leningrad and Murmansk was vital to Soviet security: hence Moscow's fear of German invasion through the Gulf of Finland.

The Finnish Government was reluctant to enter into discussions, fearing that to do so would be to compromise neutrality. The Munich Agreement of September 1938 prompted Finland to build up its defences and Mannerheim advised the Government to carry out partial mobilisation. The Soviet Union again made representations to Finland, this time suggesting that the Finns lease the islands of the Gulf of Finland to them for 30 years. Soviet pleas to Britain and France for collective security had fallen on deaf ears and Leningrad was vulnerable from the sea.

Finland was still suspicious of Soviet ambitions. By April 1939, Hitler had managed to drive a wedge through Finland's policy of joint Nordic security. (It has been said that Denmark feared Germany, Finland feared Russia, Norway feared nobody, and Sweden was never able to decide whom to fear most.) Estonia, Latvia and Denmark accepted a German plan of non-aggression, while Sweden, Norway and Finland refused.

Perilous times: After Sweden withdrew, and Germany and the Soviet Union had signed a non-aggression pact (which included a secret protocol on spheres of influence), Finland, was in a dangerous position. After the German invasion of Poland, the Soviet Union began to press the small countries within its sphere to make pacts of "mutual assistance". Delegates from Helsinki travelled to Moscow for discussions. Mannerheim now pressed for full mobilisation of Finnish forces, and the Soviet Union moved swiftly on to a war footing.

The first Soviet demand was that troops be

moved from the Karelian Isthmus. When Mannerheim refused, the Kremlin broke off diplomatic relations and launched an attack on Finland on 30 November 1939. The Winter War had begun.

Soviet forces had almost overwhelming superiority but they were untrained and ill-equipped to fight a war in severe winter conditions. Though short of heavy armaments, by contrast, Finnish soldiers had already been training for just this sort of warfare. They were used to moving in dense

forests through snow and ice, and the Finnish army's tactical mobility was on a very high level. The Finns were also accustomed to the climate and dressed sensibly when winter set in and the temperature dropped several degrees below zero. Soldiers were issued with white "overalls" – now standard in most armies for winter warfare – to cover their uniforms so that they blended into invisibility in the snowy landscape.

The most difficult problem for this kind of warfare had already been solved in the 1930s: how to camp and make shelter in a winter wilderness. Finland had developed a tent for the use of half a platoon (20 men), which could be folded into a small and easily handled bundle. A portable boxstove was enough to keep the tent warm even if the temperature fell to –40°C, and it was easy to prepare coffee and other food on top of the stove. The Finns could also operate for several weeks in uninhabited regions without tents by building shelters out of snow and evergreens.

War preparations: By copying the methods used by farmers and lumberjacks to haul logs from the forest, the Finnish army also solved a second key problem: how to operate in the forests flanking the roads. First they would open a trail in the woods using skis, avoiding gorges, cliffs and steep rises. When a few

water level to form an obstruction against the enemy advance. When the Finnish army opened the gates in the Saimaa canal in March 1940, the Russians found operations in the flooded areas very troublesome.

Attempts to raise the water level were less successful during the coldest winter period; but equally, as the ice covered the uneven features of the terrain, the enemy had less shelter and was not concealed from air reconnaissance. Later, the Finns opened lanes by blowing up the ice and eventually developed special ice mines which detonated when the Soviets approached.

Finns and Russians fought the Winter War during the darkest period of the year. In the

horses and sleighs had moved over this trail, a winter road would form along which a horse could pull up to a 1-tonne load.

Anticipating what might happen, the army had already perfected these techniques in its pre-war winter manoeuvres and, when war started in 1939, Finland had about half a million horses in the country. The army used around 20 percent of them and, as half the reservists called up to fight were farmers or lumberjacks, there were plenty of skilled horsemen to handle the horses.

During the summer of 1939, the Finns had built dams in the small rivers on the Karelian Isthmus and elsewhere which raised the

area of Viipuri, daylight lasted from 8am to 5pm. On the level of Kajaani the day was a couple of hours shorter while, at the turn of the year, Petsamo in the north enjoyed hardly any hours of daylight at all. Finnish soldiers made use of the darkness for the loading and unloading of trains, transports, and supply traffic. This prevented the enemy (with its command of the air) from noticing and disturbing operations. The troops carried out all their tactical movements in the forests, which offered even better protection.

Bottles versus tanks: To compensate for the lack of anti-tank guns, the Finns used gasoline-filled bottles and TNT-charges. This called for great courage, since to throw a bottle with telling effect the soldier had to slip alongside or behind the tank, but the Finns destroyed an impressive number of tanks in this way.

As the Soviet Army moved remorselessly west, the Finns had insufficient forces and equipment for classical air, tank, artillery and similar operations, and their aim had to be to force the enemy to attack under the worst possible conditions. But the Finnish soldiers, bred on the land, knew the terrain. The Soviet divisions, in contrast, had no choice but to stick to the roads, advancing in a tight column, strung out over some 60 miles (100 km). On either side lay a strip

longer distances, they ploughed a road over the snow-covered ice to bring troops and equipment. In any attack, surprise was the essence. Strike force commanders and their troops, all on skis, moved stealthily forward to block the road, trying to choose a time when few Russians were in the target area, so that the sappers had time to destroy the bridges and lay mines to catch the tanks before any counter-attack.

The Finns fought against great odds and during this Winter War (and partly during the Continuation War that followed) the number of Finnish anti-tank guns was so limited that the troops could use them only against an armoured attack on an open road,

around 70–140 miles (110–220 km) wide of uninhabited, forest-covered wilderness, with numerous lakes and marshes, where the Finnish troops had all the advantages of surprise and manoeuvrability.

For these attacks, the Finns either carried their ammunition, mines and explosives or pulled them along on sledges, which they also used to evacuate the wounded, often along the specially prepared winter roads running through the wilderness. At night, for

and gasoline bottles and TNT-charges were the more likely way to destroy an enemy tank. Despite that, the advantages were not always on the side of the invading army. The ill-informed, and often ill-clad, Soviet troops could not move from, or manoeuvre outside, the roads and they, too, often lacked supplies when woefully insufficient air drops left them short of ammunition and food. Throughout the war's skirmishes and more formal encounters, the "ski troops" inflicted hard blows on this ill-clad and badly deployed Red Army.

Honourable peace: Though the resourcefulness of Marshall Mannerheim's white-clad

Left, Karelians evacuate their homeland during World War II. **Above**, Finnish soldiers with a captured Soviet tank.

THE GREAT GENERAL

Carl Gustaf Emil Mannerheim was born at his family's country house at Louhisaari on 4 June 1867. The Mannerheim estate was in Swedish Villnäs, in the Turku district. The family was Swedish-speaking and of Dutch origin.

Furthermore, this great son of Finland, to whom the modern nation state probably owes its very existence, was a Russian officer for 28 years before he ever served Finland's cause. Yet Gustaf (he used his second Christian name) was not following any strong family tradition when he enlisted as a cavalry officer cadet in 1882. He was even expelled from the Cadet School, and considered becoming a sailor. Fortunately for Finland he stayed with the land forces. He was given a second chance and went to St Petersburg for cavalry training; in 1889 he was commissioned into the Czarist army, passing out in the top six, out of a total of 100.

While waiting for a Guard's commission he was posted to Poland as a subaltern in the 15th Alexandriski Dragoons. The Poles were far more restive under Russian rule than the Finns and had nothing like the same freedoms as the Grand Duchy. But Mannerheim later recalled: "The better I got to know the Poles, the more I liked them and felt at home with them."

Transferred to the Chevalier Guards, he returned to St Petersburg to train recruits. Here he came into contact with the Imperial family, and in 1892 married Anastasia Arapov, a relation of Pushkin. They had two daughters, and a son who died at birth. The marriage lasted seven years, although they did not divorce until 1919. Baroness Mannerheim died in France before World War II.

Mannerheim served as a colonel in the Russo-Japanese War, journeyed for two years on horseback through China, visited Japan, and then came back to Poland to command a cavalry regiment in 1909. In World War I, he served in the Eastern European theatre, fighting against Germans and Austrians. By 1917 he was a Lieutenant-General.

The Russian Revolution cut short his career in the Emperor's Army, and when the Czar was murdered Mannerheim considered himself released from his Oath of Allegiance. Russia was seething with revolutionary activity, and the boiling pot overflowed into Finland.

The country had seized the moment and declared itself independent. The Senate named Mannerheim Commander-in-Chief of the armed forces in the country. Quickly, he had to raise and equip an army, for none existed, and mobilise it against the revolutionary Red Guards and Russian troops still left in the country.

When the war was over and won, the Senate appointed Mannerheim Regent of Finland but he lost the subsequent Presidential election. During the inter-war years he worked for the Red Cross and for the Mannerheim League for Children.

Mannerheim's finest hour came with the onset of the Winter War against a Russian invading army in 1940, when Finland fought against Soviet Russia for three-and-a-half months under ferocious winter conditions. It came through the war with its independence intact, due largely to the deployment of highly mobile "ski troops" in winter white overalls.

Mannerheim was briefly President of Finland after the war, but retired because of ill health in March 1946. His final years were spent quietly, mainly in Switzerland, where he died in 1951, aged 83. His wartime ADC recalls the main habits of the Marshal of Finland as kindness, frugality (one drink with lunch, two in the evening), fondness for riding, and discipline. His home in Helsinki is now a museum. It is presided over by Colonel Bäckman, the retired ADC, and holds trophies and collections from Mannerheim's travels, and mementoes from the five wars in which he fought. His guns are on display, including a William Powell and a Purdey. Tiger skins and musk ox rugs cover some of the floor area, and there is a cosy library where the visitor feels he is about to meet the great man.

On the library wall is a painting of military personnel on skis and in white dress. Fluidity of movement and urgency in the human figures contrast with the great peace of a snowbound Finnish forest. Strangely the painting is dated 1890. A portent, a symbol, an idea – an idea which delivered Finland in its hour of desperate need.

troops had grasped every advantage of territory and climate to achieve several notable victories, Finland could not last long against an enemy of much greater power. The Finnish army was forced to surrender at Viipuri, and the Soviet Union set up and then abandoned a puppet government on the Karelian Isthmus. But the long front held out to the end. This guaranteed pre-conditions for an honourable peace and, in 1940, the two sides concluded an armistice. Under this, the Soviet Union's original aim – a base in Hanko, in the southwest, and the moving of the border further from Leningrad – were the only other Soviet gains.

Neverthless Finland had to surrender

appeared, however reluctantly, to have moved to the other side from Britain. On 27 January 1940, he wrote: "Finland – shows what free men can do."

The Winter War lasted exactly 100 days. But the European powers were still fighting and the inevitable result for Finland was to be swept up in yet another conflict. On 22 June 1941, Operation Barbarossa went ahead. Hitler attacked the Soviet Union, achieving complete surprise. Russian commanders signalled to Stalin: "We are being fired on – what shall we do?" Stalin replied that they were talking nonsense, and anyway why weren't their messages coded? There had been some collusion between the Ger-

around a tenth of its territory, with a proportionate shift of population and, in this respect, suffered a heavy defeat. On the other hand it was obvious that Stalin's real intention had intended to annex the whole of Finland, and their defeat in the Winter War was mitigated for the Finns by the maintenance of national sovereignty.

The British leader, Winston Churchill, was unstinting in his praise of Finnish Resistance during the Winter War, an attitude he did not lose even at a time when Finland

man and Finnish military authorities and the Finns had had to allow the west of Finland to be used for transit traffic. Partial Finnish mobilisation was ordered, and 60,000 civilians moved from front-line areas.

Alongside Germany: On the day preceding Barbarossa, Hitler had announced that "Finnish and German troops stand side by side on the Arctic coast for the defence of Finnish soil." Marshall Mannerheim was convinced that his statement was intended as an announcement of a *fait accompli.* "This will lead to a Russian attack," he said, "though, on the other hand, I am convinced that in any case such an attack would have

Left, Mannerheim's statue in Helsinki. **Above**, World War II gas masks in Hanko Museum.

occurred." The Russian High Command, taken by surprise by the German invasion, retaliated against the Finns. Russian bombs fell on Finland even before any were dropped on German targets.

Once again Finnish soldiers flocked to the colours. During the Winter War, supplies, including food, had not been lacking, although some units had been short of potatoes. Just in case, some veterans from the Winter War reported for duty carrying their kit and a sack or two of potatoes.

The Finnish army was larger, war-hardened, and better equipped than it had been at the start of the Winter War. Eleven divisions stood on the frontiers, another faced the

Russian base at Hanko, and the Commander-in-Chief had a reserve of four divisions, which he controlled from his old headquarters at Mikkeli.

Even so, Marshal Voroshilov, who was in charge of the Russian North West Army Group, had formidable numbers under his command: 13 rifle divisions, two armoured divisions, a division of frontier troops, and specialist detachments. The Hanko garrison was estimated to consist of 35,000 men, and there were many fortress units.

Many in Finland expected the army to make an advance towards Leningrad. The idea of capturing this city had at one time

attracted Marshall Mannerheim but now he informed the Finnish government that "Under no circumstances will I lead an offensive against the great city on the Neva." He feared that the Russians, faced with an advance on Leningrad, might raise irresistible forces and inflict a heavy defeat on the Finnish army.

The campaign objectives were to be the re-conquest of Ladoga-Karelia, followed by the Isthmus, and finally penetration into Karelia. All these objectives were achieved. Mannerheim had some German units placed at his disposal, but he kept them at arm's length. The Finns were co-belligerents, not allies of the Germans. When the Finns had regained all of their old frontiers, Mannerheim commented: "Here we could have stood as neutral neighbours instead of as bitter enemies."

Fortunately, Finland and Great Britain never came to the point of fighting each other, although it was a close-run thing. Mannerheim and Winston Churchill showed great statesmanship in an exchange of letters at a moment when the outcome of the war, including the survival of Britain – and for that matter Finland – was far from clear. The letters are reproduced here in full.

Personal, secret and private
29 November 1941
Prime Minister Churchill to Field Marshall Mannerheim:
"I am deeply grieved at what I see coming, namely, that we shall be forced within a few days, out of loyalty to our ally Russia, to declare war upon Finland. If we do this, we shall make war also as opportunity serves. Surely your troops have advanced far enough for security during the war and could now halt and give leave? It is not necessary to make any public declaration, but simply leave off fighting and cease military operations for which the severe weather affords every reason, and make a *de facto* exit from the war.

"I wish I could convince Your Excellency that we are going to defeat the Nazis. I feel far more confident of that than in 1917 or 1918. It would be most painful to the many friends of your country in England if Finland found herself in the dock with the guilty and defeated Nazis. My recollections of our pleasant talks and correspondence about the last war lead me to send you this purely personal and private message for your consideration before it is too late."

Personal, secret and private
2 December 1941
Field Marshal Mannerheim to Prime Minister Churchill:

"Yesterday I had the honour to receive through the American Minister in Helsinki your letter of 29 November 1941, and I thank you for your kindness in sending me this private message. I am sure you will realise it is impossible for me to halt the military operations at present being carried out before the troops have reached the positions which in my opinion will provide us with necessary security.

"It would be deplorable if these measures, undertaken for the security of Finland, should bring my country into conflict with England, and

had to be found for over 423,000 Karelians. After 1945 the Soviets insisted on show trials in Finland of the leading politicians who had given the orders to fight. These men received prison sentences, but served less than a full term and, in some cases, returned to public life with no damage to their reputation.

Finland also had to pay reparations to the Soviet Union, mostly in the form of metal products. The Soviets insisted on calculating their value according to the exchange rates of 1938, thus Finland paid almost exactly twice the price stated in the agreement.

The years of struggle and of suffering were over at long last, and a war-weary Finland set about the business of national re-construc-

it would deeply sadden me if England felt herself forced to declare war on Finland. It was very good of you to send me a personal message in these critical days, and I appreciate it fully."

Payment in full: The 1941–44 war is known in Finland as the "Continuation War" because it was understood as an extension of the Winter War and as an attempt to compensate for losses suffered in that war. In the Continuation War Finland's number of dead was 65,000 and wounded 158,000. Homes

Left, Vammala war cemetery. **Above**, like many Finnish towns, Rovaniemi was extensively rebuilt after World War II.

tion. The reparations to the Soviet Union were paid in full. This was a point of honour to the Finns.

More poignantly the dead soldiers, who had been removed from the battlefields to their home parishes, were buried with full honours in cemeteries alongside memorials to their courage and sacrifice. Unassuming, dignified and patriotic, the spirit of these graveyards and memorials is a fitting tribute to the memory of a people who had persevered and conquered. There never was and there never will be anything remotely neutral about Finland when the trumpet of war is blown in earnest.

In 1980, Finnish statesman Max Jacobson wrote that outsiders persist in viewing Finland according to the state of Western relations with the Soviet Union: "In 1939–40, Finns were idolised for their resistance against the Red Army; in 1941–44, ostracised for continuing to fight the Russians; at the end of World War II, castigated for their failure to heed Western advice to trust Moscow; in 1948, written off as lost for signing a treaty with the Soviet Union; and finally, until recently they were subjected to a kind of character assassination through use of the term 'Finlandisation' to denote supine submission to Soviet domination. Is it possible the Finnish people have resigned themselves to giving away what they were willing to die for during the last war?"

The answer, of course, is no. Yet modern Finland has a dual image. Some perceive it as an enlightened, peace-loving Nordic nation that is clean and unspoiled and heroic and healthy. Others are troubled by its position – physical and political – in relation to the Soviet Union. Finland still takes its own official line regarding the Soviet Union, following dictates of its own. In January 1991, President Koivisto called the growing Baltic crisis "an internal Soviet affair" – this despite the fact that Finland had *not* recognised annexation of the Baltics in 1940.

Baltic attitudes: Koivisto's comments dismayed some Western and Baltic leaders. Most betrayed of all, perhaps, were the Finns themselves, among whom pro-independence sentiment for the Baltics, especially Finland's ethnic cousin Estonia, ran high. One newspaper editorial remarked: "Public opinion is finding it difficult to accept the realism of this country's foreign policy leadership and its appeal to Finland's own national interest."

Defenders of the government line explained their belief that interference from the outside would only increase tensions. (A week after the Koivisto statement, Soviet

Interior Ministry troops attacked the Lithuanian TV station and more than a dozen ended up dead.) Some also reasoned that other countries could take stronger stances because they did not share a border with the Soviets, and that this border has always made things different for Finland.

As well, Finnish Communists played a big role in organising the labour force that powered early postwar industry. At one stage they held 50 out of 200 seats in the Eduskunta (Parliament or National Assem-

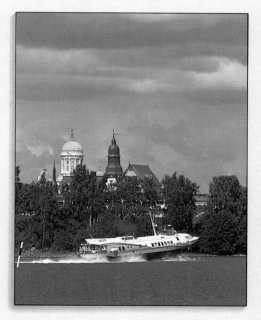

bly). The Soviets used them as a vessel through which to channel influence. This method was most effective when the Communists were most powerful. Twice, the Soviets were able to wield enough influence to lead the government to resign.

There was a flip side. Until 1947, Finland was observed by the Allied Control Commission, which included many Soviet officers. (The Commission among other tasks observed war crimes trials; the longest sentence given was 10 years, served on ex-president Risto Ryti for his dealings with the Germans.) The officers' presence was repulsive and frightening to anti-communist

Preceding pages: President Urho Kekkonen meets the Soviet leader Nikita Kruschev in 1960, at the Soviet Embassy in Helsinki. Left, Workers' Statue in Helsinki. Right, hydrofoil to Estonia.

Finns. The fear that Finland would go the way of Czechoslovakia in 1948 so rattled even the brave Mannerheim (who was president briefly after the war) that he made provisions to flee the country, just in case.

The Communist left eventually lost its grip. The Social Democrats (SDP), now barely left of centre, eventually became the dominant political party in Finland and held that position until 1991. In its last four years as majority party, the SDP was in a so-called "red-blue" coalition with the leading rightist party, the conservative Kokoomus.

Moving right: The Social Democrats' move right was emblematic of the political picture as a whole. Since the war, the sympathies of

became, eventually, rich. This accomplishment was of crucial importance to Finns, and also somewhat calmed Western worries that the country was too close to the USSR.

But long before the economic miracle happened, Finland had to carve out its political place in the post-war world, a world that rapidly began to militarise along East-West lines. Finland chose neutrality. Fathered by J K Paasikivi, at first prime minister (1944–46) and then president (1946–56) of the Finnish republic, and Urho Kekkonen, president of the republic from 1956 to 1983, the neutrality doctrine is one that shuns commitment in favour of "peace-orientated policy".

That neutrality has meant many different

the majority have moved steadily toward more traditional, "bourgeois" European values. After the 1991 parliamentary vote, Finland was ruled by a centre-right alliance that is the most politically conservative in the republic's history.

The move right kept step with the economic growth of Finland, a phenomenon of rapid change. Divested in 1917 of the lucrative 19th-century trade links it had enjoyed as a trading post of Imperial Russia, Finland had to start from scratch. Until World War II, Finland had a stagnant, subsistence agricultural economy. Post-war industrialisation pulled it out of this quagmire, and Finland

things in many different situations. In post-war Finland, the neutral Paasikivi-Kekkonen line seemed to reassure Finns that their country would not become a battleground for the USSR and its considerable enemies. To gain such reassurance, Finland had to play a tough political game, walk a narrow line. The tense mistrust that ruled East-West relations during the Cold War caused a foreign policy challenge that would have been formidable even to a nation older and more powerful.

Finland, which was was not even three decades independent by the war's end, resolved that it wanted "out" of the conflict, and bargained for postwar agreements along this line. The Soviet Union pushed hard for certain concessions, and depleted Finland had little to bargain with. Compromises were inevitable.

Soviet lease: The most controversial compromise was in the 1944 peace treaty with Moscow. In it, the Finns agreed to lease the Porkkala peninsula (near Helsinki) to the Soviets for 50 years for use as a military base. The situation was defused in 1955 when the two parties agreed to the lease's cancellation. Porkkala's return seemed to signal good things to the West, for in that same year year Finland was admitted to the United Nations; in the 1950s, the country also joined

tion, and Mutual Assistance (FCMA); it expires in 2003. This complex agreement was not a military alliance *per se*. Drawn up in clear reference to the Germans' having used Finland to attack the Russians, it demanded mutual protection; both pledged to prevent outside forces from using their territory to attack the other; and Finland promised to join no alliances hostile to the Soviet Union.

This last measure was perceived by the Finns to be in line with the neutral policy they had already decided on. Other Western nations, however, beginning to labour under sharp Cold War polarities, felt that if Finland was not for them, it could be against them. In this way began the declamations that Finland

the International Monetary Fund.

When Paasikivi began formulating his foreign policy line he stressed "correct and irreproachable neighbourly relations" with the Soviet Union. The phrase may have sounded ingratiating to Western ears but made sense to the majority of Finns, who needed to believe that the Soviet Union could be bent into the shape of benign neighbour.

In 1948, Finland and the Soviet Union signed the Treaty of Friendship, Co-opera-

Left, the Finnish Parliament (Eduskunta) in Helsinki. **Above**, Parliament in session.

was teetering on the edge of becoming part of the Eastern Bloc.

Every other nation liberated by the Western allies in World War II eventually became NATO members. Only Finland, the one country with a border with Russia to emerge outside the Eastern Bloc after World War II, and Yugoslavia did not become allies of either East or West.

Soviet fears: When Finland joined in the formation of the Nordic Council in 1952, the Soviet editorials were hysterical: "Surely this means Finland will be joining NATO?" The fact that the Olympics were set to be held in Helsinki also in 1952 added fuel to the fire.

The Soviets saw preparations for the event, such as the building of a south coast highway, as proof of more plans to include Finland in a general military threat – perhaps even war – against the USSR.

Whatever else is true of the immediate postwar period, the fact that Finland did not come into the Western fold but chose to go it alone did not endear it to the non-communist world. A lone wolf is suspect; Finland even refused the Marshall Plan.

Nonetheless, economic progress began in earnest. The Finnish-Soviet 1944 peace agreement had included demands for war reparations of over $600 million. Ironically, this demand for money helped build the new economy. Postwar Finland was low on cash but met payments by negotiating the payment of some of its debt in manufactured engineering products such as farming and forestry machinery, and ships. These items became staple sources of export income in Finland's years as a growth economy.

Before that economy got off the ground, however, most Finns lived in poverty. To this day, older Finns enthusiastically buy chocolate when they travel abroad because of post-war period memories of chocolate being impossible to obtain.

Finland had to stretch its meagre resources yet further to deal with one of the largest resettlements of a civilian population in the world. Nearly 400,000 dispossessed Karelians (and a handful of Skolt Sami) were given free land and donations of whatever the others could afford to give, which was little. Most Karelians, already poor in their homeland, arrived only with what they and what their horses could carry.

In 1950, a barter trade agreement was signed between the Finns and the Soviets. It was in force until 1990, when the Soviets abruptly announced they would not sign the next five-year extension. The reason given was that continuing it would hinder Soviet pursuit of survival on a free market economy basis. The true Soviet aim was to sell its oil for hard cash. While in force, the barter agreement was worth a fortune. It provided Finland with a completely protected market for tonnes of consumer goods each year. The heavy equipment and cheap clothes and shoes sent over were traded for Soviet oil, enough to cover 90 percent of Finnish needs.

The Finnish trade balance suffered for the treaty's cancellation by an amount that is disputed but surely significant as the USSR was Finland's fifth-largest trading partner. Its ranking has now slipped back. Soviet-orientated Finnish producers foundered or went bankrupt. The Finns had to pay cash prices for oil… and wait for the Soviets to pay them a $2 million debt.

Support for UN: In addition to economic success, another Finnish accomplishment has been its deep commitment to the United Nations since it joined in 1955. Marjatta Rasi, the UN ambassador during the 1990–91 Gulf Crisis (Finland was a 1990 non-permanent member of the Security Council) says Finland "joined the UN after the difficulties of the immediate post-war period were safely behind and the main lines of our policy of neutrality had been laid down."

Finland strongly supports UN peacekeeping functions, in which thousands (nearly 30,000 by 1990) of Finns have participated. It has also contributed a high number of UN military observers and development specialists. Involvement began during the Suez Canal crisis in 1956. There has since been a strong Finnish presence in peacekeeping operations in Lebanon, Golan, Gaza, and the Sinai. But the most outstanding efforts were made on behalf of Namibia. On a Finnish initiative, in 1970 the UN set up a Namibia Fund, and Finland also pursued and saw come to light the 1971 International Court of Justice ruling that South Africa's presence in Namibia was illegal. When Namibia finally gained independence in 1990, Finnish UN Peacekeeping General Matti Ahtisaari directed the transition.

Along with the rest of the Nordic countries, Finland contributes generously to refugee aid programmes; the total Nordic contribution equals 25 percent of the UN High Committee on Refugees fund.

Continuing crisis: While Finland was quickly able to shine in the UN arena, crises at home went on. In 1961, the USSR sent Finland a note suggesting "military consultations" regarding the 1948 FCMA. That note was probably sent because of Soviet fear of escalating (West) German militarism in the Baltic. The harm the note caused to Finland derived from the term "military consultations." Both sides had maintained the Treaty of Friendship, Co-operation and Mutual Assistance was not a military alliance, but an emblem of co-operation between two neighbours who were not allied.

Nikita Khruschev and Urho Kekkonen conferred privately, and the consultations were announced "deferred". What the Soviets had been worried about, though, was clear: that Finland was not equipped to stop the West from using it as an attack flank. The Kekkonen-Khruschev exchange was never made wholly public, but after the "Note Crisis", Finland began shoring up its military forces. Finland sought, and got, from the British a reinterpretation of the Paris Peace Treaty of 1947 allowing it to purchase missiles, forbidden by the original treaty.

The Soviets throughout the 1970s were to looked as though the pulp and paper industry's success would mean no looking back.

In 1975, the Final Act of the Conference on Security and Co-operation in Europe (CSCE) was concluded in Helsinki. It was a great public relations victory, an event that could help Finland to be seen as it wanted to be, as a place of diplomacy and enlightened neutrality. Since then, Helsinki has become a kind of Vienna of the north, full of diplomats' cars and sudden police barricades. The CSCE resumes in Helsinki in early 1992.

In the 1970s and 1980s, Finland enjoyed one of the highest gross national products in the world and pulled up its standard of living and social services to be in line with Swe-

den's. In 1989–90, Finland was the most expensive country in the world, outstripping Japan. Fantastically high agricultural subsidies, and industrial cartels which set artificially high prices, were the main culprits and brought difficult consequences.

High living: A lot of Finns, though, made a lot of money, and spent it with abandon. But it wasn't so easy to cover up the fact that they'd been poor cousins for so long. Even as late as the early 1980s one could look in shoe shop windows and gasp at the ugly, out-of-fashion footwear on display; these were the designs that had been dumped on the Soviets for the past 30 years. One could also buy

try to make life difficult for the Finns several more times. A Soviet ambassador meddled in an internal wrangle of the Finnish Communist Party. Kekkonen demanded his recall to the USSR. The fibre of Finnish society was now more firmly established and the left-wing elements were mere ragged ends. A more prosperous Finland was more difficult to "strong-arm"; by now West Germany, Sweden, and the United Kingdom were Finland's major trading partners, not the USSR. Trees had become its green gold, and it

Above, the UN Special Namibian Envoy, Finland's Markuu Ulander.

Gucci shoes, at costs that made Parisian boutique prices look like flea-market deals. There was little to choose from between the two extremes. By the end of the 1980s, the gap was closing, but prices were still wildly high, especially on imports.

Starting in the late 1980s, Finland went into economic recession. At the same time, the challenges of the "new" Europe were growing. When the rest of Europe was drawing together like a large mutual aid society, Finland seemed to repel the trend. The official word was that it had no interest in joining the European Community, but was firmly committed to continue as a European Free Trade Association member that endorsed a

strong European Economic Space. Under these circumstances, the economy was less like to improve quickly.

Finland until 1990 had few troublesome or needy immigrants; most foreigners were diplomats. The Finnish Red Cross had sponsored a few handfuls of Vietnamese, Bulgarian, and Kurdish (pre-Gulf) refugees. Finland had never opened its doors to hordes of guest workers as cheap labour, except for the odd bunch of Russian or Estonian day labourers. Nor had it ever had to deal with floods of refugees knocking at its door; its location, and reputation as a difficult place to get into, precluded that.

In early 1990, a group of Somali refugees arrived at the Finnish-Soviet border. In flight from civil war in their own country, they arrived via Moscow, the only European destination they could get to by plane via Aeroflot. By 1991 nearly 3,000 Somalis were waiting an average of nine months for their asylum decisions.

Somali influx: Lacking a comprehensive refugee policy, the Finns entered into debate about granting refugee status. The arguments ranged from generous to xenophobic. In the end, simple bureaucratic bog-downs resolved in the short term what real decisions could not; with the nine-month wait, the Somalis at least had temporary refuge. As well, they had babies in Finland and began to speak the apparently impossible language, one thing the xenophobes had been sure they would never be able to do.

Around the time of the first Somali influx came government reports showing that Finland would need – due to a brain-drain and a falling birthrate – up to 10,000 foreign labourers annually to keep the wheels of Finnish industry oiled. In the long run, according to economist Patrick Humprhreys, Finns will probably handle this better than others have handled guest workers. In his book on Finland and Europe, he says that Finnish employers will be forbidden to give foreigners different contract terms from Finns. Humphreys also predicts that there is little immediate likelihood "of an influx of European immigrants. Cultural barriers will long persist. There is also a threshold effect deterring migration to countries where there are few foreigners (25,000 out of 5 million)."

He concludes by saying: "An existing foreign community advertises a country far more effectively than recruitment schemes and official brochures can. It also eases the assimilation process and ensures the existence of important services" (such as foreign language schools). Modern Finland is still in many ways a European state in the making, and its tenuousness still sometimes shows. If Finland can learn to live well with its immigrants, diversify its economy, and take bolder stands on international issues, military neutrality notwithstanding, then it should enter the 21st century able to shed the ghosts of images that plagued it in the 20th.

Left, A ship unloads at Helsinki's busy harbour.

THE WELFARE STATE

One of the most striking things you'll notice on a first visit to Helsinki is the number of prams. They're everywhere, parked outside shops and office buildings, with plump-cheeked, sleeping babies inside them. Societies without baby-snatchers may be rare, but Finland is one of them.

The Finnish welfare system caters for almost every imaginable need of society. It offers generous state pensions, free high-quality health care, and good unemployment benefits. Promotion of a healthy milieu in which to raise children plays a very important role, and one man is largely responsible for that: Professor Arvo Ylppö.

Dr Ylppö, who lived to be over 100, was born in late 19th-century Finland, where social welfare did not exist. Malnutrition and hunger were rife among Finnish children, and only the lucky ones went to school.

One hundred years later, Maija-Liisa Salonen and her partner Risto take turns to drop off their two-year-old son at day care. They can pursue their careers while their child is cared for in a modern, state-subsidised centre close to home and with professional staff.

Maija-Liisa and Risto found the day care place easily because demand is moderate. The reason is that more parents are staying at home with their

new babies *and* keeping their jobs. Progressive laws in Finland guarantee 10 months' fully-paid leave (which can be extended) to a mother and/or father who stays at home with the baby, plus a substantial child benefit payment; the 10 months can be divided between mother and father. These laws have had the desired results: more new parents now stay at home in the crucial early stages.

Family values have traditionally been strong in Finland, for so long a poor agrarian society. The nuclear family was that agrarian society's vital unit. Not only were family members the best company for each other in often isolated farming areas but the children inherited their parents' land.

Nowadays, attention is once more strongly focused on children because the birth rate is low. Only 1.7 babies are born for every two adults. With an increased proportion of elderly people in the population and a shrinking workforce, government and society in general think it a good thing to encourage more births.

In 1887, the year Ylppö was born, and long before he started his children's revolution, 131 out of every 1,000 babies died before their first birthday. The figure is now six per 1,000, the world's lowest rate. The establishment of intensive pre- and post-natal care services for mother and child, and the growth of a children's protection society, later to become Lastenlinna Children's Hospital, are the main reasons for the improvement. Lastenlinna's founder was Sophie Mannerheim, sister of the great Finnish soldier and statesman.

Lastenlinna no longer takes in sick or poor or orphaned children because there is so little need for such care. Instead, it is now devoted to two units, the neurological and the psychiatric. New ills of society, those typical of all Western nations, have partly taken the place of the ills of 100 years ago, and have necessitated the growth particularly of the second speciality. According to a psychiatric consultant at Lastenlinna, many young patients they see are chronically in need of attention.

She calls these children the "key children"; they are given keys to their homes, the car, the motorboat, but then they are ignored. Lastenlinna attempts to restore the balance by treating the whole family together for the child's psychoses, an approach fathered by Ylppö, who believed that "the Finnish climate must in all ways be made a healthy one for our children to grow in."

Medical care for the elderly is good, and cheap, despite a shortage of beds for chronic patients. Finnish pensioners are well off financially, which helps keep illness at bay and their houses well-heated. Working Finns receive 60 percent of pre-retirement salary as a state pension. Non-salaried Finns receive, from age 65, state pensions determined by need. Meanwhile, improved lifelong health care and low birth rates have helped give Finland one of the world's most elderly populations. With over 40 percent as many pensioners as there are adults of working age, it is no wonder Finns are trying to make child-bearing more appealing.

SATA MARKKAA
100
SUOMEN PANKKI
5053193875
VIISISATAA MARKKAA
1986
7149819
02157826
2400613
4006590

WHY PRICES ARE SO ASTONISHING

Some people, when abroad, travel with pocket calculators so that they can assess costs in their own currencies. When in Finland, such travellers can be seen punching and then aggressively re-punching the numbers in disbelief, and then shaking their calculators as though the little machines have just told them some outrageous truth they refuse to accept. That's how expensive Finland is. From basics to luxury items, Finnish price tags are searingly high and, unless something radical happens, such as Finland joining the European Community, the phenomenon is unlikely to improve.

Fancy a decent bottle of Finnish vodka? Expect to lay out £20 or more. A little Marimekko T-shirt for a favourite child? £40. Tax on all cars is over 130 percent; on alchohol, it varies, but Finland is the most expensive place in the world to imbibe.

So much for luxuries, what of the basics? The strength of wages (median income, in line with UK median, around £12,000 a year) pales when faced with real costs. Finns spend 100 marks for a food basket that would cost 65 marks in Germany. This factor has helped move Helsinki ahead of Tokyo into the Most-Expensive-City-in-the-World spot. Basics like the use of a telephone line and some utilities are also extremely costly. To get a telephone line in Helsinki, you must buy a share in the phone company, at 5,000 marks (£700). To get the gas switched on in your flat costs 800 marks (£115).

Rents and income tax are more in line with the European averages (rents are controlled, and the maximum income tax is now 51 percent), yet Finnish real estate in and around the capital costs more per square metre than just about anywhere else in the world. Still, Finland has a high percent of owner-occupied housing: 65 percent. What is the reason? People borrow, for one thing. At the same time, the welfare state gives security so that it is not as urgent to build up a lot of savings, say, for one's retirement years or doctors' and dentists' bills.

Preceding pages: a Baltic ferry passes Helsinki Yacht Club. **Left**, Finnish bank notes. **Right**, Helsinki shopping mall.

Otherwise, the Finnish economy is in a mess. Although inflation was in control at about 5–6 percent in the early 1990s, there were predictions of 10 percent unemployment for the near future. These followed the wildly optimistic predictions of just a year or so earlier that Finland would have to begin importing foreign labourers, up to 15,000 a year, to keep Finnish industry going. Meanwhile the native birth rate continues to fall while the overall population ages, so that there were 40 percent as many pensioners as

people eligible to work in the year 1989–90.

The reasons why: Other countries have similar problems; what then makes Finland the *most* expensive? For one thing, the prosperity of the later 1980s sent prices sky-high. More enduringly, Finland has an agricultural policy which is the most expensive in the world, and every Finn pays dearly for it. One civil servant in the Finance Ministry, who shrank from being identified, said the policy was absolutely crazy. A British economist and author in Finland, Patrick Humphreys, describes the Finns' attempt to keep farmers' incomes in line with industrial wage earners' as "daft", while the farming policy remains as inefficient as it is; namely, farmers are paid to over-produce.

Humphreys, as author of the *Yearbook of the Finnish Economy*, is one of the best qualified people in Finland to explain the basic tenets behind the agricultural policy. The Finnish government actually pays out, according to recent OECD figures, about 50 million Finnish marks a day (that's over £7 million) to support farming. However, those government payments cover only a *quarter* of the real cost of supporting farmers.

The rest is made up by consumers who pay tax, sharp seasonal mark-ups, and the steep protective tariffs attached to all imported foods, even those foods Finland cannot

will be higher-priced. The same rule applies for tomatoes, and the other few fresh vegetables and fruit Finland can grow.

The Finnish mark is very strong, and is judged to be over-valued, another fact working against the Finnish consumer even when buying domestic products. When in the late 1980s Finnish rye flour became so high-priced that it could not compete on foreign markets, the domestic price of rye flour was increased. The export price of rye could then be lowered and the surplus sold off cheaply.

European Community: Finland's membership in the European Free Trade Association (EFTA) and the General Agreement on Tariffs and Trade (GATT) has not much hindered any

grow, so that they do not tempt consumers away from domestic stock. It's a sound Lutheran precept, and one that puts a lot of money into the government coffers.

So, you can pay as little as 15 marks a kilo for aubergines in summer, only to see the price soar to 35 marks in winter when one has to buy imported produce. Not very many Finnish aubergines are grown in summer, but those that are take priority on the stalls – imports of foreign aubergines may be stopped altogether if the Finnish supply is sufficient – and have the lowest price tag. If there are imported aubergines on the market at the same time as the Finnish produce, they

of these practices. If Finland does become a European Community member, that will be a different thing. The issue of joining the EC still raises hackles.

The first objection to membership has always been the risk of compromising Finnish neutrality, although neutral countries like Ireland have flourished in the EC and neutral Sweden wants to join. Not only is Sweden one of Finland's most important trade partners, it is also a beacon of political and socio-economic policy for Finland.

After the neutrality argument comes the protection-of-farmers argument. Deeply rooted agrarian loyalties are hard to shake in

Finland, even if full-time farmers are a dying breed. Finally, Finns have an instinctive wish to keep foreigners from buying a slice of their wealth-producing forests. For individuals, the idea of foreigners buying forest brings fears of loss of privacy, something sacred to the national character. The forest industrialists have more pragmatic fears: namely, that introduction of foreign buyers will mean the break-up of the cartel-style domestic price-fixing mechanisms which help shield the industry from real competition. Prices in this and other industries are thus artificially high, and in some sectors competition is virtually impossible.

Too much protection: The Finnish economy,

modities like oil and natural gas, Finland got a guaranteed market for manufactured goods in anything from ships to shoes. Although long a "market economy", Finland was ill-prepared for the agreement's end, and many firms involved in barter trade foundered or went bankrupt. Finland built its post-war economy on the wealth of its forests and industrial strength fostered by its agreement to pay war reparations to the Soviet Union in manufactured goods. Before the war, Finland's was an unsophisticated economy, susbsisting on its agriculture ("You have to be a little mad to practise agriculture above the 60th parallel," journalist Olli Kivinen once remarked) and textile works.

over-specialised and over-protected, has had other vulnerabilities. When its trading partners went into recession, Finland suffered too, but then had to deal with another blow. Its special barter trade agreement with the Soviet Union was called off in late 1990, abruptly, by the Soviets, and without the expected grace period.

The agreement was worth many millions in trade each year. In exchange for com-

Left, the Outokump Corporation's copper smelting plant in Harjava. **Above**, floating logs down lakes and rivers to Finland's busy wood and paper factories.

The centre-right government elected in 1991 started off with great plans for putting life back into the Finnish economy, and for making it a better integrated one. But the crucial issue is not whether Finland will survive the recession; no doubt it will. More crucial is the question of whether or not it can survive the sweeping changes in attitudes necessary to carry it into the 21st century with a viable economy.

Now that the line between East and West Europe is fading, Finland, which has all the while straddled that line, should not hesitate too long over throwing in its lot with the new Europe. If it does, it risks being lost.

ART, ARCHITECTURE AND DESIGN

When Diaghilev, founder of the Russian Ballet, divided the Finnish painters of the 1890s into two camps – "those with a nationalistic outlook and those who follow... the west" – he described a tension which has been present in Finnish art ever since.

Too close an association with the art world of Western Europe and the artistic expression of Finnish nationalism have been persistently seen as opposing forces. Taken to political extremes, artists either belonged to Europe or to Finland, not to both. Paradoxically, those who have achieved world renown were able, by creating something essentially Finnish and therefore unique, to leap over national boundaries. Today, Finnish design and architecture are among Finland's best-known products, partly because they combine a universal modernism and a recognisably Finnish quality.

Because Finland is still relatively young as an independent country, much of the art produced there during the past 100 years has been concerned with creating a national cultural identity. Until the 1880s and 1890s, the nascent Finnish cultural scene was influenced by the country's political masters – first Sweden, then Czarist Russia. The few practising Finnish artists who were able to make a living from their work either trained or lived in Stockholm or St Petersburg.

The seeds of a specifically Finnish culture were sown when organised art training began in Turku in 1830. In 1845, Finland held its first art exhibition. The Finnish Art Society was founded in 1846. But it wasn't until the 1880s and 1890s that a truly Finnish artistic idiom began to emerge and Finnish artists were at last afforded some recognition at home and, by the end of the 19th century, abroad. European artistic influences were strong as painters like Albert Edelfelt (1854–1905) utilised the style of French naturalism. Yet, while his style was initially imported from abroad, Edelfelt's subjects became increasingly Finnish.

Search for identity: In the 1880s, a motley

group of painters took up the struggle for cultural identity, which paralleled the growth of Finnish nationalism and the desire for political independence. Among those artists were Akseli Gallen-Kallela (1865–1931), Pekka Halonen (1865–1933), Eero Järnefelt (1862–1937), Juho Rissanen (1873–1950) and Helena Schjerfbeck (1862–1946). They looked to the Finnish landscape and to ordinary Finns for subjects which were quintessentially Finnish. Within that framework, artistic styles varied from powerful, harsh realism to mythology, and sentimental, bourgeois or fey naturalism.

While some painters, like Hugo Simberg (1873–1917) followed idiosyncratic, tran-

was the true Finn, and that a rural landscape was the only credible Finnish landscape – cities had been planned and designed under the sway of foreign rulers.

Still in hot pursuit of the essence of Finnishness, several painters began to go on forays to Karelia, a large chunk of which is now, ironically, under Russian control. Gallen-Kallela, often acclaimed as the most original talent in Nordic art apart from the Norwegian painter Edvard Munch, went to Karelia in 1890. His expedition started the "Karelia" movement which sent 19th-century artists and writers to the area in droves, and continued the earlier travels of the author Elias Lönnrot who compiled Finland's na-

scendental and Europe-based symbolist paths, a body of artists came to represent what was to be called Finnish national romanticism. Their focus on Finnishness – a subject dear to the heart of every Finn – meant that these artists enjoyed, and continue to enjoy, considerable popular appeal in Finland. Several artists chose deliberately to move among people whose mother-tongue was Finnish (at that time many urban intellectuals spoke Swedish) and whose traditional folk culture and rural living had, the artists believed, remained largely uncorrupted by either Swedish or Russian influences. They maintained that the Finnish peasant

tional epic, the *Kalevala*. Gallen-Kallela had gone in search of the right idiom for a series of paintings for the *Kalevala* between 1889 and 1897. *Aino*, *The Defence of the Sampo* (*Sammon puolustus*) and *Joukahainen's Revenge* (*Joukahaisen kosto*) show his transition from naturalism to a stylised, allegorical idiom which he felt lent the *Kalevala* a more heroic quality.

Undeniably a seminal figure in Finnish culture, Gallen-Kallela worked in several media, and his enormous contribution helped to lay the foundations for contemporary Finnish design, furniture-making, sculpture and wood-cuts.

Nationalist hangover: In a general sense, the legacy of national romanticism is large, and has been sometimes something of an incubus which restricted later artists, who wished to look at urban Finland, to follow European movements, or to pursue abstract styles. Finnish popular taste in art continues to be dominated by both a nationalistic and a naturalistic preference. This conservatism has frustrated many an artist who wished to forge ahead in new directions.

Groups like the October Group, whose motto was "in defence of modernism, against isolationalist nationalism", pushed hard against what is sometimes forbiddingly described as the "Golden Age" of Finnish

icked in other art forms – crafts, architecture and design. Turning their backs on the neo-classical designs of their predecessor C.L. Engel (1778–1840), whose buildings include Helsinki's Senate Square and the Cathedral, the architectural leaders of national romanticism – the partnership of Herman Gesellius (1874–1916), Armas Lindgren (1874–1929) and Eliel Saarinen (1873–1950) – used peasant timber and granite architecture as their sources.

Another leading exponent of the movement was Lars Sonck (1870–1956). Decidedly Gothic in outline, and uneasy on the eye because of the clash of smooth timber or symmetrical roof tiles with rough-hewn

art. Sculptor Sakari Tohka (1911–58) was a founding member of the October Group. Overthrowing the classicism of his Finnish forebears, he cast his sculptures in cement. They were not alone. Townscapes and urban Finland were the chosen subjects of another backlash group, the "Torch Bearers", which consisted of Väinö Kunnas (1896–1929), Sulho Sipilä (1895–1949) and Ragnar Ekelund (1892–1960).

The pattern of Finnish fine art – swinging from nationalism to modernism – is mim-

Left, Alvar Aalto Museum at Jyväskyla. **Above**, Marimekko textiles on sale in Helsinki.

granite, national romantic buildings like Helsinki's National Museum (designed 1901) and Tampere's Cathedral (designed 1899) have a gawky ugliness. The partnership trio of architects did, however, begin to draw on more soothing, elongated Art Nouveau influences too. The plans for Helsinki Railway Station, originally designed by all three, were amended by Saarinen. The building as it now stands is far more Art Nouveau than national romantic.

International architect: After independence in 1917, the driving need for a national identity diminished in the face of the need to rebuild the country. Next came a household name in Finnish architecture – Alvar Aalto (1898–1976) – who managed to fuse something Finnish with modernism and revolutionised 20th-century architecture in the process. Aalto was the prime mover in Finland in the struggle to get the principles of modern architecture, and modernism as a whole, accepted there. That done, he turned to the rest of the world, via his two Finnish pavilions at the Paris exhibition of 1937 and the New York world fair of 1939, to prove that Finland had an international contribution to make.

Aalto practised "organic" architecture, designing buildings to suit their environment as well as their purpose. Some of his

smooth, if it employs modern materials like chrome or plastic with confidence or reinvents glass or wood, and if it fits its purpose perfectly, it is likely to be Finnish. Encouraged, like architecture, by the financial and prestigious carrot of open competitions, everyday items are ceaselessly redesigned.

Finland's giant names in the plastics (Neste), ceramics (Arabia), textiles (Finlayson, Marimekko), jewellery (Kalevala Koru, Lapponia) and glass (Iittala-Nuutajärvi) industries introduce new designs periodically, adding new designer names to established reputations. Company textile designers, often working with bold colours and geometric shapes, have created products which are

buildings (the Enso Gutzeit building in Helsinki) appear to be of the archetypal, scorned "concrete block" variety – but, aesthetics aside, they are respected because they were the first to employ nakedly modern materials. His Helsinki "House of Culture" (1958) is overhelmingly contemporary, yet has a sweeping grace and elegance which are remarkable. Finland, a relatively new nation whose cities were deeply scarred in World War II, has bravely embraced modernism and made a virtue of it.

Superb designs: This applies in the field of design too. Whatever the object – a tap, a telephone, a bowl, a chair – if its lines are

identifiably Finnish alongside a handicraft culture – woodcarving, rag-rug weaving and tapestry-making – which pertains to the domestic culture celebrated by the national romantics.

Finnish art now blends more easily into a cocktail of these elements – the traditional, the rural, the modern and the urban. A sense of Finnishness has been established, and, as confidence in nationhood grows, Finland should feel justifiably proud of its cultural performance on the international stage.

Above, marking Pentik ware. **Right**, the film maker Aki Kaurismäki at work.

THE BROTHERS KAURISMÄKI

Whilst Finland may have produced such respected directors as Risto Jarva, Jörn Donner and Rauni Mollberg, and enjoyed sporadic international success with features like *The White Reindeer* (1952) and *The Unknown Soldier* (1955), it is the idiosyncratic Kaurismäki brothers who have wrenched the indigenous cinema industry from a period of stagnation and demanded worldwide attention with the rough-edged individuality and freshness of their prolific output.

Although producing an impressive average of 17 films a year over the past decade, contemporary Finnish cinema received little exposure or distribution until the recent advent of the brothers Aki and Mika. Refracting a range of influences, from the French nouvelle vague to American rock 'n' roll, through a uniquely Finnish sensibility, the brothers have created a body of work that has been seen in 65 countries, won prizes at international festivals and brought Aki the accolade of being the youngest director ever to receive a retrospective at the Museum of Modern Art in New York.

Born in Helsinki in 1957, Aki toiled as a postman and film critic before working as a scriptwriter, assistant and actor on his elder brother's *Valehtelija* (*The Liar*) (1980). The following year, the two men formed a production company named Villealfa in tribute to Jean-Luc Godard's futuristic detective story *Alphaville*. They also own a distribution company, a cinema in downtown Helsinki and were among the founders of the Midnight Sun Festival held each June in Sodankylä, Lapland.

Aki, the better known of the siblings, worked with Mika on the rock documentary *Saimaa-Ilmiä* (*The Saimaa Gesture*) (1983) before striking out on his own with a freewheeling adaptation of *Crime and Punishment* (1983). A lugubrious, taciturn figure of laconic manner and dismissive attitudes to his work, Aki has a self-proclaimed reputation as "the biggest drinker in the world". He has offered a number of explanations for his attraction to literature as source material for films, including the none too serious rationale that "it's easier if you take someone else's book – it gives you more time in the bar."

Aki's films revel in the deadpan humour of morose, hard-drinking outsiders desperate to escape the oppressive confines of a gloom-ridden country that appears to offer them little incentive to stay. It's hard to imagine that he will ever be honoured by the Finnish Tourist Board.

Frequently shot in monochrome, eschewing excessive dialogue whenever possible and rarely running to more than 80 minutes, his films range from *Calamari Union* (1985), an absurdist, unscripted comedy in which the 17 characters are all called Frank, to films based on Hamlet. *Hamlet Liikemaailmassa* (*Hamlet Goes Business*) (1987) is a modern-day version of Shakespeare set in a factory that manufactures rubber ducks, and *Ariel* (1988), which begins with a suicide, offers fulsome tribute to the little known musical delights of the Finnish tango and is described by the director as "a documentation of the destruction of Finland. Nowadays Finland tries to be like Florida and nothing matters any more except profit."

Mika, two years older, studied film in Munich and has worked in a variety of genres from the road movie *Helsinki Napoli* (1987) to the crazy comedy *Cha Cha Cha* (1988) and *Amazon* (1990), an adventure drama set in the Amazonian jungle.

More recently, Aki too has begun to distance himself from his native land, following the "Finnish existentialist rock 'n' roll odyssey" *Leningrad Cowboys Go America* (1989) and the austere *Tulitikkutehtaan Tyttö* (*Match Factory Girl*) (1989) with the Ealing-style comedy *I Hired A Contract Killer* (1990), which was filmed in London.

He has moved to Portugal and a home he shares with his wife, a few Cadillacs and a collection of 1950s bakelite objects. His exile from Finland and international aspirations may reduce the interest in Finnish cinema once more, as Kaurismäki's work is probably too personal and iconoclastic to inspire a new wave of film-makers.

Asked about his plans for the future, he recently replied, tongue-in-cheek: "Take a year off. Maybe stop film-making altogether." Besides, he playfully added, "It's a boring job."

Finnish conductor Esa-Pekka Salonen raises his black-clad arms. Then he raises his handsome boyish face. And suddenly, in striking contrast to his impish look, Salonen's downstroke plunges the hall into a feast of rich and sophisticated sound.

Is this a Finnish stage? It could be or, just as easily, the Los Angeles Philharmonic, London Philharmonic or Swedish Radio Symphony Orchestra, for whom this extraordinary young Finn is music director Designate (1992), principal guest conductor and principal conductor respectively. Born in 1958, Salonen is already one of the more notable figures in the highly competitive world of serious music.

When most people think of Finnish music, however, they still think of Jean Sibelius. The great Finnish composer, after all, sprang from a little-known country to become one of the most famous composers of all time – and Finland's most famous export. But there is much more to modern Finnish music than simply Sibelius, and audiences everywhere are finally beginning to recognise this. A startling number of Finnish musicians are winning both domestic and international acclaim.

Composers in plenty: The Association of Finnish Composers today numbers over 100 members. All have had works performed professionally, and many possess distinguished discographies. Playing their works in Finland are 13 professional orchestras, 18 semi-professional or chamber orchestras and any number of ensembles. Helsinki alone is the home of two symphony orchestras: the Finnish Radio Symphony Orchestra and the Helsinki Philharmonic Orchestra.

For a country of only 5 million people, this might be called nothing short of remarkable. But the seemingly disproportionate number of musicians is not, however, altogether coincidental. Finland takes its music seriously and has proved it through a generous policy of funding for musicians and musical institutes. Close to 130 such institutes, with a student body of 50,000 strong, offer free primary instruction, and talented graduates

Left, Esa-Pekka Salonen in action.

can audition for one of the country's seven free conservatories or the celebrated Sibelius Academy in Helsinki.

Professional opportunities for musicians are also wide. As well as holding regular concert seasons, Finland sponsors an extraordinary number of annual music festivals (with a happy preponderance during the long days of summer) attracting both native and foreign artists. Two recording companies concentrate on Finnish musicians.

At the same time, talented Finns are often lured abroad, thereby spreading the musical word. Along with Salonen, Finnish conductors are particularly in demand. The country boasts a goodly list of world-class maestros: Leif Segerstam, Paavo Berglund, Okko Kamu, Jukka-Pekka Saraste and Salonen are only a top five. In 1991, in fact, every Nordic capital had a symphony orchestra with a Finn as principal conductor.

Cello tradition: Finnish instrumentalists have also been winning global attention. Cellists, of whom Finland has an especially strong tradition, have done particularly well. Arto Noras, second prize winner at the 1966 Tchaikovsky Competition, and Erkki Rautio are renowned virtuosi. Now garnering laurels are Anssi Karttunen and Martti Roussi, both born in 1960. Cellists aren't the only ones. As a classical guitarist, Timo Korhonen (born 1965) is less known, but he looks set to fill the shoes of the legendary André Segovia. Pianist Ralf Gothoni commands a confirmed place in Europe, and celebrity should not wait long for pianist and composer Olli Mustonen (born 1967) – "Finland's Mozart" – who performed a concerto of his own composition with the Radio Symphony Orchestra at the age of 12.

After Sibelius and Salonen, however, it is Finland's singers who have gained the most fame. Foreign audiences adore Finnish basses: Matti Lehtinen in the 1950s, Martti Talvela before his premature death in 1989, and now Matti Salminen and Jaakko Ryhänen. Baritones Jorma Hynninen, Tom Krause and Walton Grönroos grace houses like the New York Metropolitan, and tenor Peter Lindroos is a familiar at London's Covent Garden and Berlin's Deutsche Opera. Nor have the sopranos missed out; Ritva Auvinen, Anita Välkki, Taru Valjakka and Karita Mattila have all attained stardom, and newcomer Soile Isokoski, winner of the

1988 Elly Ameling contest, is rapidly joining their ranks.

Unfortunately, in contrast with other countries where successful musicians usually continue to favour home stages, Finland has had trouble in holding on to its singers, especially the sopranos. The current National Opera House – a charming but nowhere near adequate house in size or acoustics – is undoubtedly a large part of the problem. Everyone expects things to change after a new opera house opens in 1993.

Famous festival: Even the most recalcitrant sopranos come home for the annual Savonlinna Opera Festival. Held in a 500-year-old castle, Savonlinna ranks among the foremost opera festivals in the world. Though its sopranos seek fame overseas the Finnish National Opera Company doesn't suffer too much, and it made operatic history in 1983 as the first foreign company to be invited to perform at New York's Met.

Vocal works have always been the backbone of the Finnish musical tradition, which may, perhaps, help explain why over 60 Finnish operas have been published since 1970 alone. Of them, at least three have already been performed in leading houses outside Finland: Aulis Sallinen's *Ratsumies* (*The Horseman*) and *Punainen Viiva* (*The Red Line*), and Joonas Kokkonen's *Viimeiset Kiusaukset* (*The Last Temptations*).

These operas offer additional proof that Finnish composition, too, lives on beyond Sibelius. Joonas Kokkonen might be called the country's pre-eminent living composer but, among so much excellence, it is hard to choose just one. Erik Bergman and Einojuhani Rautavaara, for example, are two other acclaimed senior composers. Among younger composers, Magnus Lindberg (born 1958) and Kaija Saariaho (born 1952) are of special note. Lindberg's *KRAFT* (1985) has won the music award of the Nordic Council and the Koussevitzky disc award and, after the premiere of *JOY* in 1991, *Le Monde de la Musique* called him "doubtlessly one of the best composers in the world of his age." Saariaho, an electro-acoustic innovator, has also received much acclaim.

Clearly, behind the blinding radiance of Sibelius stands a small country graced with an incomparable musical genius. It seems only a matter of time before a new Sibelius appears – or is recognised.

SIBELIUS

It cannot be easy for a man to find himself a figurehead in his country's search for an identity, yet it was this label rather than the simple genius of his music that many Finns tied on to their most famous composer, Jean Sibelius (1865–1957), during the years before Finnish independence. His tone poem *Finlandia* in particular became an emblem of everything Finnish, and this aura of reverence must have sometimes irked the composer.

Yet Sibelius did embody many things Finnish; even his ancestry took in areas of Finland as far apart as the coastal town of Loviisa, almost on the Russian border, the Swedish influence of Turku, the northwest coast of the Gulf of Bothnia and, nearer at hand, Häme province where he was born on one of the coldest days of December 1865. The family already had a daughter but Jean Sibelius was the first son of Hämeenlinna's doctor, Christian Gustaf Sibelius, and his wife Maria.

Though his father's family in Loviisa was wealthy, Dr Sibelius was better known for his medical care than as a financial manager and when, three years later, he died looking after his patients in the typhus epidemic that raged during Finland's last great famine, Maria Sibelius had little choice but to file for bankruptcy.

The family remained in Hämeenlinna. All three children (Christian was born after his father's death) showed musical talent, displaying their concert skills on family visits to Loviisa. The birthplace has a photograph from that period which shows the young Jean (violin), Linda (piano), and Christian (cello) during a recital.

Although it is simplistic to think of Sibelius as being solely influenced by the Finnish landscape, he was undoubtedly part of the late 19th-century movement of artists, writers and intellectuals who turned for inspiration to Finland's landscape and people, and its past. Yet, after the first performance of his early Kullervo symphony, which was based on Finnish folklore at the height of the national romantic movement, Sibelius withdrew the work from performance and it was not played

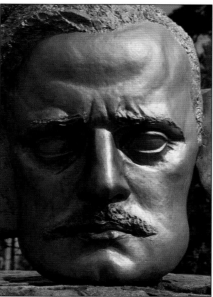

again until after his death. The great Sibelius scholar Erik Tawaststjerna insists that Sibelius moved in the mainstream of European music and was influenced by Beethoven, as well as Bruckner and Tchaikovsky. His relationship to Wagner's music could be described as love-hate.

Certainly Sibelius travelled to Bayreuth and Munich in the 1890s and planned an opera, something he did not achieve though some of its proposed music went into *The Swan of Tuonela*. He wrote his *First Symphony* just before the turn of the century and followed it with the popular *Second* in 1902, around which time he started to plan the *Violin Concerto*, now regarded by many as his greatest work. Its first performance in 1904, arranged hurriedly because Sibelius, who liked to live well, had financial problems, was not a success. Sibelius withdrew the work for revision.

Not long after, the family moved to Ainola, overlooking Lake Tuusula near Järvenpää, close to the retreat of his friend the artist Pekka Halonen. The site for Ainola (named after his wife Aino) was located by the painter Eero Järnefelt, Aino's brother, who skied out with the composer to see it. Another friend, the architect Lars Sonck, designed the house. By autumn, the composer, his wife and three young daughters had moved in, and Sibelius wrote some 150 works there, including the remaining symphonies.

Sibelius lived for 53 years at Ainola until his death in 1957. Life at Ainola could be sociable, and the small artistic colony spent much time in one another's houses. The atmosphere of Sibelius's home is quiet, as it was in his day.

To compose, Sibelius needed no musical instrument – though, for pleasure, he would play the grand piano with which his friends marked his 50th birthday. Music came from within, and he needed silence. His young daughters went away to friends and the servants crept around on tiptoe.

In the end, even the composer himself grew silent. From the final years of his life, Sibelius left no music. Until his death, there were constant rumours of one more symphony; but, though many believe Sibelius continued to compose, nothing can have satisfied him. The *Seventh Symphony* was his last.

"Literature is the country's interpreter. Literature is the nation's mirror. Without literature the nation is like a blind man, like a deaf mute."

– *Eino Leino, poet, novelist, playwright, 1910.*

The story of the past two centuries of Finnish literature is the story of a country struggling to find its voice and its identity. Mimicking Finland's political development, there have been peaks and troughs, high expectations and disappointments. Writers have expressed the fortunes of their country by veering from excessive romanticism to cynicism and realism. The written portrait of the Finn has covered the spectrum from noble hero to drunken buffoon.

The high expectations came first, partly fuelled by the blank canvas on which the first writers of the 19th century worked. Until that time, Finland's literary tradition had been primarily an oral one. Because there was no written precedent, writers had a free hand to invent the Finn on paper, and many made him a hero.

Johan Ludvig Runeberg (1804–77), Finland's national poet, offered just such a romantic vision of his countrymen. In his three collections of Swedish-language poems, *Dikter I–III* (*Poems*), and in his patriotic ballad series, *Fänrik Stål Sägner I–II* (*The Tales of Ensign Stål*), he created loyal, gracious and noble Finns. They were readily, even eagerly, embraced.

In the 1820s, Elias Lönnrot (1802–84) began a project which was to generate yet more national pride. Lönnrot travelled through Finland recording folk poetry, taking it from a potentially finite oral arena to a more permanent written state. The result, adapted and added to by Lönnrot himself, was the *Kalevala* of 1835 (now commonly called the "Old Kalevala"). A new, far longer version was published in 1849.

The *Kalevala* is often called "Finland's epic poem", which somewhat heightens readers' expectations. This poem is not a heroic epic on the scale of *The Odyssey* or *The Iliad*. It is a rag-bag of narratives, some sustained through several "poems". Others form light interludes, existing apparently

just to preserve old customs and old songs. The narrative line, where maintained, is itself interrupted by poetic "charms", some of which belong to the realms of a Shakespearian romantic comedy (a charm to stop a dog barking, a bee charm, a seed-sowing charm).

Lönnrot's real achievement is not so much the quality of the *Kalevala*, but how it raises the status of the Finn. Lönnrot's legendary Finn is portrayed as a participator in the creation of the world. The characters are larger than life, epic and modelled on classical figures with a Finnish twist. The context – the sea, farm, forest – is entirely Finnish.

The *Kalevala* managed to enact a national fiction-cum-history which stretched back to the beginning of time, and which did not include the humiliating details of real life – seemingly never-ending domination by foreign rulers. In Lönnrot's mythical Finland, power lay with the good and the just. Lönnrot compiled the work in the mid-18th century, yet it reads like a piece of literature which is as old as the classics or, at the very least, as old as the Norse sagas. It is trickier still for, because it is drawn from an oral tradition which is without date, it is impossible to question its veracity while under its spell.

At the same time, other Finnish-language writers like poet, novelist and dramatist Aleksis Kivi (1834–72) were celebrating the virtues of rural life, casting the ordinary people in the role of hero: true Finns led simple, virtuous lives among the forests, living harmoniously with nature.

By the early 20th century, real events began to cast doubts on this unimpeachable national character. Political achievements – especially that of independence – were quickly soured by subsequent developments and crises. It became the job of writers to find explanations and to come to terms with, or make sense of, events like the civil war, or the effects of industrialisation, that lay heavy on the nation's conscience and presented nothing but confusion.

During this time, although their forebears had laid the bedrock of the Finnish literary tradition, Swedish-language writers drifted away from the main pulse of Finnish writing, becoming more isolated and less politicised.

Some, like the poet Edith Södergran (1892–1923) nonetheless enjoyed considerable popularity and have been read widely in Scandinavia. Others, among them Christer Kihlman, author of *Den Blå Modern* (*The Blue Mother*) and *Dyre Prins* (*Sweet Prince*), and the creator of the Moomin troll books, Tove Jansson, show just how idiosyncratic and how diverse Swedish-Finnish writing has become.

Throughout the 20th century, mainstream Finnish writing continued to concern itself were imprisoned during World War II for, as the textbooks have it, "political reasons". Where now was the unifying vision of the faultless Finnish hero?

The years after the war expurgated many people's consciences. The fate of several hundred thousand refugees from Karelia was one literary theme. Undiluted criticism of the war appeared in Väinö Linna's hugely successful and controversial novel *The Unknown Soldier* (*Tuntematon sotilas*) as well as in the writing of Antti Hyry. Linna's book

with events in the world at large. The rise of the Nazis, combined with Finland's World War II allegiance with the Germans against the Russians, pricked literary consciences. In 1936, a Finnish-speaking literary group called The Wedge (*Kiila*), which counted among its members poets Viljo Kajava and Arvo Turtiainen, and prose-writer Elvi Sinervo, was formed. Much in the vein of their Finnish-language predecessors, the group wove working-class heroes and socialist principles into their writing. Many

Above, the Kalevala, Finland's national epic comes in many languages.

promotes the ordinary soldier as a near-innocent, the victim of his political masters and of his army superiors.

National therapy in such a public form has raised inevitable furores and discussion. By the 1960s, the general trends in writing were those of the rest of Europe – protest poetry, working-class novels, middle-class angst and, because of rural depopulation, a closer scrutiny of rural life.

Today, Finnish heroes are not paragons and they no longer have to act as vessels for the nation's pride. They are as troubled and beset by worries, as ludicrous and as human as the heroes of other literatures.

Swedish-speaking parents in Finland face hard choices. If their own Swedish mother tongue is to continue, their child will have to be bilingual. Should the child go to a Finnish-language nursery school? A Swedish-language secondary school? Or what? But places at schools may be limited, so there could be no real choice at all.

Some parents succumb to the harsh facts of life. Finnish, they argue, is the dominant language, the language of power, so their children should be brought up to speak only

is described as a "bilingual" nation, it means that Swedo-Finns can speak both Finnish and Swedish. Finnish-speaking Finns more often speak English than Swedish.

At first glance, nevertheless, it would appear that the linguistic minority is adequately catered for. Swedo-Finns can attend Finnish schools and be taught in Swedish; they can read Finnish newspapers published in Swedish and listen to Swedish-language programmes on Finnish radio stations. But there are problems. Swedish-speaking

Finnish. Equally, the children of Swedish-speaking parents may opt to be more involved with Finnish than Swedish, through their choice of friends, youth clubs, and colleges of further education.

This is something visitors to Finland find difficult to understand. Swedish-speaking, or Swedo-Finns as they are described by the government, are not immigrants, nor are they Swedes. They may not even have any family connections with Sweden. They are Swedish-speaking Finns whose first language is Swedish but who can also speak Finnish, and who are usually obliged to do so at work and outside the home. When Finland

schools are few, and are often some distance from the Swedo-Finnish home.

Linguistic roots: Swedish speakers are a throwback to the 700 years when Finland was the eastern part of the Kingdom of Sweden. Then, and even during the time when Finland was a Grand Duchy of Russia, from 1808 to independence in 1917, Swedish was the official language, the language of the civil service, of the law, of higher education, at the University of Turku (Åbo in Swedish), and of the monied classes. There was also a sizeable Swedish-speaking rural population, largely in the west and south.

Fed by students from the university, Finnish cultural life was dominated by Swedish-speakers too. It was not until 1828 that Turku University established a Finnish language lectureship, and not until 1850 that a professorship of Finnish was introduced.

Because the Swedish language held sway in this way, it was the principal language of the nascent Finnish mid-19th century cultural and political life. Early political activists like the Fennomen, who supported the Finnish language and campaigned for its recognition as an official language, often faced the paradox that they themselves were Swedish-speakers whose love of their country was paramount. A considerable number of 19th-century cultural ambassadors, painters and writers, who searched for an artistic expression of Finnish nationalism, were also Swedish-speakers.

It was not surprising, therefore, that when Finland gained its independence, the 1919 Constitution decreed that Finland should have two offical national languages: Finnish and Swedish. At that time, Swedish-speakers accounted for 12 percent of the Finnish population. Today, the figure has shrunk to 6 percent. Only 300,000 people are now Swedo-Finns, whose mother tongue is Swedish and who speak Swedish at home.

The Swedo-Finnish town of Porvoo (Borgå in Swedish) was, and continues to be, a hub of Swedo-Finnish life. Its links with pre-Independence Finnish nationalism are strong. The student, Eugen Schauman, who assassinated the hated Russian Governor General Bobrikov in 1904, is buried in the town's graveyard. Porvoo was the birthplace of Swedo-Finnish painter Albert Edelfelt (1854–1905), one of the earliest and most successful Finnish painters. Finland's national poet, the Swedish-speaking and writing Johan Ludwig Runeberg (1804–77), taught there for 20 years. The opening words of his Swedish-language *Fänrik Ståls Sägner* (Tales of Ensign Stål) became Finland's national anthem (*Vårt Land*, or *Maamme* in Finnish). Runeberg is the perfect illustration of the fact that Swedo-Finns consider themselves as Finnish as Finnish-speaking Finns.

Left, the League of Nations in Geneva meets to decide Åland's disputed status in 1921. Right, Gallen-Kallela's scenes from *The Kalevala* in the National Museum.

The compiler of the epic poem the *Kalevala*, Elias Lönnrot (1802–84), was born in Nyland in the southwest and has a Swedish name. Yet he was a great champion of the Finnish language and folklore and went on to become Professor of Finnish at Helsinki University. He also produced a Swedish-Finnish dictionary, which is credited with establishing a Finnish literary language.

With encouragement from individuals like Czar Alexander II, who made it official in 1863, Finnish gradually became the dominant language and the language of power. Political disputes over the two languages and their relative prominence flared up from time to time, especially in the 1920s and

1930s when it became a central political issue. Accusations that Swedo-Finns were wealthy or disproportionately powerful have rumbled on over the decades. It is noticeable, however, that Finnish history books often play down the national and cultural contribution made by Swedo-Finns.

Definite decline: Sadly, the population of Swedo-Finns is dying out. There are signs that stalwarts of Swedo-Finnish culture – general-interest newspapers, for example – are on the decline. In 1960, there were 21 Swedish language newspapers (182 Finnish); in 1988, the figure was 14 (with 374 Finnish publications). Helsinki's Finnish newspaper *Helsingin Sanomat* has a circulation of 457,000, while the Swedish-language Helsinki equivalent, *Hufvudstadsbladet*, manages 67,000.

Because the definition of a Swedo-Finn within Finland tends to be linguistic rather than broadly cultural, there has been little alarm at the prospect of the Swedo-Finnish population eventually dying out altogether. Yet the danger is there. Factors such as the growing number of "mixed marriages" between Finnish and Swedish speakers speed the decline, primarily because Finnish-speakers often do not have the will to learn Swedish. They prefer English, the glamorous language of movies and pop songs.

The dwindling numbers of Swedo-Finns cluster around four main regions in the southwestern and western coastal areas – Nyland, Åboland and its principal city Turku (Åbo) and Österbotten. Here, Swedo-Finns account for about 20 percent of the population and the law requires that they are adequately catered for.

Unique situation: The case of the Åland Islands, which lie off the southwest of Finland almost halfway to Sweden, is unique. Though this is Finnish territory, the roles are reversed. When Finland became independent in 1917, the Ålanders' background and culture were (and are) Swedish and they

voted overwhelmingly in a referendum to become part of Sweden. After much wrangling, the matter went to the infant League of Nations in the early 1920s and, in the way of international bodies, it complicated what could then have been a relatively simple settlement by deciding that the Åland Islands remain Finnish but that the islanders' Swedish language would be safeguarded.

The official language, therefore, is Swedish, and Swedish culture is preserved by law. The 24,000 Ålanders have their own parliament and government to rule their internal affairs, using an appropriate proportion of the Finnish budget. They also send a member to the main Parliament in Helsinki.

In terms of political representation for mainland Swedo-Finns, the Swedish People's Party (SFP) was founded in 1906. Other political parties claim to be multilingual or bilingual parties, but the SFP is the most obvious repesentative of Swedo-Finns. Its power base has been constant in recent years. It won 5.3 percent of votes cast in the 1987 parliamentary elections (13 seats) and 5.4 percent (11 seats) in 1991.

Cabinet office: Frequent coalition governments have resulted in some Cabinet prominence for SFP Members of Parliament. Ole Norrback has held a number of ministerial posts, including that of Minister of Transport and Communcations in 1991. A source of some curiosity because of the perceived paradox of her sex and her job, the SFP's Elisabeth Rehn was appointed as Minister of Defence. Both are obviously obliged to conduct Finland's cabinet business in Finnish.

Talk to Swedo-Finns about the personal problems of being a linguistic minority and they will often tell you of the difficulties of not being able to express themselves fully in both languages. Although technically bilingual in Swedish and Finnish, they know the frustrations of fishing for a specific word to convey a meaning in one language and being able to recall that word only in the other language. The plus side is that some Swedo-Finns, used to switching from Swedish to Finnish, become very able linguists, taking on board German, English, French, Danish and Norwegian without too much effort.

Left, Swedish Folk Partiet leader, Ole Norrback addresses a rally. Right, road sign, giving Swedish language first.

GÄLLER EJ
KYRKOBESÖKARE
EI KOSKE
KIRKOSSA KÄVIJÖITÄ

THE SAMI AND THEIR LAND

For the Sami (Lapps), who on the whole prefer to mind their own business and hope other people will mind theirs, the second half of the 20th century has brought mixed blessings, putting further pressure on a fragile ecology already under threat. Against that, the many and huge changes have also triggered among them a much greater awareness of their own identity.

Most specialists agree the Sami descend from a people who, following the retreating edge of the continental ice, reached Finland and East Karelia in the latter millennia BC. Their contacts with an indigenous proto-Sami people gave birth to the earliest Sami culture. Later came the Finns, also speaking a Finno-Ugric tongue, and thus sharing with them a common if remote linguistic heritage originating in the Ural mountains.

The cornerstone of early Sami society was the *siida*, a community of several families and the territories in which they co-operatively hunted, trapped and fished. Place names in southern and central Finland suggest that Sami communities thrived until the Middle Ages. But as the Finnish settlers moved in, so the Sami – those who were not assimilated – moved on, ever northwards. In Finland today they are concentrated in northern Lapland around Utsjoki, Karasjoki, Inari and Enontekiö. Based on language criteria there are an estimated 5,700 Sami people in Finland, considerably fewer than in neighbouring Sweden and Norway.

The Sami home in Lapland (Lappi) is Finland's northernmost province and covers nearly a third of the country's total area, most of it north of the Arctic Circle. Away from the few towns and scattered communities its extraordinary beauty is still predominantly primeval wilderness. Extensive swamps and forests of conifer and birch rise in the far north to bareheaded fells, the highest topping 4,270 ft (1,300 metres); all this is laced by swift rivers and streams and punctuated by lakes and pools.

You may think of it as the land of the

midnight sun which, depending on latitude (and cloud cover), is visible for up to 70 summer days. In winter there is an almost equivalent sunless period, tempered at times by the flickering veils of the Northern Lights; or, around midday, by the lingering dawn effects from the invisible sun; or the inescapable, all-pervading whiteness of the snow. Spring is a swift green renaissance in the wake of the big thaw. And autumn flares in colours so spectacular the Finns have a special term for it: *ruska*.

You may also think of it as the land of the Lapps. They, however, prefer their own name for themselves: Sami (pronounced *Sah-mi*) a preference which is being increasingly respected. Today the Sami's territory extends across northern Scandinavia and into the northwest corner of Russia.

Early development: Inevitably the Sami's more fragile, less structured society was increasingly threatened by rivalry with the Finnish newcomers over natural resources, by growing contact with Finnish social organisation and, not least, the effects of Finland's innumerable wars. The nomadism associated with the Sami people of northern

Norway and Sweden has never been so widely practised among the predominantly Forest Sami of Finland's Lapland and, gradually, an economy based almost exclusively on hunting and fishing evolved into one dominated by reindeer husbandry as the wild herds once vigorously hunted were semi-domesticated. Quite early on, many Sami adopted the more settled life of the Finns, often keeping a few cattle and tilling scraps of soil to grow oats and potato, the only viable crops in these latitudes. In reverse, many northern Finns have also opted for the reindeer economy.

This versatile beast has always represented very much more than a meal on four

legs, its skin contributing to bedding and winter clothing, antlers and bones raw materials for tools and utensils. It also provided a major means of transport, sledge-hauling across the winter snows, only recently ousted by the noisy and unbeautiful motorised skidoo. So, even now, the annual cycle of the reindeer – rutting, herding, separating, slaughtering, calving, marking – to a large extent moulds the north Lapland calendar. The winter round-ups are among Europe's most colourful events, resembling nothing so much as scenes from a Wild West film transposed to an Arctic setting.

Integral to early Sami culture were the

shamanist beliefs deeply rooted in the power and mysteries of nature which so profoundly affected all aspects of their lives. Everything it was believed, whether living or inanimate, had a soul and the spiritual world was as real as the material one. The wise man skilled in interpreting one world to the other was the *noaide*, and the magic drum with its pictorial symbols was the instrument with which he achieved a state of ecstasy, thus enabling him to enter the spirit world.

Fire and brimstone: Not surprisingly, as soon as they began to penetrate these remote regions, religious missions made every effort to discourage such goings-on; yet, despite compulsory drum-burning and other deterrents, shamanism survived well into the 19th century. Its eventual submission was largely due to the teachings of Lars Levi Laestadius whose emotion-charged, fire-and-brimstone form of Christian worship must have struck a familiar chord among the Sami. The old gods gave way to the new and today many of the brightest events on the Lapland calendar are associated with church festivals – notably Lady Day and Easter: popular times for Sami weddings, traditional activities such as lasso competitions and reindeer races, and a general get-together for widely scattered families.

In addition to God, the religious missions brought education. The Sami's rich oral tradition ensured that a plentitude of tales and legends as well as centuries of acquired wisdom were passed from one generation to the next. There was also their simple brand of pictorial art. Very special to Sami culture – and surviving still – is the yoik, a kind of yodelling chant, each a unique improvised tribute to an event, a landscape, an emotion, a person.

Sami culture has always lacked early written sources, and the first books in Sami were exclusively of a religious nature. Later came grammars and dictionaries and, finally, though not until well into the 20th century, the beginnings of a Sami literature.

No century has left a greater impact on Lapland than this one. The rebuilding programme following the devastation wreaked by World War II marked the beginning of changes that have altered its face forever. Since 1945, Lapland's population has soared to nearly 200,000 (predominantly Finns), though in an area of nearly 38,600 sq. miles

(100,000 sq. km) this is hardly overcrowded.

The administrative capital of Rovaniemi has been virtually rebuilt and expanded to take in a satellite sprawl of light industry. A score of communities has burgeoned from scattered hamlets into modern mini-townships. A network of new or improved roads penetrates regions only accessible a few decades ago by foot or ski. Rivers, notably the Kemi, have been tamed for their hydroelectric power. Two large man-made lakes, Lokka and Porttipahta, add new permanent patches of blue to the Lapland map. And a trickle of visitors has grown into a steady stream, spawning a whole range of facilities.

Working together: Organisations dedicated

tion for the first time acquired an assembly – the Sami Parliament – elected by them from among themselves. Its role remains limited since it has no legislative mandate, but it does provide a forum for promoting Sami concerns. Paramount among these are their rights to territory and its traditional usage in northern Lapland – age-old rights which have been eroded (though never legally removed) over the centuries.

Ironically, education has brought its own threat to Sami culture as youngsters increasingly abandon traditional occupations to enter almost every branch of trade and the professions. On the other hand, Finland's Sami today have their own publication

to Sami interests go back to around the turn of the century but their efforts were relatively uncoordinated until the 1950s. In 1956, the Nordic Sami Council was founded to "promote cooperation on Sami issues between Finland, Norway and Sweden." It was the first body to provide all Sami with a common platform from which to coordinate their aims and inform the world at large. A few years later a State Commission for Sami Affairs was established by the Finnish government and in 1973 Finland's Sami population

Left, Sami man wearing traditional costume.
Above, reindeer round-up at Vuotso, Lapland.

(*Sápmelias*, founded 1934) theatre, arts and crafts organisations. In the field of music, the yoik has begun to make strange alliances with modern music forms. And in 1991 for the first time a Finnish Sami writer, Nils-Aslak Valkeapää, was awarded the Nordic Council prize for literature.

One may regret the inevitable adulteration of a culture increasingly under pressure as the 21st century draws closer. One may, on the other hand, prefer to notice that the influences can work both ways. Perhaps people outside Finland are only just beginning to realise the enriching potential emerging from the Sami's ancient culture.

FROM RALLY DRIVERS TO RUNNERS

Take any group of rally drivers – men and women who drive their cars into a pulp through forest, desert and farm tracks – and among them you are likely to find a puzzlingly high number of Finns. The top Finnish rally stars, Ari Vatanen, Hannu Mikkola and Markku Alen, may be known only to lovers of motoring sports, but it's still true that more people outside Finland could probably name one of them than could identify the country's current prime minister.

The British magazine *Motoring News* has

(which certainly comes in useful in the more circuitous rally routes) and must have a distinct advantage over someone who comes from a more "civilised" country.

Finally, one must look beyond the physical features of the country and examine the Finnish personality. There is one feature of the Finnish character which the Finns themselves call *sisu*, a quality so central to their being as to make a dictionary definition nearly impossible. Roughly speaking, it conjures up an enigmatically tough, independ-

called the Finnish rallyers "devils from the backwoods". Rally enthusiasts, from fans to the competing drivers, have marvelled at the way the Finns seem to give their heart and soul to the sport.

No one has satisfactorily explained why Finns should excel in this particular field, but the answers perhaps apply to all successful Finnish athletes: the fact that Finns come from a quiet northerly country that feels a need to make its mark on the world must have something to do with it. Another reason is the landscape: anyone who can orientate himself or herself in the Finnish wilderness already has a built-in sense of navigation

ent personality. Hand in hand with the toughness is staying power under the most adverse conditions.

Sisu has certainly played its role in Finland's most important pursuit: independence itself. From the republic's very early days – in fact, even before Finnish independence – sport and freedom were inseparably intertwined.

Outstanding performance in sport is a point of national pride which dates back at least to the Stockholm Olympics of 1912 (the last before World War I), when Finland was still part of Russia. During those games, the Finnish medal winners far outstripped the

Russian winners, gaining 23 medals against the Russians' three, although officially Finland and Russia were competing under the same flag.

At the 1912 Games, the Finnish competitors made a point of leaving a 50-metre gap between themselves and the Russians in the Games' opening ceremonies. They also dared to raise a Finnish flag at the medal ceremonies, the first sign that the yearning for Finnish independence was not to be taken lightly. The gesture was not in vain: the breaker and medal winner (with four golds), Nurmi first competed in the 1920 Olympics. He died in the 1970s. Variously known as the Flying Finn, the Phantom Finn, and the Phenomenal Finn, he is still remembered for his extraordinary running style, his speed, and his tough character. That great champion of the Olympics movement Avery Brundage said of Nurmi: "No one seeing Nurmi's running style can ever forget him. His running rhythm was his endurance secret; it went beyond majestic movement, and the

world took notice. Five years later, Finland was an independent republic.

As proof of their durability, Jalmari Kivenheimo, was still exercising and running every day even after his 100th birthday. His more famous, but not quite as long-lived running mate, Hannes Kolehmainen, scored gold in 1912. But the Finnish runner whose name has been famous for most of the 20th century was just under competition age in 1912: Paavo Nurmi. A multiple world record

Left, Hannu Mikkola, winner of China's first Road Rally. **Above**, ski-jumper Matti Nykänen flies over the crowd.

mathematical use of time."

John Virtanen, one of Nurmi's biographers, adds the observation that Nurmi seemed to disregard gravity as he ran. One reason for this was his incredibly long stride, which was measured, during a one-mile race, at 88½ inches (225 cm).

Nurmi had running in his blood from an early age. Although his father, a religious man, didn't approve of running, believing it to be a frivolous pastime, Nurmi exerted his independence and spent every spare moment running with boys in his neighbourhood. He ran in competitions at school, too, and also alone in the woods. John Virtanen suggests that sports competition between Finnish-speaking Finns and Swedish-speaking Finns was particularly keen in Turku, Nurmi's home town in southwest and heavily Swedish-speaking Finland.

If indeed some of Nurmi's determination was spurred by local ethnic competition, it is interesting to note that later, according to Virtanen, "no ambassador could have been more effective than Nurmi" in attracting positive attention and even investment to the fledgling Finnish republic while it struggled to build a political and economic life for itself.

Nurmi's father died when Paavo was in his early teens, and from then economic circum-

stances forced the boy to work to support his family while he was still attending school. But, as he lifted heavy loads and worked under what were no doubt appalling sweatshop conditions, Nurmi used to tell himself that all physical labour was good for his dream of being a champion runner.

Later on in his life, when asked about the relationship between Finnish independence and the performance of Finnish athletes in the early part of the 20th century, Nurmi said: "The higher the standard of living in a country, the weaker the results often are in the events which call for work and effort. I would like to warn this new generation: Do

not let the comfortable life make you lazy! Do not let the new means of transport kill your instinct for physical exercise! Too many young people get used to loafing and driving in cars even for short distances. I believe that I must thank sports for the fact that I am an independent, self-supporting man."

Despite his warnings, Finns still perform remarkably well in sport. There is the ski jumper Matti Nykänen, the javelin thrower Seppo Räty, and the rower Pertti Karppinen, all gold medalists in recent Olympics. However, some old-timers hold with Nurmi's views and believe that, because of the complacency of the generations that succeeded him, Finland will never produce another athlete in Nurmi's class.

The Finnish sport tradition is unlikely to die out, though, because it is honoured and well established, engrained in every child from the moment he or she is put on skis at the age of two. In the centuries before motorisation, Finns often invented athletic ways to get across their great distances and traverse their vast forests and lakes. The best known was the church boat race, a rowing competition between villagers to see who would arrive at church first.

Sport was associated with religion at other times of the year, too. At Easter, there were competitions in tug-of-war and high and long jumping, while Christmas was for shows of strength by weight lifters and plough pullers. Finland has always produced healthy crops of cross-country skiers. Even now, cross-country skiing is as much a form of transportation as an enjoyable winter pastime.

Finnish schools today have rigorous sports programmes and, as Finnish officialdom likes to say, sport is the country's biggest youth movement. Whether or not this is true, anyone visiting Finland will be amazed and impressed by the number of sports institutes scattered around even the remotest districts of the country, not to mention the skiers practising on roller skis throughout summer and windsurfers converted to ice surfers in the winter.

Left, Eero Mäntyranta – three times gold medallist in the Winter Olympics of 1960, 1964 and 1968. **Right**, the great athelete Paavo Nurmi lights the Olympic flame at the 1952 Helsinki Olympics.

FOOD FROM SEA AND FOREST

Not so long ago, there was a saying that the Finns' salad was a sausage. Although the Finnish diet has come a long way in the past few decades, fresh fruit and vegetables are a relatively recent event on the table. Nearly all are expensive imports or hothouse products, save for the brief, if abundant, appearance of summer berries and mushrooms.

If lucky, you'll find homes and restaurants where unbeatably fresh country fare is served. The enormous expanses of Finnish wilderness yield up reindeer, pheasant, snow grouse, and hare. The forests and fields are the source of the wild berries and mushrooms from which countless sauces, compotes, garnishes, and fresh salads are made. Wild raspberries, strawberries, and blueberries take over the markets in summer. Mushrooms include the cantarelle, morel, russula, and boleti. Finnish cuisine bursts into glory in these late summer months when the earth and sea finally warm up enough to produce a bounty of edibles to delight the most discriminating of palates.

On more mundane tables, alas, some unembellished form of beef or pork and the ever-present boiled potatoes dominate the hot dishes. Luncheon is for many the main meal; dinner may consist simply of dark bread with sausage or cheese. Even the less imaginative cooks, though, can be wonderful bakers. Homemade bread is commonplace. Cakes and pastries are nearly always included in any offer of coffee, the drinking of which is practically a rite.

Fabulous seafood: Fish and shellfish are wonderful, especially if you can get to a market or restaurant where it is fresh. Smoked cod, shrimp rolls, gravlax (salmon cured in a special way), and marinated rainbow trout are some of the ways fish is eaten cold. Warm, there's charcoal grilled herring (*hiilillä paistetut silakat*), salmon basted in butter in the oven (*uun issa paistettua lohta*), warmed trout and boiled egg served in a delicate pie crust (*kalapiirakka*), and a dozen other varieties of fresh and saltwater fish.

Preceding pages: smoked fish is a Baltic delicacy. **Left**, crayfish celebration. **Right**, preparing traditional food.

One of the most delectable of these foods is the crayfish (*rapu*), appreciation of which is heightened by the fact that its season is so fleeting. The fishermen always know when it is about to begin; others must watch the newspapers and the markets to know when the season has officially opened. It begins in late July and goes on to the end of August, fortunately, a time when a lot of visitors are around to indulge alongside the Finns, who use the *rapupäivät* as an excuse to see out the summer in great festivity. For there is no such thing as merely eating a crayfish, An entire ceremony, nay a ritual, is involved.

Celebrate crayfish: A crayfish feast usually begins in late afternoon or early evening. In both restaurants and private homes there are always armloads of fresh dill to accompany it. The crayfish are steamed and then brought out on giant, warmed dishes, claws akimbo.

Then out comes the inevitable partner: schnapps. Like schnapps anywhere, the Finnish version is lethal, especially when drunk in quantities, which it always is during *rapupäivät*. There may also be vodka, wine, and beer, but the schnapps is crucial. It is especially hard to come away from the feast sober because you spend so much time at table working to get at the meat of the crayfish. You will probably hear the virtues of female crayfish extolled over those of the male. Females reputedly have more meat on their posteriors but, whether this fable is apocryphal or based on sound biological fact, few have dared ask. In any case, the end result is the same: one is truly sated, and truly hung over the following day.

What you'll probably need then is a good breakfast to help recovery. Breakfast at home is usually simple; tea with bread and butter, or ham. The restaurant version of the breakfast, lunch, brunch or smörgåsbord is called *seisova pöytä* or *voileipäpöytä*, and

Ethnic choices: If you eat out in Finland, you'll find the variety of ethnic cuisines limited. Russian and Chinese are probably the most popular, though recently a more diverse variety of Asian restaurants have sprung up. As well, you'll find some fanciful hybrids: at one restaurant in Lapland, the chef claims to serve French, Lappish, and Israeli fare. Then there is pizza. Finns adore it, and consume it at home (homemade) and in restaurants in quantity.

One dish you'll find in homes but probably never in a restaurant is the *maksalaatikko* or liver casserole, delicately spiced and served hot with *perunalaatikko*, a puréed sweetened potato casserole.

can be outstandingly bad or outstandingly good. Marinated fish, fresh ham, and a good assortment of cheeses can make it a delight; processed meat and stale bread and cereal may occasionally be all that's on offer.

Whatever the choice, if a meal is included at your hotel, you should make the most of it as Finnish food is the most expensive in the world, with retail food prices 45 percent percent higher than elsewhere in the West and restaurant prices considerably more so. The reasons for the high cost are high agricultural subsidies to farmers, restrained by the shortest growing season in Europe – and steeply protective taxes on imported foods.

Other variations will depend on where in the country you are, the most notable deviation being Lapland, where you will find quite a large variety of dishes based on reindeer. *Poronkäristys* is a rich reindeer stew, and *poron piiras* is braised reindeer, onions, and mushrooms on a flaky crust.

Don't miss yoghurt and other cream and dairy products which are excellent and fresh here; the quarks, crème fraîches and smetana creams are especially good. And whatever the season, Finns will always eat ice cream.

Above, rooftop café in Helsinki. **Right**, Finnish barmen can loom large.

WHY DO THE FINNS DRINK SO MUCH?

One cannot walk through the streets of Helsinki without noticing the drunks. Holding wobbling court in the railroad station tunnel, in parks, at street corners, or outside bars they have been forbidden entrance to, they are omnipresent.

Finns drink to get drunk. Or at least that's what the Finns themselves say. Where getting smashed is possible, getting tipsy just won't do. It's a chronic problem, and recent statistics show it is not going away. Young Finns are drinking more and starting to drink earlier, and sociologists have not yet come up with a plausible explanation as to why. Popular theory has it that the new generation of alcoholics got hooked into the materialism and wealth of the 1980s in a serious way and, now that wealth is declining, they have large empty holes that badly need filling – with alcohol.

Countering the drinkers, there are also a lot of teetotallers. One can see their point. If you grow up in a place where an average bottle of whisky costs well over 140 Finnish marks (£20) and the result of imbibing seems to be to crash to the floor with a thud of skull on concrete, drinking might not appeal. Some blame strict Lutheran mores – the belief that there's no such thing as sinning just a little – for

the go-all-the-way attitude toward drink. But Finns are lackadaisical churchgoers, so at best this is only a partial explanation.

There *are* Finns who drink socially, and in moderation. The average Finnish consumption of alcohol may not even hit alarming levels by international standards and comparisons. But the persistent drunks are *determinedly* drunk, regardless of alcohol prices that should be prohibitive – double what they are in most Western countries – but clearly are not.

Ten percent of state revenue is raised through alcohol sales, a statistic which reflects a sharp business acumen on the part of the state. For high prices have never dampened Finnish alcoholism; they merely impoverish the determined drinkers and, if anything, encourage more "booze" cruises

to Tallinn and Stockholm, where alcohol is duty-free (though even then expensive by most world standards) and drinking continues unabated.

Since the early 1950s when prices were set to rise to counter each consumption surge, the average per capita consumption of alcohol increased by nearly four-fold. High prices will never cure the ills of alcoholism, yet the government continues to take the drinker for everything he or she has.

No one has ever clearly determined what it is that makes the Finn drink such lethal quantities, a habit shared by compatriots who live at equally high latitudes, the Norwegians, Swedes, and Russians. The finger has been pointed at hereditary inclination. It has also been pointed at weather and darkness, although there are no indications that drinking lessens any in the summer when the days are sunny and long.

Another twist of logic in this unending debate on how to curb relentless drinking is that Alko, the state liquor monopoly, has no opening hours on summer Saturdays, but is open Monday–Saturday in the winter. (The off-licence does not exist in Finland, but grocers sell medium beer; then there is always the pricier option, bars and restaurants.) So people stock up even if it costs them a king's ransom to do so, for drinking outdoors on a summer Saturday is after all one of life's great pleasures. Note that Labour Day (1 May), Midsummer (late June), and the crayfish season are all red-letter drinking occasions.

In the end, it seems that the only effective control is the Finnish doorman, as ever present as the drunk. Usually young and strong, these men keep the already-soused out of bars and restaurants, and rapidly deport anyone who becomes zealously drunk while within. They have a lot of power, these chaps, and you learn to both love and resent them – depending on which side of the breathalyser you are.

With this wash of alcohol, what about drunken driving? Finns rarely attempt to drive after having a drink – a case of official discouragement having the desired effect: the law hands out stiff prison terms for the offence, with almost no hope of appeal. That's the silver lining: in Finland, you are more likely to trip over a drunk in the street than be overtaken by one on the motorway.

IN DEFENCE OF GREENNESS

Finns have long looked to their country's natural environment for a sense of national identity. The national anthem celebrates the country's summer landscape; its blue and white flag is said to represent the white snow of winter and the blue lakes of summer; literature, fine art, design and architecture have all drawn on the environment for a Finnish idiom.

As the environmental campaigner Martti Arkko put it in 1990: "We depend on nature and the environment for everything. If we allow our forests and lakes to become polluted, our Finnishness will disappear too. The hearts of the Finnish people lie in the lakes and forests. They are our identity, our capital and riches."

The defence of Finland's lakes is high on the political agenda, looked on as a battle to preserve nationhood and to save the country's greatest assets and, as a race, Finns really care. Surveys in the late 1980s indicated that more than half of the population was willing to support civic action to protect the environment. Outstripping education, health and housing, the environment came second only to employment on the list of subjects of major public concern.

Enter the politicians: The environment became a political issue in the 1980s and has continued so into the 1990s. In 1987, the Green League won four parliamentary seats (or 4 percent of the votes). In the 1991 general election, this figure rose to 10 seats (and nearly 7 percent of the votes). Although they won no seats, two other parties, the Ecological Party and the Party for Pensioners and Green Mutual Responsibility, also stood on an eco-ticket. For other parties, too, a "green" Finland became a crucial element.

Public concern for the natural environment is nothing new in Finland. Like other Nordic countries, civic organisations have been committed to protection for many years. The Finnish Nature Conservation Association, which became the Finnish Environmental Protection Association (FEPA) was founded in 1938, taking as its brief the

creation of nature reserves and the preservation of rare plants. In its present form, the FEPA has around 16 regional and 170 local branches. A sister organisation, Natur och Miljö (Nature and the Environment) exists for Swedish-speakers.

Alarming incidents: As long ago as the early days of national independence, the young republic introduced legal protection for the forests and threatened species, and the Forestry Act of 1886, which was intended to curb wasteful uses of the forests, pre-dated the republic by 30 years. Later laws prohibited the devastation of forests and defended threatened forests areas. Yet, when the owners of the private Lake Koijärvi decided to drain it, people who protested were prosecuted for civil disobedience.

The Ministry of the Environment was set up in 1983, and the 1980s was the decade when the government surveyed, theorised, and made policies and assessments. Their conclusions appeared in the 1987 National Report on Environmental Protection in Finland, a substantial overview of the state of the environment. It identified many problems and put forward suggestions for controls, concluding: "General environmental protection goals have been comparatively little considered in Finland, especially from a long-term perspective."

Finland's problems are the basic ones shared by industrial nations everywhere: air and water pollution, energy conservation, the despoilation of the natural landscape, endangered species and waste management. Doom-laden though this may sound, it is well to remember that, by comparison with the really polluted areas of Europe, Finland is a model of purity. Where the country does suffer, perhaps more acutely than others, is from the atmospheric and water pollution of its near-neighbours. The Soviet Union is the principal offender, but Poland and what was the German Democratic Republic have also contributed to the pollution of the Baltic Sea.

Since the 1987 report, the government has acted on some of its suggestions. There has been more talk – conferences and summits on the state of the Baltic, on the Arctic and on acidification – and Finland has put its clean-

__Preceding pages__: at the heart of Finland's forests. __Left__, Pyhähakki National Park.

air and clean-water industrial technology at the disposal of the USSR and Eastern Europe. Finland has also agreed to waive some of Poland's debt if, instead, that country re-invests in anti-pollution measures. In the wake of pollution from the Chernobyl tragedy, which Finland was the first Western country to detect, a multi-country early warning charter has been signed.

Driving through Finland, you might feel there is little cause for concern about its endless green forests and lakes, but the Finns nevertheless brought a Wilderness Act into force in February 1991 to defend the areas which remain in their natural state. The Act designated as "wilderness" 12 areas in

Lapland, each roadless and some 380,000 acres (150,000 hectares) in size. Protected zones now account for nearly one-third of Lapland's area. Forestry will be restricted here and limited to "natural forestry" only – that is forestry where operations are adapted to the natural development of the forest. No extensive felling, no clearing, and natural regeneration are the prime components.

Finnish forestry accounts for 78 percent of the total land area (90,000 sq. miles/230,000 sq. km). It is Finland's largest resource and the country's major export, and forestry and mining provide a considerable proportion of the country's income. Yet, potentially, for-

estry, timber processes, and mining can do the most environmental damage.

Planting, bog-draining for plantations, fertilising, and felling have all had severe consequences, changing natural habitats and the balance of Finland's water courses, and over-exploiting the soil. Responsible forest management, planned on a national scale, has been the government's solution but, as the state owns only some 27 percent of the forests, it has also had to offer incentives for private owners to subscribe to the national plan. The government hopes that by the end of the 20th century, state-initiated plans will cover 90 percent of privately-owned forests.

While afforestation and exploitation of the forests have spoiled some habitats, the trees are themselves threatened by air pollution, or acidification ("acid rain"). Like other countries, Finland has legal limits designed to control industrial emissions. Effective policing of these emissions and the question of whether the limits are pitched at an acceptable level are the nub of the issue. Environmentalists push for tighter controls, setting the environment before economics. Industry argues for economically "realistic" targets.

The green sanctuaries of Finland's forests are also Finland's playgrounds. The right of common access permits free access and allows the picking of berries and mushrooms, which is a national summer pastime. But greater use of the forests for recreation brings more litter and different forms of pollution, such as the noise of too many vehicles, and the selfish drivers who thoughtlessly plough their vehicles through uncharted territory.

In Lapland, there is a different cycle of difficulties and paradoxes. The cultural traditions and the livelihood of the Sami, or Lapps, at one and the same time contribute to environmental damage and are threatened by it. Their reindeer herds are a fundamental part of the Sami's lives. Chernobyl was a disaster and meant that hundreds had to be slaughtered. Yet, in that same summer of 1985, the Sami reindeer herds exceeded reindeer quotas (introduced to prevent overgrazing and the destruction of young trees) by almost 100,000. Another contradictory factor is the predators – wolves, lynx, eagles, wolverine – which are protected by the government but seen by the Sami as a threat to their reindeer and so best killed.

"Green" policies have for some time been part of everyday Finnish life. Recycling schemes and attempts to improve house insulation continue, and the government has repeated its commitment to public transport. If you want to cause a heated argument, try a casual mention of a subject such as the construction of a fifth nuclear power station – a proposal which has been resisted powerfully in the wake of the Chernobyl disaster. New worries, such as the damage salt on winter roads may do to the water courses, also rear up regularly. The Baltic Sea is an ongoing concern, and global environmental catastrophes continue to preoccupy Finns, as they do people everywhere.

resurfacing. Other experiments have involved research into biodegradable plastic – especially biodegradable carrier bags – for plastics, as a sideline of Finland's oil refineries, are a Finnish speciality.

In the world of design, too, specialists have been applying their minds to ecological considerations. Juha Valtanen, Hannu Kalhonen, and Jukka Vaajakallio have together formed the Oljenkorsi Group, or Straw Group. They argue that product design should strive for the minimum use of raw materials, the maximum use of recycled and recyclable materials, the minimum use of energy during the manufacturing process, and the longest possible life for the product.

Small-scale Finnish projects which could solve some of the Western world's most pressing ecological problems, hit the headlines from time to time. The pioneering idea of building a road out of chopped-up rubber car tyres was intended to have a dual "green" purpose. Firstly, it gave a use for tyres, which are notoriously difficult to dispose of. Secondly, the experiment was an attempt to find a durable road surface able to resist the strains of the fierce winter ice, which calls for frequent road maintenance and endless

Left and <u>above</u>, everything that a Finnish family needs for summer.

From a visitor's point of view, Finland may already represent a supremely unspoilt environment. The main selling line of the Finnish Tourist Board has been the country's landscape, supported by photographs of summer Finland's green places, its blue waters and its leafy towns. Human habitation appears in its proper context, dominated by vegetation, a tiny sprinkling of buildings in a vast forested terrain.

This is a true picture of Finland, nevertheless. In a country which is the fifth-largest in Europe, the 5 million inhabitants are just a blip on the map, highly influential but outnumbered several thousand to one by trees.

Mrs Alec Tweedie would be amazed could she revisit Finland today. Her vivid account of several weeks journeying *Through Finland in Carts* was published in 1897, all but 100 years ago. In fact, the "carts" were by no means the only methods of transport she and her companions experienced though these horse-drawn contraptions, and the roads along which they travelled, certainly left the greatest impression.

The Tweedie party coincided with one of the hottest summers on record. "The roads, although well marked by signposts and milestones, are certainly not good," she pronounced. Later she added more detail. "The heat was so great… two or three inches of dust covering the roadways… that we determined to drive no more in day-time… On future occasions we started at six in the afternoon, drove till midnight, and perhaps did a couple or three hours more at four or five in the morning; think of it!"

Happily, today's traveller need not go to such extremes. Several hundred kilometres of motorway and many thousands more of well-surfaced trunk and secondary roads now probe into the remotest reaches of forest and lakeside. In a country of such huge horizons this still leaves plenty of what the Finns call "gravel" roads (a gravel foundation surfaced with oil and sand); but these are clearly indicated on the excellent and regularly updated motoring maps. The spring thaw (late April to early June, depending on latitude) is the only time to be wary of them, when signs announcing *kelirikko*, translating as "bad state of the roads", forewarn that a section ahead may have temporarily become an impassable quagmire.

Otherwise, two hazards loom. The first is represented by elk or reindeer: warning pictorial signs depicting these animals along stretches of road where they are most likely to be encountered, especially at dusk. Take heed, for it is no joke to collide at speed with 500–600 kilos of elk in the middle of nowhere. The second hazard is more insidious: a state of inattention into which it is all too

easy to be lulled on roads that, outside main towns, are blessedly uncongested. But at least you will not be obliged, as was the stalwart Mrs Tweedie at the end of each dusty day, "to see how completely our hair was powdered, and note the wonderful gray hue our faces had assumed, eyelashes, eyebrows and all."

About 90 percent of all Finland's public roads carry regular coach services, including the admirable yellow postbuses which reach deep into areas where few visitors penetrate. Though slower than their more commercial rivals, they provide a closer contact with the Finnish ethos. The driver is also the ticket-collector – and guide, mentor, friend to country ladies struggling back from market, and postman. You may admire how the post is delivered by a flick of the wrist into rows of roadside postboxes, sometimes far from any visible habitation, as the bus slows down but rarely stops.

Gentle waterways: Even before Mrs Tweedie's adventurous journey, the labyrinthine waterways of Finland's often interconnected lakes (187,888 at the last count) provided a gracious mode of travel. "One can travel nearly all over Finland in steamers, and very comfortable steamers they are too, with nice little cabins and good restaurants," Mrs Tweedie tells us. And so they are still.

There are regular passenger routes on several of the lake systems but the oldest and probably the most romantic are those across Saimaa's vast expanses. Steam first came to Saimaa, wheezing and belching its thick black smoke, in the 1830s. It revolutionised the timber business until then reliant on sailing vessels – and their dependence on the vagaries of the wind – for the transport of Finland's "green gold" from forest to factory during the short summer.

The heyday of passenger steamers was in the early years of the 20th century, especially pre-World War I, when the well-to-do of St Petersburg arrived by the night train at Lappeenranta for a leisurely 9-hour steamer trip to Savonlinna, then a new and fashionable spa. In due course the steamers covered the four points of the Saimaa compass, picking up and dropping off the lakeland's scat-

Preceding pages: fishing, sailing and ferrying in the Baltic. **Left**, braving the white water.

tered inhabitants, along with livestock and every imaginable form of cargo, at communities of all sizes and no size at all. One of the great sights of Savonlinna each morning and evening was the departure and return of the Saimaa fleet of wooden double-deckers. Several still survive.

Despite the changes, it still presents a highly photogenic scene today. Gone, of course, are the trailing plumes of black smoke though even into the 1960s some engines were still wood-fired. Indeed it was part of the adventure to stop off at designated lake-side depots to watch – even assist if you felt so inclined – as logs were hurled on board to fuel the next few hours' journeying.

Finland's railway age the country was a Grand Duchy under Czarist Russia, and thus had the imperial gauge bestowed upon it.

Railway buff's delight: Until well into the 1960s, Finland was a railway buff's paradise for many of its trains were still steam-powered by those two pre-eminently Finnish natural resources: wood and water. Some of the most venerable survive in Hyvinkää's Railway Museum, or from time to time one will emerge on to the open railroad.

Today, rail travel is still not always the most obvious means of getting from one place to another in a land whose topography often precludes straight lines and whose lakes have obliged railway engineers to seek

Now all are diesel-powered. Scheduled services to a large extent have also been replaced by sightseeing cruises, though certain traditional routes like Lappeenranta-Savonlinna (now 7½ hours) and Savonlinna-Kuopio (11½ hours) still survive.

In Mrs Tweedie's time, the railway network, though more comfortable, was a lot less comprehensive than the dusty roads. "There are not many railways in Finland, the first being laid in 1862;" observed Mrs Tweedie, "they are all narrow-gauge." In this, in fact, she was wrong because the gauge was, and is, 10 centimetres wider than in the rest of Europe, for at the dawn of

more tortuous routes. Otherwise, today's rolling stock along 4,000-or-so miles (about 6,500 km) of railway lines is as streamlined as you will find anywhere, gaining in comfort and efficiency what it has lost in nostalgia. You can cover the 600 miles (1,000 km) between Helsinki and Rovaniemi in 10 hours, comfortably tucked up in a sleeping car after a good meal. You can also take your car along with you.

So much for summer, but what about winter's totally different challenges? Those of us who live in countries where communications grind to a halt at the onset of a few inches of snow or a few days of heavy frost may well marvel at the apparent ease with which Finland's airports, roads, railways and harbours are kept open under all but the most exceptional conditions. It was not always thus. "For four or five months during every year the harbour is solidly ice-bound," comments Mrs Tweedie, referring to Helsinki. Indeed at that time, little Hanko, then a fashionable spa on a south-western island, was Finland's only winter port.

Today it needs a very exceptional freeze-up to close shipping routes to Helsinki – even more so Turku, also in the southwest – whose sea lanes are kept open by the powerful ice breakers of which Finland is a leading producer. Nevertheless, even Helsinki has ice

ternative to the sledge so favoured by Mrs Tweedie. In the far north opportunities for reindeer sleigh safaris are rapidly being outnumbered by snowmobile and even dog-sledge tours. The traditional and once-ubiquitous *pulkka* – a boat-shaped sledge on one runner drawn by a reindeer – is fast becoming a museum piece.

High above the forests and tundra, the year-round sky is busy with sights and sounds that would have baffled Mrs Tweedie. Ever since air travel literally took off – and Finnair, Finland's national airline was among the pioneers – it has been a prime means of communication throughout the country. Many Finnish youngsters have

enough to provide pedestrian and even motorised traffic routes across the harbour ice from mainland to islands. Throughout Finland's winter, short-cuts over frozen lakes and rivers can substantially reduce distances between communities and bring islands out of their summer isolation.

Off the beaten track, skiing is still second nature to most Finns. But for speed or distance the snowmobile, its noise and fumes rather doubtfully outweighed by its convenience, provides a modern if unattractive al-

Left, snowmobile – the modern way. Above, Finland makes the world's best ice-breakers.

taken air travel for granted long before encountering their first train.

The most recent newcomer to Finland's skies is Concorde, now a regular midsummer and midwinter visitor to the Arctic Circle with its full complement of passengers eager to meet Santa Claus on home territory. It is still enough of a novelty to attract a large number of Rovaniemi's citizens. As arrival time approaches, a steady stream of traffic heads out to the spacious acres of the airport. There is an appreciative murmur as a distant speck materialises into that unmistakable shape and the jet slips elegantly down from the sky. Mrs Tweedie would be amazed.

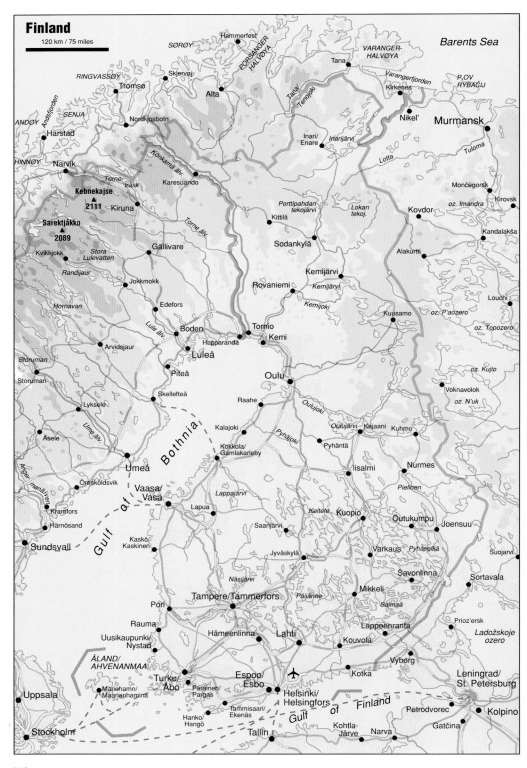

Finland

120 km / 75 miles

Barents Sea

SØRØY
Hammerfest
PORSANGER-HALVØYA
VARANGER-HALVØYA
Tana
RINGVASSØY
Skjervøj
Alta
Varangerfjorden
Kirkenes
P.OV RYBAČIJ
Tromsø
Nikel'
Murmansk
ANDØY
SENJA
Andsfjorden
Nordkjosbotn
Harstad
Inari/Enare
Inarijärvi
Lotta
Tuloma
HINNØY
Narvik
Könkämä älv.
Karesuando
Mončegorsk
oz. Imandra
Kirovsk
Torne-träsk
Kebnekajse
2111
Kiruna
Porttipahdan tekojärvi
Lokan tekoj.
Kittilä
Kovdor
Kandalakša
Sarektjåkko
2089
Stora Lulevatten
Gällivare
Torne älv.
Sodankylä
Alakurtti
Kvikkjokk
Randijaur
Jokkmokk
Kemijärvi
Kemijärvi
Louchi
Hornavan
Edefors
Rovaniemi
Kemijoki
Kuusamo
oz. P'aozero
oz. Topozero
Lule älv.
Boden
Tornio
Kemi
Arvidsjaur
Happaranda
Luleå
Storuman
Piteå
Oulu
oz. Kujto
Storuman
Skellefteå
Raahe
Oulujoki
Voknavolok
oz. N'uk
Lyksele
Kalajoki
Oulujärvi
Kajaani
Kuhmo
Åsele
Ume älv.
Kokkola/Gamlakarleby
Pyhäjoki
Pyhäntä
Iisalmi
Nurmes
Örnsköldsvik
Umeå
Lappajärvi
Lapua
Keitele
Kuopio
Pielinen
Vaasa/Vasa
Outukumpu
Joensuu
Kramfors
Kaskö/Kaskinen
Saarijärvi
Varkaus
Pyhäselkä
Suojarvi
Härnösand
Jyväskylä
Savonlinna
Sortavala
Sundsvall
Näsijärvi
Mikkeli
Saimaa
Tampere/Tammerfors
Päijänne
Pori
Lappeenranta
Prioz'ersk
Ladožskoje ozero
Rauma
Hämeenlinna
Lahti
Kouvola
Vyborg
Uusikaupunki/Nystad
ÅLAND/AHVENANMAA
Kotka
Leningrad/St. Petersburg
Mariehamn/Maarianhamina
Turku/Åbo
Parainen/Pargas
Espoo/Esbo
Helsinki/Helsingfors
Petrodvorec
Kolpino
Uppsala
Tammisaari/Ekenäs
Hanko/Hangö
Gulf of Finland
Kohtla-Järve
Gatčina
Stockholm
Tallin
Narva

Gulf of Bothnia
Angermanälven

112

PLACES

Nobody has managed to count with any degree of certainty how many lakes and islands there are in Finland – almost enough, it seems, for every Finnish family to have an island or lake of its own, with plenty of space for visitors too. No wonder that an ideal Finnish summer is based on a wooden cabin at the edge of lake or sea and a wooden smoke sauna house nearby. With some fishing, swimming, and a small boat tied up alongside, this is Finnish perfection.

There are hundreds of thousands of square miles of untouched landscape, crossed by endless straight roads running between tall trees. Roads like this eat up the distances, though beware in case the sheer ease of navigating the long avenue stretching ahead does not encourage a tendency to doze off at the wheel.

As the road heads ever further north, you scarcely realise at first that the rolling farmland of the south has moved into those boundless forests and that, gradually, the dark green gives way to the peat and tundra of Lapland and the north where the midnight sun gives the landscape a red glow in the late evening. This is the territory of the great herds of reindeer, and the animals of the wilderness areas – bear, wolf and lynx – though their numbers have declined in recent years. In the northwest the ground rises to peaks over 3,000 ft (1,000 metres) as it reaches out towards the Norwegian mountains. Along the west coast of the Gulf of Bothnia, the lesser-known beaches and dunes and the surprisingly warm water are ripe for exploration.

Even the cities are interspersed with green. Parks and trees run between the houses and rocky knolls protrude above street level to make possible a church such as Temppeliaukio Church in Helsinki, scooped literally out of the rock, under a beautiful domed roof.

For a country of five million, Finland has produced an astonishing number of architects, artists, sculptors and designers – and it shows. In Helsinki, in particular, almost every corner reveals another intriguing detail: an elegantly carved facade on a block of flats, a statue, a curved window, or a small figurine full of humour that you nearly miss but laugh when you spot it. In older cities such as Turku or Porvoo (Borgå), where the Swedish influence was strongest, some of the oldest buildings remain. Nowhere else in the Nordic countries has so many cultural festivals. No other Nordic city offers such an assortment of theatre, music, and artistic events.

Even the seasons seem more distinct. In winter, it is time for snow and skiing and also for the great reindeer round-ups in Lapland. In summer, sea and lake are full of sails and swimmers. Between the two are a sudden bursting spring when everything turns green in a week, and autumn, full of reds and browns as the leaves swirl over the city squares. Finland is a land for all seasons.

Preceding pages: Sami life pictured by the Sami artist Alariesto, Sondankyla Museum, Lapland.

HELSINKI

Throughout the city, the sea follows you, its salty tongue lapping at the sides of metropolitan bridges and boulevards, pressing its way into residential areas, creating natural harbours and sudden bays.

In summer, the sea glistens and preens under a tireless sun, driving the light-starved locals wild with its shine. Autumn arrives and, as darkness encroaches and the rains begin to fall, it begins to churn, creating a world of wet and grey where the borders between sea and land are no longer distinct. Only during the long cold winter does the sea finally rest, freezing into an endless expanse on which weekend promenaders can walk dogs or try out their cross-country skis.

To understand Helsinki is to accept that kitschy title "Daughter of the Baltic." It is to the Baltic that Helsinki owes its fortunes, its weather and perhaps even the massive, undulating nature of its architecture. It is also to the Baltic that the city owes much of its relatively short but difficult history.

Helsinki was founded in 1550 by King Gustav Vasa of Sweden-Finland to compete with Tallinn, whose port was controlled by the Hanseatic League. A first fledgling city was erected on the mouth of the Vantaa River at the innermost point of the Helsinki Bay – a bit northeast of where Helsinki stands today. To fill it, Gustav Vasa simply ordered citizens from Porvoo, Ulvila and Rauma to move to the new town.

The new port of "Helsingfors" proved, however, to be not only unpopular but was not even lucrative as the shallow inner bay became shallower and impossible to navigate. It languished for nearly a century until a visiting governor general named Per Brahe recommended it be moved further down towards the open sea. In 1640, a second site was designated on the section of present-day Helsinki called Kruununhaka and the citizens

were once again ordered to move. On this new site, Helsinki finally began to grow, though it still wasn't much more than an outpost for fishermen and farmers. But the Russian Empire was also stirring, particularly against Sweden and the town's fortunes soon began to go downhill. After battling against the Great Famine in 1697, the Great Northern War between 1700 and 1721, and the Great Plague in 1710, Helsinki was reduced to ashes and the population to some 150 hardy souls.

The fortress: Sweden's decision in 1746 to build Suomenlinna Fortress off the shore of Helsinki, to protect what remained of its Finnish territory, proved to be the city's saviour. Construction of the Baltic fortress drew attention to the port and brought its first taste of wealth. Newly rich merchants constructed a handful of stone houses and, although streets were still unpaved and many houses turf-roofed, an interest in European cultural life took root.

The city was given new life. Russian money and the talents of German archi-

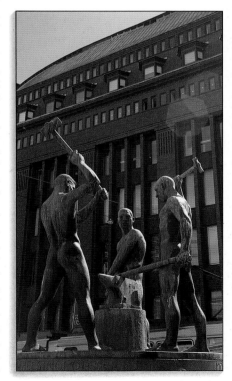

tect Carl Ludwig Engel, whose neo-classic work can also be seen in Leningrad and Tallinn, were poured into the creation of administrative halls and a cathedral. As the city began to enjoy steady prosperity from around 1850, even workers' homes were mostly replaced with stone.

By the year 1900, Helsinki was a new place. Half a century saw it grow from a small port with some 20,000 inhabitants and an equivalent number of cows and cabbage fields into a bona-fide capital city. The population soared to 100,000, a railway was built, and gasworks, electricity and water mains all laid down.

At the same time, Helsinki became the seat of the nationalist movement and, with it, of a new self-consciousness. Native architects, such as Eliel Saarinen and then Alvar Aalto, emerged and, after independence in 1917, the more Finnish functionalism replaced Jugend (the German version of Art Nouveau) as Helsinki's predominant architectural style.

Massive air attack: Unfortunately, nothing could completely protect the city from the massive Russian air raids of 1944 – nor from fervent, not-always-lovely postwar reconstruction. But Helsinki's position on the sea resurfaced to help Finland's capital regain and then increase its stature, not only as a major port but eventually also as the important site for shipbuilding and international meetings it is today.

Modern Helsinki is a tranquil but still growing city with some 900,000 occupants in its total metropolitan area – many of whom are only second-generation city dwellers. Gone are the marshes and wooden houses of yesteryear, but the faces of the fishermen who sell their catch from the docks are palpable reminders of the city's so-recent urbanisation.

Helsinki isn't an overtly frivolous city but, whenever possible, the Finns have let their innate artistry flavour their capital. Statues crop up on every other corner, and even the most functional of buildings can present itself as a notable monument to Finland's architectural history.

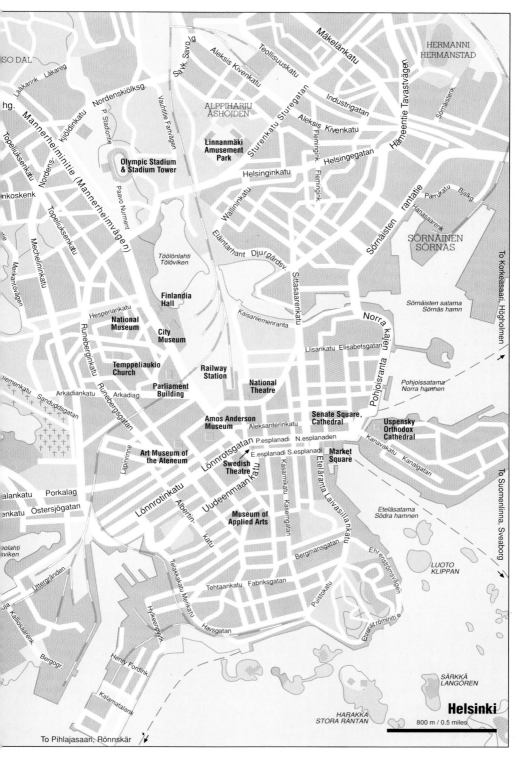

Helsinki

800 m / 0.5 miles

133

Consider the **Railway Station**. A busy place that connects Helsinki with numerous commuter cities as well as the rest of Finland, it also contains both a metro station stop and an underground shopping mall. At the same time, the station is a strikingly stylish, round-edged structure in pinkish granite with green trim, a black roof and a 160-ft (48-metre) green clocktower. Designed by Saarinen in 1905 but not completed until 1919, it links two of Helsinki's most prevalent styles: national romanticism and functionalism. It also incorporates work by other well-known Finns. Thanks to Emil Wikström, pairs of solemn-faced, bemuscled giants hold translucent lanterns on either side of the station's impressive front doors. A large painting by Eero Järnefelt looks over the **Eliel Restaurant**.

The railway station has replaced the harbour as the metropolitan focus in Helsinki life. It is also a good reference point for making a city tour and, weather permitting, most places of interest to visitors are within walking dis-

tance of here. An extensive network of urban transport also uses the station as its base. The metro stops beneath it, many buses stop beside it and almost all trams stop in front of it.

The first thing to do before beginning a tour of Helsinki, however, is to find your directional bearings. These are not immediately obvious because much of central Helsinki lies on a peninsula, jutting southward into the Baltic. Being by the sea, therefore, doesn't automatically mean you are in the south of the city. In fact, the peninsula has only a brief southern shore but extended longitudinal coasts – on both its eastern and western sides.

Deceptive titles: Don't rely on names either, which (if they belong to the time not so long ago when the city was much smaller) can be deceiving. The "South" Harbour actually lies on the peninsula's *eastern* side. It is, however, *south* of Kruununhaka – the city centre when it was built. Just keep in mind that the railway station is pretty much right in the middle of the peninsula; the tiny

Wikström's massive figures at the railway station.

Keskusta, or centre, runs east-west below it; and the other sections of central Helsinki radiate out around them.

More confusing, probably, is a visitor's initial glance at the city. Helsinki doesn't follow any of the rules of European capitals. It isn't quaint; it isn't regal; it isn't even terribly old. Little more than a century ago, there were still animals wandering in the streets, and almost everything predating 1808 was burnt to the ground.

Don't be surprised to step out of the railway station and find yourself face to face with two monolithic commercial complexes side-by-side; one, modern and bedecked with neon signs, called **Kaivopiha**, and the second, nicknamed **Makkaratalo**, or "Sausage House", because of a long tubular balcony winding about its facade. Helsinki is a pragmatist – and for good reason. But Helsinki can also be compelling, not in a flirtatious way, but in a quintessentially Finnish way: reserved, modest and wry. Make an effort and you can come to know it.

The **National Theatre**, to the immediate east of the station and at the northern head of the cobbled railway square, is a charmer. This little castle in whitish granite with green trim and a red roof was conceived in purely national romantic style. Productions are generally in Finnish but the pensive **statue of Aleksis Kivi**, Finland's national writer, in front of it, transcends language.

Directly across the swirling reddish square from the theatre is the **Ateneum**. Built in 1887, the Ateneum's gilt yellow and white facade might seem reminiscent of St Petersburg but is the site of Finland's National Gallery of Art and one of the first manifestations of Finland's struggle for independence. The museum's collection of Finnish paintings, sculpture, drawings and graphic art covers the years 1750 to 1960 and includes well-known works by such famous Finns as Akseli Gallen-Kallela and Albert Edelfelt.

The Ateneum lies on the east side of Makkaratalo. Wedged in between Kaivopiha and the north-south running

The statue of Aleksis Kivi glimpsed through the banners outside the National Theatre.

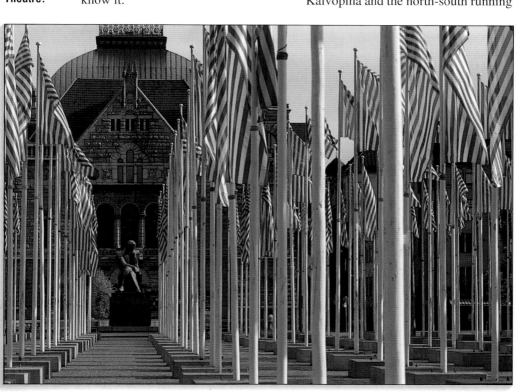

Mannerheimintie (Helsinki's main thoroughfare and the longest street in all of Finland) is the handsome **Seura-huone Hotel**. Inside, the red-velveted, high-ceilinged **Café Socis** is a perennial favourite with locals and resident foreigners, especially late at night.

Bootleg vodka: Behind these buildings stretch three blocks containing one of Helsinki's most important shopping districts. **Aleksanterinkatu** (better known as Aleksi), running parallel to the street the railway station is on, is the main thread of this, but intersecting streets also contain shops. Kaivopiha's fountain-crowned square has its own special shopping identity; it is the number-one spot for buying and selling bootleg Russian vodka and, supposedly, the city's tiny handful of narcotic contraband.

Steps from this square lead up to Mannerheimintie and the **Old Student House** (or Vanha). Built in 1870, Vanha's own stairs are a favourite meeting-place for young trendies in leather jackets, and its interior now houses a "progressive" performance hall, smoky drinking room, exhibition quarter and library. Student organisations, as well as a cinema and ticket service, have been moved to the **New Student House**, on the other side of the Kaivopiha steps.

Vanha lies on the intersection of Aleksi and Mannerheimintie, and a trio of naked men with nice pectorals – the **Three Smiths' Statue** – dominate the triangular square beneath it. As soon as the snow melts, musicians use this square to serenade the passing crowds, ice cream stands open their windows and even some café tables appear.

Finland's largest department store, **Stockmann's**, lies on the other side of Three Smiths' Square from Vanha. Beside it on Keskuskatu, is Scandinavia's largest bookshop, **Akateeminen Kirjakauppa**. The latter is a fabulous place to lose oneself – though a fairly expensive one, given the exalted price of books in Finland. Its upstairs has a stylish but pricey café that was designed by Alvar Aalto.

Esplanadi.

The Akateeminen Bookshop faces a second important Helsinki landmark, **Esplanadi Park**. Planned by J. A. Ehrenström (the Finn responsible for the 19th-century new city plan), it was first laid out in 1831 and runs east-west between Mannerheimintie and the **South Harbour**.

The **Swedish Theatre**, an elegant semi-circular stone building dating from 1866, commands Esplanadi's western head on Mannerheimintie. Back to back with it and facing into the long and narrow park is a family-type restaurant called **Happy Days**. Its *terassi*, in warm weather, is always filled with boisterous beer drinkers.

Place to meet: An old-fashioned promenade leads from here the length of the park; between well-sculpted patches of lawn, past the central statue of J. L. Runeberg, Finland's national poet, to the **Kappeli Restaurant** at its eastern end. This park is still a very popular meeting place and is often the scene of animated fairs, such as the Christmas Fair in December or Night of the Arts in August. On May Day Eve it is given over to general lunacy.

Kappeli is also an important spot for a rendezvous. A very different sort of place from Happy Days, tall lacy windows and a whimsical roof give it a Chekhovian, gazebo-like feel and, indeed, the older parts of the café date from 1867. Like all self-respecting restaurants in Helsinki, Kappeli has a summer terrace. This mars its beauty but gives patrons the important chance to enjoy fresh air, drinks and music from the facing **bandstand** (active from June to September) simultaneously.

Flanking the bandstand are two pretty little "ponds" graced by statues of cavorting fish boys and water nymphs. They cannot, however, compete with the **Havis Amanda Fountain**, which stands on the small square that separates the eastern end of the park from the South Harbour amidst a constant swirl of traffic and trams. This square is also the site of a flower market as soon as spring comes.

The sensuous bronze Amanda created quite a stir when she was first erected in 1908. Surrounded by four sea lions spouting water, she represents the city of Helsinki rising from the sea, innocent and naked. On May Day Eve, at least, she gets something to wear – a white student cap – while a champagne-happy chaos of clustering human cap-wearers cheer.

Two esplanade boulevards stretch east-west alongside either side of the park. Nowadays, the fine 19th-century stone buildings along **Northern Esplanadi** mostly house tourist shops like **Marimekko** and **Aarikka**, the latter featuring, among other things, Aarikka's distinctive wooden jewellery. Number 19 is an exception. The **Helsinki Information Office** and the **City Tourist Board** occupy its first floor; both offer extensive selections of maps and brochures.

More venerable houses line the **Southern Esplanadi**, most of which function in some type of official or commercial capacity. The oldest is Engel's Empire-style former **Council of State**, dating from 1824. During the

The Kappeli Restaurant, a favourite summer haunt.

period of Russian rule, it was the palace of the governor general.

Going to market: The **Central Market Square**, across from Havis Amanda on the South Harbour, exudes a much earthier type of appeal. A busy market makes its home here year round, from 7am to 2pm Mondays through Saturdays and, again, from 3.30pm to 8pm during summer weekday evenings. Going to market is still an important part of daily routine in Helsinki, partly because agrarian life is a comparatively recent experience for many residents. Shoppers, baskets tossed over their arms, wander from stand to stand looking for the perfect new potato or bunch of dill.

Peninsular Helsinki has no less than four open-air markets. Of these, the Central Market is both the one most aimed at visitors and the most expensive, but locals on lunch-break from nearby shops and offices and housewives from the affluent southern suburbs still favour it. A multitude of ruddy-faced merchants gather to serve them and, after the ice melts, boat owners also get involved, tying their vessels to the end of the harbour and selling fish and root and other vegetables straight from their prows.

The north part of the market square is reserved for Finland's delicious fresh produce. Offerings very much follow the seasons and, in summer, become irresistible: sweet baby peas and mounds of deeply flavoured berries. No wonder that, by July, every good Helsinki dweller can be seen clutching a small paper bag filled with something juicy and colourful.

Further down, around the bellicose **Czarina's Obelisk** – whose imperial, doubled-headed golden eagle was ripped off during the Russian Revolution and not restored until 1972 – the market turns away from food. Some of these stands proffer interesting goods and handicrafts, but if you are looking for authenticity you should know that even most Finns stopped wearing furs quite a while ago. Women wearing high heels might also want to keep in mind that the spaces between the cobble-

Street musicians.

138

stones are particularly treacherous here.

The water in this part of South Harbour is overrun by gulls and geese and not all that clean, but don't let that stop you from sitting with the locals and a pint of Finland's fabulous strawberries on its storied docks in the sun. However, if it is cold or raining, you might prefer to duck into the yellow and red brick **Old Market Hall**.

Having traded for more than 100 years, the Old Market Hall is not only Helsinki's most centrally located *kauppahalli* but its oldest. It knows its advantage. The interior is polished to the gills, and the price of even simple *piirakka* can be sky-high. As well as reindeer cold-cuts and rounds of Oltermanni cheese, you can buy ready-made snacks from an excellent Russian-style kebab stand or a small café.

The Central Market sprawls like a spectre of the masses before some of Helsinki's most important administrative buildings. An austere row lies directly across at the end of Northern Esplanadi: the long blue **City Hall**, designed by Engel in 1833, with a Finnish flag flying above it; the sensible brown **Swedish Embassy**, importantly placed, and with a Swedish flag; the **Supreme Court**, dating from 1883; and the **Presidential Palace**.

Czarist palace: The Presidential Palace was designed in 1818 as a private home and turned into a czarist palace by Engel in 1843. The Finnish president lives here now, but a new official residence is currently being raised outside the centre.

Like the palace, the City Hall also started out with a different purpose. Until 1833, it was the elegant home of the Seurahuone Hotel (now across from the railway station). Its first opening was celebrated by a grand masquerade ball – so that women, who were usually prohibited, would be able to attend. The female guests had to leave by 4.30am, but, record has it, the champagne continued to flow.

Helsinki's third major landmark – **Senaatintori**, or Senate Square – stands one block north of here, back along

Gypsies at the harbour market.

Aleksi. There seems to be something fateful about Senate Square. As early as the 17th century, the same spot housed a town hall, church and central square. It was flattened by the next century's continual battles, but the merchants made rich by Suomenlinna soon rebuilt it, erecting the city's first stone buildings about its southern perimeter. The 1808 fire destroyed everything wooden, but Russia straightaway commissioned architect C.L. Engel to rebuild the square as the municipal centre of their new city plan for Helsinki. Eventually, so many important institutions made their home here that Senate Square became a sort of national centre.

The square is still a very impressive spot as well. Some 2,700 sq. miles (7,000 sq. metres) in size, it is covered by no less than 400,000 grey and red cobblestones of Finnish granite.

Nowadays, the Senate Square functions more than anything as a byway. The main building of **Helsinki University**, which occupies the entire western border of the square, has a new entrance at the back that lures student activity away. The current **Council of State**, directly opposite, receives few visits from the average citizen. The former **Town Hall**, on the south side, is used for entertaining official guests, and the flux of boutiques around it cater mostly for visitors.

But the city remembers. Senaatintori becomes the centre of activity on many important occasions, such as Independence Day in December, when the wide wind-swept square becomes a sea of candles held by students who march here from Hietaniemi Cemetery in the mid-winter dark. More locals gather again one month later to listen to the mayor's traditional New Year's Eve speech and watch fireworks and again for May Day. The University often uses it for commemorative events.

An extremely self-important statue to **Czar Alexander II**, erected in 1894, stands in the centre of all this. At his feet, four additional figures tell the square's story: *Lex*, or law (facing the government palace); *Lux*, or light (fac-

Yesterday's trams cope with today's traffic conditions.

ing the south and sun); *Labour* (facing the university); and *Pax*, or peace (facing the cathedral).

The **Helsinki Cathedral**, up a bank of treacherously steep steps on the northside, is a point of pride for Finns, and the exterior – with its five greenish cupolas, numerous white Corinthian columns and sprinkling of important figurines posing on its roof – is certainly impressive. The interior, however, is startlingly severe. Apart from the gilded altarpiece and organ, only statues of Luther, Agricola and Melanchthon disturb its airy white symmetry.

Engel's triumph: A walk around the square can also reveal a lot about Helsinki's history. The city's oldest stone building, dating from 1757, is the small blue-grey **Sederholm House** on the corner of Aleksi and Katariinankatu. Across the street is the **Bock House**, also 18th-century, which became the meeting place for Helsinki's City Council in 1818, as a plaque by its door proclaims. It also served briefly as the governor general's residence after

Engel had it embellished with Ionic pillars and a third floor. In most cases, Engel was also responsible for additions to the other patrician homes on the south side.

The rest of the square is pure Engel, making it not only a beautiful but unusually consistent example of neoclassical design. In 1832, the oldest part of the main building of Helsinki University (it was extended later to cover the entire block) was completed under the architect, on the western side of the square. Ten years earlier, he had designed the Council of State, along the entire eastern side of the square. The Finnish Government still has its seat here. Engel drew the plan for the cathedral as well, although he died 12 years before its completion in 1852.

Across Unioninkatu, the **University Library** is decidely ornate. Not only do white Corinthian columns line every inch of its yellow facade, inside the splendour continues. In the central room, more columns (now marble with gold tips) support a dark-wood second

The University of Helsinki Library.

tier, beneath a painted cupola ceiling. This is still very much a working library, and visitors are expected to leave their coats at the door, sign in and, above all, respect the quiet. Nor are all the rooms open to visitors – look out for some prohibition signs. But don't let this discourage you from enjoying what the public parts of this most beautiful of Engel's works, dating from 1844.

Outside the centre: After exploring Helsinki's Keskusta (centre), venture into one of the surrounding districts, each of which has its own very particular character, though borders are not always clearly defined.

One of the most attractive is **Katajanokka**, which lies on a small promontory sticking out into the sea, a few blocks east from Senate Square. Katajanokka is connected to the centre by two short bridges but manages to maintain a remarkably remote atmosphere. After a snowstorm or on a brilliant spring day, its elegant streets are the picture of serenity. Unfortunately, the first thing you see crossing the **Kanavakatu Bridge** on to Katajanokka is one of Alvar Aalto's least successful efforts: the dirty white marble **Enso Gutzeit Office Building** (known as the "sugarcube"), dated 1962. Do as the locals do and pass by. Katajanokka has much better sights to offer.

The **Uspensky Cathedral**, across the street at the top of a sudden grassy knoll, gives supreme proof of this. Russian Orthodox, built in 1868, dedicated to the Virgin Mary and undeniably glamorous, Uspensky makes a striking exception to Helsinki's generally sensible architectural style. Its red-brick conglomeration of cross-tipped spires and onion-shaped domes has undoubtedly helped to convince many filmmakers to use Helsinki as a surrogate Moscow (for example, in *Reds* and *Gorky Park*).

Uspensky's interior is also both impressive and atmospheric, with a glittering iconostasis – but frustratingly difficult to see. The cathedral only opens for short periods, though services in Church Slavic are held at least twice weekly. It is best to check times.

The interior of Uspensky Orthodox Cathedral.

Appropriately enough, a fine Russian restaurant, called the **Bellevue**, waits at the base of the cathedral, across from **Katajanokka Park**. The Bellevue, however, has a slightly unorthodox political history. The restaurant was founded the year Finland declared independence from Russia (1917). It also displays on one of its golden walls a thank-you note received in 1990 from America's First Lady, Barbara Bush.

The Russian motif is echoed elsewhere on Katajanokka, and flirtatious basilic motifs appear over many doorways. Red brick also gets more use, particularly in the recently built residences on the tip of the promontory. But central **Luotsikatu** is one street where Jugendian style rules. Many of the buildings on this and nearby streets were designed by the architectural team of Gesellius, Lindgren and Saarinen at the turn of the century and abound with little pleasures. Don't miss the charming griffin doorway on No. 5.

Turning north from Luotsikatu onto **Vyökatu** takes you to the northern waterfront. A narrow flight of stone steps leads down to an ageing gateway, which until 1968 blocked the way to the **Naval Barracks**. These long, mostly yellow buildings have since been restored and now house the Finnish Foreign Ministry. Some have been completely reconstructed but follow Engel's original design. The public is welcome to stroll along the pleasant avenues that run between them.

The southern side of Katajanokka sees more public activity. This is where the huge Viking Line ships come in from Stockholm three times a day, disembarking crowds of passengers. Conversions have already been completed on the block of old warehouses at Pikku Satamakatu, beside the Viking Line Terminal and the so-called **Wanha Satama** now entertains a clutch of eating spots (including the cheerful **Café Sucre**), exhibition halls and stores. Two more warehouses nearby have also been earmarked for renovation but the **Customs and Bonded Warehouse**, however, should not change. Even if you don't have any business to attend to here, it's worth passing by to view its inventive Jugendian style, as designed by Gustaf Nystrom in 1900.

Following Kanavakatu back west will return you to Helsinki's oldest district, **Kruununhaka**. Senate Square is actually at the lower end of this area, whose name means "the King's Paddock" and not so many centuries ago was primarily a home for cows. It is now favoured by the well-heeled and boasts a large collection of antique furniture and clothing shops.

Central Helsinki's second oldest building lies in the southeastern corner of this district, at the juncture of Aleksi and Meritulli Square. The modest squat structure was erected in 1765 as a **Customs Warehouse**, but now houses normal offices. Other venerable left-overs hover nearby, such as the deep red **Lord Mayor's Residence** at No. 12 Aleksi (next to Helsinki's **Theatre Museum**) with its gorgeous blown-glass window-panes and the mid-19th century, neo-Gothic **Ritarihuone** ("House of Nobility") one block north on Hallituskatu.

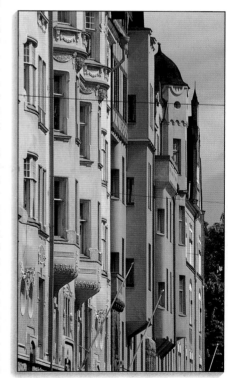

A few particularly nice pedestrian streets crown the crest of hilly Kruununhaka. Solid stone buildings in yellow, brown, rust and grey cut into exposed rock cliffs, insulating the end of the district from the **Siltavuori Strait** flowing directly below. They also shelter the city's oldest extant wooden buildings at Kristianinkatu 12, the Burgher's House.

The **Burgher's House** was built in 1818 shortly after the great fire, by a wealthy merchant who wasn't quite wealthy enough for stone. A high wooden fence encloses it with a second mustard-coloured house and a weatherbeaten red shed, all cuddled round a small earth-floored courtyard filled with the scent of wood smoke.

In structure, the main house remains exactly as it was when first built, and its beautiful wooden floors are completely original. The furniture, however, is from different periods starting with 1860 and, to complete the atmosphere, guides dress in old-fashioned garb.

Summer sunning: If it's a warm day, you may want to head east down to **Tervasaari**. This little island, now connected to Kruununhaka by a man-made isthmus, used to be the city's storage place for tar – one of Finland's most important early exports. Tervasaari literally means "tar island". Modern times have turned it into a nice park for summer sunning, with a dog run and laid-back *terassi* restaurant.

Walking west instead brings you down to **Kaisaniemenkatu**, the same street that begins in front of the railway station and more or less frames the western edge of Kruununhaka. An attractive park squeezes between it, the station and **Kaisaniemi Bay**.

Kaisainiemip Puisto is a sort of multi-purpose park, with sloping stretches of grass, a variety of playing fields that turn into ice-hockey rinks in winter, an open-air restaurant and the **University Botanical Gardens**. Designed by a landscape gardener from St Petersburg in the 1830s, these gardens form a very peaceful place to stroll right in the middle of the town.

The Burgher's House, one of Helsinki's oldest wooden buildings.

A long bridge separates Kruununhaka and the park from tiny **Hakaniemi** and larger **Kallio**, traditionally Helsinki's "worker" communities. Indeed, Lenin briefly lived beside spacious **Hakaniemi Square** before the Russian Revolution. Today, ironically, unemployed drunks lord over it.

From 7am until 2pm, Monday through Saturday, however, a no-nonsense market takes over the square and the **Hakaniemi Market Hall** on its edge. Both are noticeably more natural than those at the Central Market, and the hall has an upstairs devoted to dry goods including stands run by the ubiquitous Marimekko and Aarikka.

Kallio was first built up in haphazard fashion during the early 19th century. It was eventually given a city plan and rebuilt after the fashion of St Petersburg, but you still need to know where to wander to find attractive areas. One of its prettiest blocks, **Torkkelinkatu**, rises above the whimsical **Kallio Library** on Viides Linja. The nearby **Kallio Church** is an important struc-

ture in grey granite from 1912. Its bells ring a tune presumably from Sibelius.

The northern border of Kallio hides Helsinki's **Museum of Worker Housing**. This special museum comprises four wooden tenements built by the city for its workers and used from 1909 until as recently as 1987. Household scenes have been recreated with great effect within eight apartments – using intimate knowledge of the former inhabitants. In flat C-6, for example, where an abandoned wife and her trouble-making illegitimate son lived, a bottle of alcohol stands in a traditional spot beneath the man's seat at the table.

All the apartments displayed are single rooms that housed entire families. This meant that, by day, the beds had to be tucked away in some fashion, but, in flat 9-E in 1925, those of a poor widow and five of her six children are left unmade. Only the eldest daughter had already gone to work, folding her bed against the wall and leaving steel hair curlers on the table. This family's story is particularly poignant; after the wom-

A 1920s room in the Workers' Museum.

an's husband died (it is said by suicide), she saved and saved until she was able to buy a cross for his grave and, with no money left to hire a car, carried it on her back all the way to Malmi Cemetery.

Helsinki's amusement park, **Linnan-mäki**, perches on a wooded hill just a short walk north from here. This isn't the raciest tivoli in the world, but it is supposedly the most-visited attraction in Finland.

Kallio lies north of the railway station along the east side of **Töölö Bay.** Several other of Helsinki's 50-odd museums lie on the bay's western side, in a neighbourhood called **Töölö**. Like Kallio, Töölö came into its own after the turn of the century. Though it is not especially chic today, many of its streets offer priceless examples of Jugendian architecture.

To get to Töölö from Kallio, you can follow a pleasant park around the bay's north end, over the train tracks. This way takes you by some important places for locals: the **City Theatre**, the **City Conservatoire**, the **Olympic Sta-**dium (beside which is an overly popular outdoor swimming pool) and the site of the future **Opera House** (to be opened 1993).

The **Piekka**, Helsinki's one restaurant specialising in Finnish cuisine, stands near the end, at No. 48 Mannerheimintie. It is a surprisingly refined but unaffected place that eschews all imported ingredients.

To take the alternative route to Töölö, start by walking one block west to Mannerheimintie, as far as the four-storey mall – with shops, fast-food restaurants, a bar and two cafés – called **Forum Shopping Centre**. Turn north, and one and a half blocks further on a bronze statue of **General Mannerheim** himself, on horseback, lords over the busy inter-section between Manner-heimin, Arkadian, Postin and Salomon streets. Töölö lies directly over the traffic bridge from here.

Beneath the bridge, the old **Railway Yard** has been converted into a fashionable art gallery and a clutch of whole-world food and goods stores. The **Par-**

The Ilmatar and Sotka Statue in Sibelius Park.

liament Building, directly across the street, atop an important row of steps, is decidely less casual. Fourteen columns of grey granite mark its stern facade, built between 1925 and 1930 after J.S. Sirén's design.

Architectural trio: Statues of former Finnish presidents scatter the area between the Parliament Building and Finland's **National Museum**. The Gesellius-Lindgren-Saarinen trio designed this museum in 1906 to reflect Finnish history in its very construction. Although national romantic in overall style, the heavy grey building also manages to incorporate snatches of old Finnish church and castle architecture. The main tower, for example, imitates that of the Turku Cathedral.

The museum's decoration and collection offer more on Finland. The stone bear by the entrance is the work of Wikström and the frescos on the foyer ceiling, depicting scenes from Finland's national epic, the *Kalevala,* are from Gallen-Kallela. The entertaining jumble of artefacts inside runs from early archaeological finds up to present-day items.

The **City Museum**, across the road, is also somewhat disorganised but doesn't manage to carry things off quite so well. Uninformed visitors especially may find it less than riveting. It does, however, have one of the cosiest of Helsinki's many cafés on its front lawn: the **Café CaraMelle**.

Finlandiatalo (Finlandia Hall), next door, is undoubtedly the most famous building in Töölö – if not all of Helsinki. Alvar Aalto designed it both inside and out, completing the main section in 1971 and the congress wing in 1975. It now houses both of Helsinki's symphony orchestras as well as any number of other concerts and events.

The stylish white building was specifically devised to blend environmentally with the backdrop of **Hesperia Park** and Töölö Bay, especially in winter. Ironically, Finlandiatalo is having ecological troubles. The Carraran marble of its facade has not just greyed; it is warping disastrously from the Finnish

Left, *Attack* **by Ectu Istu (1899), a protest against Russification. Right, detail of the Barbara Altar from Kalanti Church (both National Museum).**

winter. Before long, it is estimated, the hundreds of marble slabs that form its facades may even slip off.

Whether or not to replace the marble with something more suitable for Finnish weather has set off a raging battle between architectural pragmatists and purists. Meanwhile, the hall has a second, less-pressing but equally well-known problem: the acoustics of the concert hall are poor. Electrical experiments are underway to try to improve them. Regardless of their success, the hall serves as an indisputable bastion for modern Helsinki culture.

A number of other important cultural spots cluster around the Parliament House. The **City Art Hall**, which shows regionally orientated exhibitions of varying success, lies directly at the back of it, and the **Sibelius Academy**, Helsinki's famous musical conservatory, stands around the corner. Across the street, the **Zoological Museum**, whose numerous glass showcases and imaginative (if often gruesome) dioramas offer a colourful lesson on Finn-ish wildlife, is one of Helsinki's most underestimated museums and well worth a visit. Its pretty neo-baroque building is easily identified by the bronze cast of an elk on its lawn.

A perennial tourist favourite nestles, literally, into a small hill behind all of this on the winding streets of Töölö. The ultra-modern **Temppeliaukio Church** is not only an architectural oddity – built as it is directly into the rock cliffs, with inner walls of stone – it is also the site of many good concerts, sometimes avant garde. A service for English speakers is held here weekly.

Another district in southwestern Helsinki which is worth exploring is **Punavuori**, a plush area beneath Töölö towards the end of the peninsula. The main street here is **Bulevardi**, which begins at a perpendicular angle from Mannerheimintie (just a couple of blocks before its end) and leads down to Hietalahti shipyard.

Gracious avenue: Bulevardi is one of Helsinki's most beautiful avenues. Most of the buildings date from be-

Left and right, architectural styles along Bulevardi, one of Helsinki's most distinctive streets.

tween 1890 and 1920 and were formerly home to Helsinki's turn-of-the-century patricians. The **Old Church**, however, between Annan and Yrjön streets, is a stray from Engel. Dating from 1826, it was the first Lutheran church to be built in the new "capital". The outcrops of crumbling gravestones sprawled across its large front lawn are even older – one goes back to 1710.

The **Finnish National Opera House** lies a few blocks further west on Bulevardi. This delightful red building was erected in 1870 as a theatre for Russian officers. The inside is plush and ornate, and the performances are often excellent. The problem is the building is much too small, and plans for it after the opera has been moved to a new and more suitable home in 1993 are still unresolved.

As you reach the end of Bulevardi, you will probably begin to notice a strange tea-like smell in the air. The heady fumes come from **Sinebrychoff Brewery**, established in 1819 and the oldest brewery in Finland. They seem to fall especially over the **Hietalahti Market** which functions as a regular market with fish and fruits and vegetables for sale but is best known for its **flea market**. The goods themselves are usually just unwanted records and clothes, but this is one of the best places in Helsinki to watch locals of all types in action and in large numbers during the day.

Bulevardi does, however, harbour many of the most fashionable art galleries in Helsinki, and many types of boutiques spill over neighbouring streets. Two blocks south and parallel to Bulevardi, the **Iso-Roobertin** pedestrian street has a particular concentration of youth orientated shops and restaurants. Helsinki's main gay bar, **Gambrini**, can be found here. Another two blocks further on, still parallel to Bulevardi, is the **Johannes Church**. This rather regal affair with important stiletto spires is the largest church in Helsinki and a particularly popular place for choral concerts, with excellent acoustics. Across the street, the **Museum of Applied Arts**, is an essential

The small boat harbour.

stop, as it is a showcase for Finland's famed skills in design. Heading directly south from here will bring you into **Eira**, perhaps Helsinki's most exclusive neighbourhood.

Small boats' harbour: On the southernmost end of the peninsula the coastline below Eira is lined by parkland and is an extremely pleasant place to walk during sunny days. After the ice melts, small boats dock all along the coastline and half the world seems to be cycling by. While the sea is still frozen, you can actually walk out to some of the closer offshore islands.

Towards the northeast and the centre, this strip of green grows into Helsinki's best park: **Kaivopuisto**. In summer, the city sponsors numerous free concerts here and Kaivopuisto overflows with happy suntanning locals. But, unlike almost any other municipality in the world, even on occasions when they reach the tens of thousands, this crowd mingles politely and peacefully, leaving little litter behind.

Kaivohuone, a former spa in the park, is also one of the city's most popular places to meet and hear music, especially for trendy youngsters. The recently refurbished nightclub features hot Finnish bands and has a noisy garden terrace. However, the well-heeled local residents of Kaivohuone have been battling virulently against the club's existence. It can currently rock 'n' roll only on summer evenings!

Many of these locals come from the embassies that fill the **Ullanlinna** district. The **Soviet Embassy** is the most noticeable, commanding almost a solid block opposite **St Henrik's**, one of Helsinki's two Catholic churches. Above them rises **Observatory Hill** (the Finnish equivalent literally means "star tower"). From this high outcrop, you can look down over the centre and **Katajanokka** to the north. Directly below to the east is the **Olympia Quay**, from which the huge Silja liners to Stockholm and other cruise ships come and go across a sea that has brought prosperity to Helsinki, and given the city the title of "Daughter of the Baltic".

Helsinki's energetic night life.

ROCK 'N' ROLL, FINNISH STYLE

You may not find anything Finnish on the international rock 'n' roll charts, but it doesn't mean you'll have to – or even be able to – forget rock 'n' roll while visiting the country.

Walk around any Finnish town, and you will see dozens of people in leather, looking like archetypal rockers. You might think that these poor Finnish rock fans, speaking a language that couldn't be further from the roots of rock, would have to import anything they wanted to dance to. But you would be wrong. Finland has a broad field of original rock music and a good handful of the leather wearers may themselves have made a small-label recording.

The best way to learn about the Finnish rock scene is to attend one of the summer rock festivals. The biggest can draw up to 25,000 people, in a wide range of ages and hairstyles. They usually last for two days. Things get going late Saturday morning, and by evening the bottles are piling up fast. On Sundays, however, the atmosphere is mellower.

Provinssirock, held in Seinäjoki during the start of June, traditionally marks the opening of the summer rock festival season. A four-hour train trip north from Helsinki, Seinäjoki turns into a rock

heaven for this one weekend. Bands play on three different stages, set up in a beautiful camping spot just outside the city. As well as the best of the Finns, Provinssirock attracts quality names from abroad, such as R.E.M., the Fine Young Cannibals or Iggy Pop. As elsewhere, there are beer tents selling brew to the thirsty. (Drugs are very low-profile in Finland and you are unlikely even to find anyone smoking pot.)

The other important summer rock festival is Ruisrock at Turku. The oldest rock festival in Finland, Ruisrock faded for quite a few years but was recently revived and attracts some of the biggest names in rock. Recent guests have included Bob Dylan, Billy Idol and Midnight Oil.

Rock travellers should also visit Kuusrock in Oulu and Saapasjalkarock in Pihtipudas. Even

Finnish President Mauno Koivisto favours the interesting blues and rock artists often featured in the huge Pori Jazz Festival. After listening to Stevie Ray Vaughan perform, he took the now-late Texan guitarist on a private boat ride.

The other festival where families with babies can go without fear of drunken mishaps is Puisto Blues in Järvenpää, a small city just north of Helsinki. Visitors to Puisto Blues, which takes place at the beginning of June, are clearly more interested in music than bottles.

Rock hardly stops with the end of summer. There are rock clubs in almost every town, and every part of the country has its own particular style of local bands.

Helsinki has, of course, the largest number of bands and clubs. *Rumba*, a local rock paper, is a good source for finding more information on them, but the Tavastia Klubi, close by the Kamppi subway station, is one good bet.

English is more or less the language of choice for Helsinki bands. But, though this suggests a determination to appear international, it doesn't keep them from producing very original material. If you want to hear interesting songs in Finnish, however, look for Tuomari Nurmio, Sielun Veljet or Nelja Ruusua. You may not understand their words, but the music is universal and all three groups possess very charismatic performers.

Another currently popular style in Helsinki may seem a little unnatural to foreigners: Finnish rap. The best Baltic rappers are Raptori and Rapatti. Equally curious are the incomprehensibly popular Clifters. Don't be fooled by them. Although they may appear to be singing Beatles songs (and other hits from the 1960s), they actually have a songwriter for their own lyrics.

Generally, the further north you travel, the louder the music gets – and, some say, the more interesting. Windy and cold Oulu in northern Finland has the most intense rock population. The best word to describe the Oulu sound is extreme. Oulu also has the only male choir in the world that doesn't even try to sing: *Huutajat* (literally, "the Shouters"). Dozens of long-haired men in black suits and gum ties shout their hearts out in perfect order – Arctic hysteria at its best.

HELSINKI'S ISLANDS

Literally hundreds of islands dot the Helsinki coastline. Some, like Lauttasaari and Kulosaari, have been so integrated by bridges and metro lines that they are almost indistinguishable from the mainland. Others are reserved for weekend cottages, reached over the ice in winter or by motorboat in summer.

Suomenlinna ("Finland's castle") is undoubtedly the most important of this last type. In reality it consists of five islands, over which the ruins of a naval fortress and its fortifications are spread. Suomenlinna has played an integral part in Helsinki's life since its construction started in 1748, under Count Augustin Ehrensvärd.

Suomenlinna has a complicated identity. It began as a naval post, and still houses Finland's Naval War Academy, but it is hardly just a military enclave. A thriving local artists' community, which uses restored bastions as studios and showrooms, is more visible. Fishing boat repairers and restoration workers also live on the island.

Getting to the island is both cheap and easy. Water buses leave from Market Square every half hour, year round, and cost the same as a metro ticket. They dock on Iso Mustasaari and from here, a hilly path leads up through **Jetty Barracks**, past wooden houses, towards the rambling remains of the **Ehrensvärd Crown Castle** and gardens. The castle courtyard is the best preserved section of the fortress and contains the 1788 sarcophagus of the Count himself. His former home is now a museum.

The rest of Suomenlinna is split between residences and the fortress fortifications, which spread across **Susisaari** and the southernmost island of **Kustaanmiekka**. From the highest outcrop on this windswept last island, it is sometimes possible to see Estonia, 50 miles (80 km) away. The **Nordic Arts Centre** is also here and an atmospheric summer restaurant called **Walhalla**.

Korkeasaari is another "tourist is-

Preceding pages: Karelian costumes at the Open-Air Museum on Seurasaari. Below, a good way to see Helsinki, from the harbour.

154

land" but has neither Suomenlinna's complexity nor its charm. Finland's only zoo completely dominates this rocky outcrop just metres away from the mouth of Sörnäinen Harbour. You can reach it by boat from Hakaniemi from the Market Square.

Korkeasaari Zoo is not one of the world's greatest. Although it specialises in "cold climate animals", if you want to learn about Finnish fauna, you'd probably do just as well at the **Helsinki Zoological Museum**. Still, kids always seem to like the baboons and bears and free-roaming peacocks.

Seurasaari is also strictly a visitors' island, but eminently more atmospheric. A pretty, forested place, its northeastern side has been made into an **Open-Air Museum** of wooden buildings from provinces all over Finland. The other side is a national park.

The transplanted houses on Seurasaari date from the 17th to 19th century and include farmsteads and a church. Bonfires near here celebrate traditional festivities for Midsummer and Easter for which local Finnish children dress up as "Easter witches".

This is one island that does not call for a boat. Just take either bus No. 24 from the centre or bike along the Meilahti coastal drive (which takes you past **Sibelius Park** and the silvery tubular **Sibelius Monument**). A wooden footbridge connects the island to the Helsinki shore.

Helsinki's favourite island for swimming is undoubtedly **Pihlajasaari**. Literally *Rowan Island*, Pihlajasaari actually comprises two islands, with a sandy beach, café and changing cabins on the larger island's western shore.

A fifth, very special, island is now a wildlife reserve but, up until 1990, was reserved for military purposes and is still in an absolutely pristine state. A network of paths (marked by signposts giving information in Finnish and Swedish) circle the tiny island and visitors are begged not to stray or pick any flowers or remove plants. You can reach Harakka by boat in the summer or, in winter, by crossing the ice from Eira.

Part of the old fortifications on Suomenlinna.

ACROSS THE BALTIC

They are known as the "Finland Ferries," even though they ply the Baltic sea lanes to and from Sweden and several sail under the Swedish flag. Any preconceived ideas about what a passenger-car ferry is, or should be, will quickly vanish as soon as you board one of these magnificent ships operated by either of the top players, Viking Line (red) and Silja Line (white).

These vessels are a generation or two ahead of ferries operated by any other company on international routes, and are truly luxurious vessels comparable to Caribbean cruise ships. The main difference is that the swimming pool is covered or below deck rather than open-air in the stern.

They were not always so sumptious. At one time, the cabins were so small that cabin-mates were almost obliged to take turns standing, and no-one wanted to spend more time in one than was absolutely necessary. The choice of things to do was, however, limited to looking out of the window or sitting in the bar, where the band was a three-man combo from – it always seemed – Bulgaria or Albania.

Smörgåsbord or cafeteria: When it came to dining, the choice was a crowded smörgåsbord restaurant or a rather sterile cafeteria. Shopping was more or less limited to tax-free booze, cigarettes, and sweets. Nevertheless, it was fun and it was value for money. Moreover, the route was through the beautiful archipelagoes of Stockholm, the Åland Islands, and Finland's west coast.

Today, times have changed. While still noted for good times on board, the Finland ferries are no longer floating singles bars. Ship construction has also greatly improved with better insulated cabin walls and doors that fill the frame. But they are still fun, still value for money, and still cruise through the most beautiful seascapes in the world.

Over the past three decades, both Silja and Viking Lines have introduced new ships at regular intervals. The competition between them is strong and each new christening offers more in the way of comfort. Cabins are bigger, berths stand side by side instead of being double bunks and, though basic things like shower and WC in the cabin became standard long ago, the shower-rooms are now more spacious.

The sea-going smörgåsbord restaurant is still a must but the premises are better designed, to make it easier to get to the herring, salmon, meatballs and all the other delectable Finnish, Swedish and international dishes. The ships also include a remarkable number of first-class à la carte restaurants, from seafood and oyster bars to gourmet dining.

You can dance in multi-deck night clubs with top bands and often international floor shows. There are casinos with blackjack and roulette as well as row upon row of one-armed bandits. For the younger set, or those who think they are young, there are hi-tech discos and video game arcades.

Bargain alcohol?: The limited tax-free shop has given way to a multi-outlet shopping complex with fashions, accessories, toys and electronics, as well as the usual tax-free array. But a warning for the non-Finn, non-Swede: the term "tax-free alcohol" is a misconception since the prices, while lower than in either country, are often higher than the retail price in many others.

Saunas were standard from the very beginning. Now they have become "relaxation centres" with solarium, physical fitness rooms, swimming pool and whirlpool. Children get special consideration and can enjoy themselves in miniature fun parks and well-equipped play centres, looked after by qualified assistants.

As the Finnish economy started to grow stronger in the 1970s, affluent Finns and already-affluent Swedes enjoyed more leisure time and discovered the 24-hour mini cruise and the opportunity to take a "quick" foreign holiday with packages that included attractively priced hotels. For foreign visitors also, the ferries now make an easy and unusual way to combine a visit to both countries. As well, both Finns and

Swedes have a tendency to gather in groups to discuss any topic imaginable and the companies hit on the idea of providing meeting facilities for the ever-growing conference-at-sea market. The chance to meet in luxury away from the office has strengthened this Finnish and Swedish "groups" tendency.

Environmental doubts: All this, and the mirror-smooth Baltic, make for a comfortable trip for the passenger but it is the ever-growing size of the Finland ferries that is likely to cause rough sailing ahead for the ship owners. It is not the vessels' sea-worthiness that is in doubt but the growing complaints of the environmental lobbies. In some respects, the Finland ferries are a model of environmental friendliness since no waste of any kind is dumped into the sea and sulphur emissions from the newer vessels have been reduced by using more expensive low-sulphur fuels.

Nevertheless, all ships create wakes and, when they are as huge as the Finland ferries, there is valid concern for the erosion of the shorelines especially on the islands of the inner archipelago, as well as the havoc caused to small boats, piers, and even the seabed. Another environmental concern is the air and noise pollution caused by heavy traffic in areas near ferry terminals. The ferries carry over 900,000 passenger cars, almost 30,000 coaches and nearly 170,000 trailer trucks a year.

But it would not be easy to replace the Finland ferries. They are a vital link in Finnish-Swedish trade and one of Finland's main lifelines to Europe. Travellers for pleasure or business benefit from the very fact that so much of Finland's foreign trade goes by trailer trucks on to the ferries. In the same way, reasonable freight rates are maintained by ticket and on-board sales to pleasure and business passengers.

But on a still summer night, as pinpoints of light appear on the islands on either side of the ferry's white wake, not many of these practicalities are likely to figure much in the mind of a passenger leaning over the deck rail to gaze out to the darkening sea.

The ferries' route weaves in and out of thousands of islands. Right, young Astonian in national dress.

THE BALTIC STATES

Luxury ferries from Helsinki regularly cross the Bay of Finland to some of the most attractive cities of the former Soviet Union. Most popular of all is the two-day excursion to St Petersburg; visas are not needed, accommodation is provided on the boat and there are no money worries; Russians would rather have your dollars, pounds or yen than there own devalued rouble. St Petersburg is the creation of Peter the Great, founded as a window into Europe in 1703 on 40 islands in the Neva river delta. Largely built by European architects, it is the least Russian of Soviet cities. Italianate palazzi line the long embankments, their pastel-painted facades reflected in the numerous waterways; inevitably comparisons have been drawn with Venice and Amsterdam.

It is European art, too, that draws crowds to the Hermitage for, despite all the statistics – 1,057 rooms, 2 million items – the highlights of the collection are concentrated in the rooms devoted to Western Painting, most of it from private collections nationalised after the Revolution: 26 works by Rembrandt, Poussin's neoclassical scenes, masterpieces by Cezanne and Van Gogh and the huge, colourful and vivacious *Dancers* by Matisse.

St Petersburg is a rewarding city for walking and absorbing the street life, which is particularly lively during the "white nights" of June, when everyone comes out to watch the lingering sunsets. A walk from the Hermitage, through the archway of the General Staff building, will take you past what used to be the Fabergé workshop in Herzen (Gertsena) street to Nevsky Prospect, the city's main thoroughfare.

Drop in at the Kafe Literaturnoya (18 Nevsky) for Viennese atmosphere, excellent coffee and cakes, and occasional poetry readings for chamber concerts. This is a much-revered institution because Pushkin ate his last meal here, in 1837, before he went to fight his fatal duel. Arts Square, round the corner, is the place to spend an evening listening to music at the Philharmonic, or watching opens and ballet at the Maly Theatre. Gostiny Dvor (35 Nevsky) is the city's largest department store and will show you all that Russia produces by way of consumer goods.

The trip out to Petrodvorets (18 miles/28 km west of the city) is a must. This is Peter the Great's answer to Versailles and he invited all the European rulers to attend its gala opening. The centrepiece of the Great Cascade is a statue of Samson tearing open the jaws of a lion which shoots a jet of water 50 ft (15 metres) into the air: it symbolises Peter's victory over the Swedes at Poltova in 1709. Equally revealing of Peter the Great's character are the trick fountains: be careful when choosing a seat to rest upon – some will suddenly send up a shower of water to soak your backside.

Tallinn, the capital of Estonia, is the other ferry destination, and from here you can set off to explore all three newly independent Baltic states – the other two are Latvia (capital Riga) and Lithuania (capital Vilnius). Tallin lies directly opposite Helsinki, 50 miles (80 km) across the water, and large numbers of Finnish tourists (many of them former refugees from Estonia who fled in the final years of World War II) visit the city: more, it has to be said, for the lively nightlife than for its unspoiled medieval old town. Cobbled alleys ascend from the 14th-century castle and the Gothic architecture reminds you that Tallinn was once an important port of the Hanseatic League.

Riga, a city founded by merchants, has a similar history. The 13th-century Romanesque cathedral is lined with the tombs of Teutonic bishops, Prussian knights and Westphalian *landmeisters*. The organ, German too, is the fourth biggest in the world, and most evenings you can hear performances of Bach or Mozart.

Vilnius, by contrast with its Lutheran neighbours, is Catholic, thanks to long association with Poland. Three things impinge on every visitor: the ubiquitous jewellery shops selling amber, for which Lithuania has been famous since antiquity; the warren of medieval streets clustering below the castle on Gedimas hill where you will find many a courtyard or basement restaurant serving food, surprisingly good food – game a speciality; and the festive, almost disbelieving atmosphere that prevails here now that the long-dreamed of independence has finally become a reality.

THE ESSENTIAL TRIANGLE

In many countries, a city conjures up a picture of busy streets clogged with cars, and tall buildings. A Finnish city certainly has its motor traffic but it is also a spreading area of lake, forest and green spaces between the buildings that sometimes feels as though it were in the heart of rural Finland.

This makes a triangular tour, some 300 miles (500 km) between the three largest cities one of the best ways to get a feel of Finland in a couple of weeks. From the capital Helsinki, the road leads to Turku, the old capital in the centre of Swedish-speaking Finland, and then on to Tampere, the industrial capital, where water set the first 18th-century mills arolling, then back by the old road to Helsinki.

Along the route are most of the elements, past and present, that make Finland what it is today. In the south, there are coasts and lakesides, some lakes so vast that it is difficult to decide whether they are lake or sea. Beautiful old houses restored as museums and hotels lie along the route, as do historic castles with magnificent banqueting halls and dungeons too, and statues that reflect Finland's history, sometimes warlike, sometimes at peace.

Further north, the lakes become more frequent, and it is tempting to leave the car and travel as the Finns of old did, using waterways such as the Silverline route which winds through the lake system between Tampere and Hämeenlinna. You can go north by the Poet's Way to Virrat, and everywhere can swim, fish or sail on lake or sea.

This is a good opportunity to get to know something about Finland's arts and culture, remarkable in a country of only five million, and see the Finns' famed skill in design at glassworks and studios that welcome visitors and offer distinctive articles that could only be Finnish. Above all, between the cities lies the long Finnish road through dark green forests and old villages, to make it a tour filled with flowers and fresh air.

EN ROUTE TO TURKU

The 19th-century search for a national Finnish identity out in the countryside has left a selection of museums and buildings all round Helsinki. First along the route to Turku is **Tarvaspää**, the home of the flamboyant painter Akseli Gallen-Kallela, whose illustrations of the *Kalevala* are among his best-known works. He was already well established when, between 1911 and 1913, he organised the building of a studio-home around Linudd villa on the old Alberga Manor ground.

Today, Helsinki reaches almost to Tarvaspää yet it is still set in forest and field. Though it was designed by the architect Eliel Saarinen, much of the painter's forceful personality also found its way into Tarvaspää, along with his own hard physical work.

It is a peaceful tree-shaded place. The studio, still in its original form, has some 100 of the paintings for the *Kalevala* which decorated the Finnish Pavilion at the Paris Exhibition in 1900. Also on view are paintings for his frescoes in the Jusélius mausoleum in Pori (*see page 214*), which commemorated Sigrid Jusélius, the 11 year-old-daughter of a Pori businessman. Working on these frescoes was a poignant task for the painter, whose own young daughter had died only a few years earlier. There are also many traces of the journeys of this inveterate traveller, such as a Japanese home altar, and relics of times in Africa, Paris and elsewhere.

Tarvaspää consists of a studio wing, tower and main building, and the original Linudd Villa holds a coffee house and a terrace restaurant; there is also a daily guided tour. To get there, leave road 1 (E3) 250 yards (200 metres) past Turunväylä (Tarvontie). Almost at once, a road marked Tarvaspää takes you to the museum. The assistants at Tarvaspää will advise on a cross-country route to Saarinen's home at Hvitträsk, some 14 miles (20 km) west in Kirkonummi municipality, but it is simplest to return to road 1 (E3), take junction 3 left for Jorvas, and follow the signs for Hvitträsk.

Natural blend: You would expect the studio home of three of Finland's most famous architects to be at one with its surroundings but **Hvitträsk** surpasses the term. The stone and timber buildings seem to blend into the forest, the great cliffs and the lake (White Lake) that gives the house its name. Inside, architecture, interior designs and furniture are also a whole. The partnership of Eliel Saarinen, Herman Gesellius and Armas Lindgren was responsible for many important buildings and, in all, the big, main studio, now a museum, saw the planning of 70 projects.

Hvitträsk celebrated one of the architects' earliest triumphs, the Finnish Pavilion at the Paris World Exhibition in 1900 (decorated by Gallen-Kallela's *Kalevala* frescoes). The dining-room ceiling is also Gallen-Kallela's work. Saarinen, who disliked long meetings, designed the hard black table and chairs. What his dinner guests said is not recorded but new productions of

Saarinen's furniture designs are still on sale today, mostly distinctive straight backed chairs and settees or round tables. Don't miss the heavy metal rings in the drawing room's "whisky corner". Every time Saarinen won a prize he held a party where guests could drink as much whisky as they liked, as long as they could clutch the whisky rings and stay upright.

The early working harmony did not always extend into the private life of the little community, however. Propinquity, perhaps, turned the gaze of Saarinen's first wife, Matilda, towards his partner Gesellius and she simply crossed the garden and changed houses. Apparently bearing no grudge, Saarinen married Gesellius' sister, Loja, two years later. But the triumvirate broke up in 1906 and by 1916 Saarinen was working at Hvitträsk on his own.

In 1922, after gaining a major prize in a competition in New York, Saarinen moved to America, became Dean of the Cranbrook Academy of Art and as well known as he had been in Finland. He continued to visit Hvitträsk each year until his death in 1950, and his grave overlooks the lake.

Leased to Russia: The whole Kirkkonummi municipality was once a large rural Swedish-speaking area, with a spectacular coastline on the Baltic Sea, and is still a favourite for summer cabins. At the end of World War II, Finland was forced to lease the Porkkala Peninsula in the south to the Soviet Union as a naval base (a lease prematurely ended in 1956). The Russian cemetery, on a typical Soviet scale, is an ageless reminder of that 12-year period, when 7,000 Finns had to leave their homes at 10 days' notice.

Today Porkkala has a Finnish naval garrison in Upinniemi, with a remarkable Sea Chapel, designed by Marianne and Mikko Heliövaara, shaped like a boat with open sails and overlooking the sea. Some of the best bird migration routes pass over the Porkkala Peninsula and spring and autumn draw ornithologists galore to watch flocks of cranes, swans and geese. In summer, sailing

Far left, a coat of arms shows the Swedish influence.

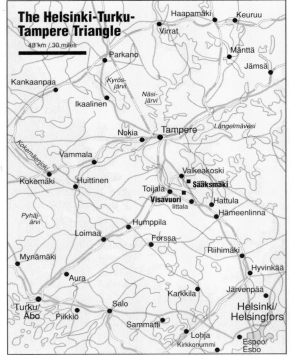

The Helsinki-Turku-Tampere Triangle

48 km / 30 miles

Haapamäki · Keuruu · Virrat · Mänttä · Jämsä · Parkano · Kankaanpaa · Kyrös-järvi · Näsi-järvi · Ikaalinen · Nokia · Tampere · Längelmävesi · Kokemäenjoki · Vammala · Valkeakoski · Kokemäki · Huittinen · Sääksmäki · Toijala · Visavuori · Iittala · Hattula · Hämeenlinna · Pyhäjärvi · Humppila · Loimaa · Forssa · Riihimäki · Mynämäki · Hyvinkää · Aura · Järvenpää · Karkkila · Helsinki/Helsingfors · Turku/Åbo · Piikkiö · Salo · Sammatti · Lohja · Espoo/Esbo · Kirkkonummi

Grefve Armfelt till Åminne

boats by the hundred take over as the main attraction.

Back on road 1 and heading west, the area of lake and ridge is part of the **Salpausselkä Ridge**, formed at the end of the Ice Age. The next major stop is Sammatti, just south of the road. Look out for the sign to **Paikkari Cottage**, (Paikkarin Torppa) the home of Elias Lönnrot, who collected the old legends and tales for the *Kalevala*. The building is typical of a worker's home in 19th-century southwest Finland. Outside, his statue is by Halonen and **Räsänen**. A couple of miles away stands Lammi House where Lönnrot died. At **Salo**, some 80 miles (115 km) from Helsinki in the heart of the apple-growing Salojoki Valley, it is worth turning off the main road to go into the town centre, which has old houses and beautiful gardens, **Uskela Church**, another of C.L. Engel's works, and a fine valley view.

Tyrant's carriage: At Piikkiö, only some 10 miles (15 km) from Turku, turn right for the **Pukkila Manor House Museum and Vehicle Museum** (Pukkilan kartano-ja ajokalumuseo), where the rococo-style mansion is furnished as the home of a state official. The Carriage Museum in the former byre has 30 different carriages, including that of the notorious Governor General Bobrikov, assassinated in 1904.

The town church dates back to 1755, built partly of stones from the ruins of Kuusisto Castle. This medieval bishop's castle is worth a detour to the **Kuusisto** peninsula. (Just west of Piikkiö, take the road to Pargas [Parainen] and branch on to a secondary road to the ruins.) The castle was built in the 14th century and stood stoutly until Gustav Vasa ordered its demolition in 1528 but enough remains to have encouraged recent attempts at restoration.

Having come this far, you may like to continue to **Pargas** (**Parainen**), which has a beautiful view over the islands of the archipelago, and is most famous for its large limestone quarries. From here it is a short drive northwest to Turku or Åbo, Finland's principal city during the Swedish centuries.

Hvitträsk, home and studio for Saarinen and his architect partners.

TURKU

Turku is the other face of Finland, the view from the southwest, closest to Scandinavia and the rest of Europe, not just for trade but also in culture. Its atmosphere is a mixture of river and sea: the River Aura divides the modern city in two; the Baltic, curling round the river mouth, has countless islands in an archipelago that stretches mile after mile southwest until it runs into the Åland Islands, half-way between Finland and Sweden.

It is also a city of paradoxes. Turku, Åbo in Swedish, feels like a capital even though it never held that title in a sovereign country but only as the principal city and home of the Viceroy in the Finnish part of the Swedish-Finnish kingdom. It is Finland's oldest city and yet many of the buildings go back only to the Great Fire of 1827 which destroyed a town then largely made of wood. Islands, river and sea make Turku a summer paradise of sunning and swimming, yet it is also the birthplace of Finnish culture and the country's religious centre.

The Swedes were the first known nation to arrive at the mouth of the Aura River when King Erik sailed in with an English bishop, and an expeditionary force in 1155. As Bishop Henrik, the bishop later became the first Finnish patron saint. Even earlier, Finnish tribes from the southeast had settled and traded along the river valleys of southwest Finland, and sailors and merchants came and went to the first settlement, up river at Koroinen.

The Swedes called their growing town Åbo and in 1229 Pope Gregory IX agreed to transfer the See of the Bishop of Finland to Koroinen. By 1300, a new Cathedral a little downstream on Unikankare (the "Mound of Sleep") east of the river was ready for consecration, and Turku became the spiritual centre of Finland.

Around the same time, the solid lines of a castle began to rise near the mouth of the River Aura as the heart of royal power in Finland, where the Swedish governor lived and visiting dignitaries paid their respects. It was also a fighting castle, standing firm under a winter siege in the mid 14th century in one of the bloody struggles for the Swedish throne. In all, the castle was besieged six times. In the 16th century, Gustav Vasa, father of the Swedish Vasa dynasty, survived a winter siege and proclaimed his young son (later Johan III) as the Duke of Finland.

After Duke Johan returned in 1552, with his wife, the Polish princess Katarina Jagellonica, Turku Castle entered its most colourful phase of royal glory. Katarina brought glamour, in her Polish courtiers, her velvet and lace, and even her spoons, forks and knives, and introduced a splendid court life that was already common in most of Europe but had not yet reached Finland. In summer, the court visited the island of Ruissalo, just off the coast, as Finns do today. But this gracious life did not last. After Gustav Vasa's death, feuds broke out between his three sons, and the

eldest brother, Erik XIV, besieged the Duke. The castle surrendered in three weeks and Johan and Katarina were bundled into captivity. Though later, as Johan III, Duke Johan gained his revenge on Erik whom he captured and imprisoned in Turku Castle, castle life never again achieved such heights.

Castle renewed: Today, the castle's massive faces, honey-coloured under the sun, grey when the weather is grey, look towards the modern town centre, some 2 miles (3 km) away. Many of its great rooms have been preserved as **Turku Historical Museum** with portraits of Duke Johan and his wife. The old chapel has regained its original purpose and the magnificent banqueting halls are the scene of civic celebrations.

Turku had the first university in Finland, founded by the 17th century Governor General of Finland, Count Per Brahe. He travelled the length and breadth of his governorship and his name is commemorated in many towns and buildings. His greatest contribution to Turku, however, was Åbo Akademi which, after its ceremonial opening in 1640, made Turku the centre of culture and learning as well as religion. When Finland became a Russian Grand Duchy, the Czar ordered the Academy to be transferred to the new capital to become the University of Helsinki but the **Old Academy Building** remains. In 1918, independent Finland created a second Akademi as Turku's Swedish language university, and also founded the University of Turku.

After the Great Fire in 1827, market and town moved away from the Cathedral to the west bank of the Aura, much of it designed and built to the plan of that industrious German, Carl Ludwig Engel, who visualised a city of rectangular blocks intersected by broad streets, a plan still clear in modern Turku. The way to start a walking tour is among the bright stalls, piled with fruit and flowers, in the market square. On one side, the Hotel Hamburger Börs is one of Turku's best, with bars, cafés, and restaurants packing its ground floor. It is busy all day and up to mid-

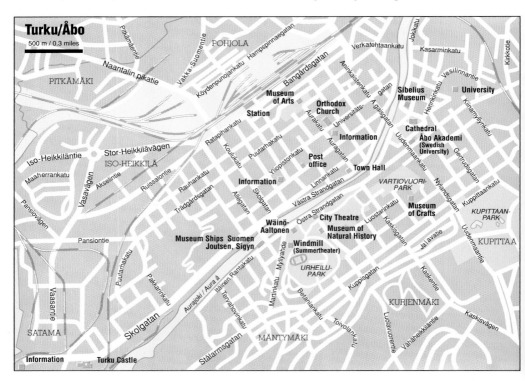

night, not just with visitors but as a local meeting place. The hotel faces across to the green, cap-like dome of the Orthodox Church, an Engel design built in 1838 on the orders of Czar Nicholas I. The yellow building to the southwest is the **Swedish Theatre**, also by Engel.

Orthodox community: During the days of the Grand Duchy, the **Orthodox Cathedral** served a Russian community but it is now attached to Constantinople. Its present congregation of 2,000 includes some converts and one or two families who moved from Finnish Karelia during the World War II resettlement. Inside, it has all the rich beauty of an Orthodox Cathedral, the dome held up by ornate pillars. Paintings show the story of St George and the Dragon, and Empress Alexandra (martyred wife of the Roman Emperor Diocletianus) to whom the church is dedicated.

A selection of shops such as Pentik, Aarikka, and Sylvi Salonen, along Ylliopistonkatu (Universitetsgatan) to the west, is a happy hunting ground for gifts and mementoes, with a selection of handcrafts, wooden and chinaware and other typically Finnish goods, and most will post and pack under the duty free scheme. Between here and Eerikinkatu (Eriksgatan) is the **Hansa Shopping Centre**, enticingly weatherproof in a Finnish winter.

More exciting is the 19th-century **Indoor Market**, across the street in Eerikinkatu. There is something about the very smell of a market hall that lures you in, a mixture of cheese, meat, fish, sweets, and a tang of exotic spices. The small stalls stretch along the entire length, with tempting arrays of *munkki*, a sort of doughnut, and *pulla* a cake-like bread. At Turun Tee ja Mausta you can smell the tea before you buy and pick up interesting oddities such as ginger tea for Christmas or one spiced with cloves – good for cold weather, the Finns say – more than 200 in all. Nearby, a stall sells typical wooden tulip flowers and leaves, painted in mauves, greens and yellows. Made by a sheltered workshop, they are half the usual cost.

The Market Place below Turku's Orthodox Cathedral.

Summer dancing: Turning down Aura-katu towards the **Aurasilta** (bridge) you pass the Tourist Information Office, and the bridge gives the first view of the sleek white hull and complicated rigging of the *Suomen Joutsen*, the Swan of Finland, which once plied between South America and Europe. Along the banks, people sit at open-air restaurants and, below the bridge, there is dancing every summer Tuesday from 6 to 8pm.

Over the bridge, on the right hand side, the **statue** is **Paavo Nurmi**, claimed to be the greatest long-distance runner of all time. He lived from 1897 to 1973, won a total of nine gold and three silver Olympic medals, and set 31 world records. You may already have seen a replica of this statue of Turku's most famous son in front of the Olympic Stadium in Helsinki where he carried the Olympic Torch in the 1952 Games.

The entrance to one of Turku's most interesting areas is just a short walk from here. This is Luostarinmäki, Cloister Hill, the site of an early convent. There's a certain rough justice in the fact that the only part of the wooden city to survive the Great Fire of 1827 was this hill. For it housed those too poor to buy houses in the 18th-century city who moved away from the centre to build their own community. That escape has left an inheritance that, unlike most Nordic open-air museums, stands where it was founded and is not a collection of typical buildings moved in. The name is the **Handicrafts Museum**, which is a pity because this old area is much more; the woman spinning today in the dark interior of a wooden house is a museum worker but she is spinning in the same way and in the same place as the early inhabitants, and the 18th-century costumes seem quite natural.

There are traditional sweets, every sort of craft, tin, copper and goldsmith's, and a baker's which sometimes sells pretzels made in the traditional way. Seamstresses sew and tailors tailor and the old way of life is revealed in the community houses where different families lived in the same building, sharing their kitchen and their bath-

Turku Cathedral, once the focal point of old Turku, after its most recent restoration in the 1980s.

house, or by the truckle bed of a university student who lived with a family, giving service in return for his keep. The main house near the entrance has an excellent self-service restaurant with good homemade food.

Coming down from the hill, detour via the Observatory on Vartiovuori Hill, another Engel building, now the **Maritime Museum** and **Astronomical Collection**. Nearby is an anti-aircraft gun memorial from World War II, when ordinary Finns raised money for defensive guns. Turku bought nine.

Old centre: Turku Cathedral, also on this side of the river, was the focal point of old Turku. Look down from the balcony for the best view of the high arches of the main aisle, with its side chapels. The balcony also has the Cathedral Museum, with valuable collections opened to the public in the 1980s after the most recent restoration. Among the most interesting chapels is the Kankainen Chapel where the stained-glass window by Wladimir Swetschkoff shows Queen Karin Månsdotter, wife of the luckless Erik XIV, who was eventually poisoned after his imprisonment.

Don't miss the statue of **Mikael Agricola** near the Cathedral's south wall. The architect of the Reformation in Finland, he was born on a farm in North Finland and took the name Agricola meaning "farmer's son" when he went to study in Rome. In the Cathedral Park **Governor Per Brahe** stands in a classically proud pose, not far from **Åbo Akademi**, a block or two to the north. The main buildings of the present Swedish language university and the University of Turku are also nearby.

In Turku you are never far from the River Aura and can cross and recross its four main bridges or take the little ferry that still carries pedestrians and cycles across free of charge. For a riverbank tour, the first stop is **Qwensel House**, Turku's oldest wooden building, named after, and built by, Judge W.J. Qwensel who bought the plot as long ago as 1695. From the waterside, low bushes trace the name TURKU/ÅBO, and Qwensel House is now the **Pharmacy**

Traditional dress in the Pharmacy Museum.

Museum. A recent innovation, leaving from the front of the museum, is the horse cab Musta-Hilu which provides a leisurely and unusual view of the city. (Children also have the Koiramäki tour of the city in a special red and yellow bus with guides in costume. This daily summer tour is, as yet, so far conducted only in Swedish and Finnish.)

Walking towards Myllysilta (Mill Bridge), the red granite statue is "Sheltered Growth," by Jarkko Roth and, just past the bridge in Borenpuisto Park, the dramatic "Icy Sea," is dedicated to Turku's seamen. August Upman (inscribed on the pedestal) was a pioneer of winter navigation. Below on the river is a former Lake Saimaa steamer *Pikinytky* which once carried timber and, past the next bridge, Martinsilta, the s/s *Ukkopekka* was the last steamship to sail Finland's coastal waters. Depending on how far you care to walk, you can continue on this side as far as **Turku Castle** (easily reached by bus for a separate excursion) and the modern harbour areas that show how important the sea

still is to Turku, with workaday merchant tugs and tankers, and the terminals of the Viking and Silja Lines.

Mannerheim's Day: Otherwise, cross over Martinsilta to the *Joutsen* (Swan of Finland). Built at St Nazaire in 1902, the ship is today a popular place for visitors and locals alike, particularly on 4 June, the anniversary of Field Marshal Mannerheim's promotion to general. Green pea soup is on offer, free, and people queue up for it all day. Don't miss the old picture of a traditional "Crossing the Line" ceremony. Almost next door, the smaller barque is *Sigyn*, launched in Gothenburg in 1887, and sailing as far as the East Indies and South America. Her last home port was the Åland Islands and her last voyage from there in 1949 but she still shows signs of the past and those who know about sailing ships will realise *Sigyn* is unique as the last barque-rigged ocean-going vessel.

Heading back towards the centre you come to the austere outlines of the **Wäinö Aaltonen Museum**. Designed by Aaltonen's architect son and daugh-

River walk beside the Aura.

ter-in-law, the building contains much of his work including the massive statue of Peace, hands raised, and Faith, a mother and child. In a self-portrait, this very private man placed a text in front of his face to hide his feelings. Further along, outside the **City Theatre** is Aaltonen's statue of Aleksis Kivi, one of the first authors to write in Finnish.

The windmill on **Samppalinnan-mäki** (hill) overlooking the river is the last of its kind in Turku. Here also, stopwatch in hand, Paavo Nurmi trained against his own best times, and the polished granite stone on the slopes is Finland's independence memorial, unveiled in 1977 on the 60th anniversary. On this river walk, you will notice the waterbuses by Auransilta Bridge and below Martinsilta Bridge. Be sure not to miss a sight-seeing cruise, the best way to get a feel for this water city.

Some of these boats go to **Ruissalo Island**, also reached in a few minutes by crossing a bridge. It is a green and leafy island, a place for botanists and bird-watchers as well as cyclists and walk-

ers. Ruissalo has the area's best beaches, including a recently opened nudist beach, something still rare in Finland, not because of any national prudery but because the Finns, with their lonely cabins on isolated lake-sides, had not realised one might need permission to bathe without a swimsuit.

Art and rock: The island is also a surprise place for art lovers for Ruissalo boasts one of the best art centres in Finland. The 19th-century **Villa Roma** is typical of the so-called "lace villas" (because of their latticed balconies and windows) built by wealthy merchants. Its present owner, Marjo Brunow Ruola, a Turku businesswoman, has dedicated her talents to providing a summer exhibition of top-quality Finnish art, from glass to painting to textiles. There are toy and home museums, and a café which the energetic Mrs Ruola supervises. Another good restaurant is **Honkapirtti**, a Karelian-style pinewood building built in 1942–43 by infantry soldiers near the front during the Continuation War. In summer also, this

The children's sight-seeing bus.

multi-faceted island is home to Ruisrock, the world's oldest annual rock festival (*see page 211*).

One of the most civilised ways to see the archipelago is a supper cruise aboard the S/S *Ukkopekka* which retains something of its steamship past and its original engine. As the passengers strive for window tables, the *Ukkopekka* moves smoothly down the river and out to sea. The bearded skipper, Captain Oskari-Pentti Kangas, is everyone's picture of a sea captain and a couple of musicians sing old Finnish sailing songs as the islands glide by. If the timing is right, from one a fisherman sails out to the *Ukkopekka* with the fish he has caught and smoked that day. The steamship cruises to different islands and towns, including Captain Kangas' home town of Naantali, north of Turku, where there is dancing on the quay.

Naantali is now a famous sailing harbour, packed with visiting boats. It is also a historic town, with an "old town" from 200 years ago; no museum piece but a place with houses that are still lived in today. There is a beautiful greystone convent church, with a new organ that attracts famous organists, particularly during the **June Music Festival** when some 15,000 visitors crowd into the tiny town. At its start in the 1980s, the sceptics thought that little Naantali's festival "would die in 10 years." Now into its second decade, the Festival is proving them wrong. The harbour is also popular with artists, and galleries include the Purpura, which specialises in Finnish artists and supports an artist-in-residence.

The Presidents of Finland also have their summer residence nearby, at **Kultaranta** – "the golden shore" – whose gardens and parkland are open to the public. Many foreign dignitaries visit Kultaranta and take a sauna in former President Kekkonen's unusual sauna house above the rocky coast.

Naantali, around 20 minutes by the new road from Turku, could also be a detour on the way to Tampere but the more direct routes leave the city on road 40 (motorway at first). This leads to Aura, some 20 miles (30 km) north where from road 9 you have a fine view of the **Aurakoski** (rapids). Road 9 is one of two alternatives, continuing northeast through rich farmland with a possible detour right at the Helsinki-Pori crossroads (road 2) for a short drive to the **Humpilla Glassworks**, which have a glass-walled demonstration forge where you watch glass-blowers at work. The **Glass Village at Nuutajärvi**, a little further north on the left of the road, was formed around Finland's oldest glassworks from 1793, and is also worth a stop.

The alternative route, road 41, slightly to the west goes through Oripää, a gliding centre, where the Moorish style building is the studio-home of sculptor Viljo Syrjämaa, and from Vammala, the road goes through the flat, fertile land of the Loimijoki valley. A 3-mile (5-km) detour on the secondary road to **Ellivuori** is well worthwhile. It is both a winter and summer centre. Just north of **Noki** are more magnificent rapids at the start of the waterway system that leads to Tampere.

Left, Captain Oskari Pentti-Kangas, skipper of the *Ukkopekka*. **Right**, Naantali.

TAMPERE

Tampere people call their city the Manchester or the Pittsburgh of Finland, depending on whether they are talking to someone from Great Britain or the United States, yet anything less like a classic industrial city is hard to imagine.

The city lies on a narrow neck of land between two lakes, great stretches of water so large that you feel you are close to a sea rather than scores of miles inland. Linking the lakes, the rushing waters of the Tammerkoski river first brought power, industry and riches to Tampere. Though it still provides some energy, the Tammerkoski is so clean nowadays that it attracts growing numbers of anglers, out for trout. At weekends, the two lakes are bright with rainbow sails, and the white wakes of motor boats, packed with picnickers, track their course to one of the islands or to a summer house along the lakeside.

Despite a changing pattern of industry, Tampere has managed to retain many bygone factories and workers' houses without allowing them to turn into slums, and the tall red-brick chimneys that do remain are symbols of both past and present, for Tampere's factories are still high on the list of Finland's leading manufacturers and exporters.

Romantic waterways: There are some 200 lakes in and around the city. The two largest, Näsijärvi to the north and Pyhäjärvi to the south, are the meeting point of two famous waterway routes. To the south, the Silverline threads its way though a labyrinth of lakes towards Hämeenlina, passing Valkeakoski, another industrial town in a splendid rural setting, and stopping at Aulanko Forest Park among other places.

The romantically named Poet's Way boat, *S/S Tarjanne*, steers north through narrow, winding waters to **Ruovesi** and **Virrat**. The whole journey takes nine hours and gives a two-day taste of Finland's lakes, with an overnight stay at either Virrat or Ruovesi. A little further north, **Ähtäri** has one of Finland's best native zoos. The national poet, J. L

Runeberg began his best-known work, *Tales of Ensign Ståhl*, in **Ritoniemi Mansion** at Ruovesi and, near the village, Akseli Gallen-Kallela built his first "**Kalevala**" studio-home, which is occasionally open to the public. By water is also a fine way of city sightseeing, though there are also bus and coach tours.

Tampere was officially founded in 1779 by King Gustav III of Sweden-Finland but, since the Middle Ages, the **Pirkkala** area to the south of the centre had been settled by farmers, attracted by the good waterways which made transport easy. From around the 13th century, when the Swedes granted them rights to collect taxes from the Lapp people, they prospered richly. These earliest Tamperelaiset (Tampere people) are commemorated on the Hämeensilta Bridge in four statues by Wäinö Aaltonen, *The Merchant*, *The Hunter*, *The Tax Collector*, and *The Maid of Finland*, characters who come from the ancient legends of the Pirkka. Also clear from the bridge is the tall

chimney of one Tampere's earliest industries, the paper-makers Frenckell from 1783. The old mill is now a theatre with two stages.

The Tammerkoski has largely lost its working factories, and hotels and shopping centres have taken their place. The venerable and well restored Grand Hotel Tammer, the Cumulus Koskikatu and Hotel Ilves all have splendid views of the Tammerkoski rapids, and from the top of the Ilves' 18 storeys, the panorama takes in the quay where the Silverline boats berth, the tiny toy leisure craft, the red-brick of the old factories and the magnificent stretches of lake. A minute or two away on the riverside, the **Verkaranta Arts and Crafts Centre** displays and sells good-quality craftwork. Above it on the town side is the Tourist Information Office. Below the hotel, the **Koskikeskus** covered shopping centre has some 100 shops. There are also various open-air markets and a **Market Hall** at Hämeenkatu 19.

Wartime memories: Across a foot-bridge over the rapids one of the oldest factory areas stands on Kehräsaari (Spinning Island). In the Independence (Civil) War, the victorious White Army crossed the Tammerkoski here to capture Tampere. Today, its factories and boutiques are grouped around cobbled courtyards. Nearby, the only factory still working on the river, Tako, makes carton paper. Keep an eye out too for the old factory chimney with a bomb shield on the top, a reminder that Tampere was bombed fiercely in the 1918 Civil War, when it was an important "Red" stronghold, and again during World War II with eight heavy raids.

Another reminder of World War II on Kehräsaari is **Bunkkeri** (Bunker Restaurant). The Bunker's wartime look includes World War II pistols, rifles, submachine guns and other paraphernalia, and guests eat from tin mess plates and drink "Molotov cocktails". The Bunker is popular with young people, a paradox in a country that talks but rarely and with difficulty about war.

Culture and education centre on

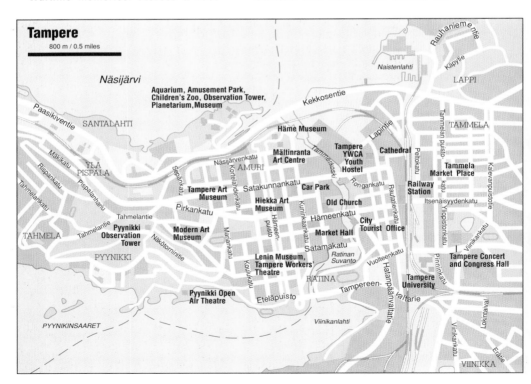

Tampere but it is modern culture and scientific and technical education. The architecture is also largely 20th-century, typified by the **City Library**, an astonishing building said to be based on the open wings and spread tail feathers of a wood grouse, though you might see it more as a series of mushrooms. In the mid-1980s the Library won several awards for its architects, Raili Paatelainen-Pietelä and Reima Pietelä (wife and husband) and the Tampere City Building Office. Finns are great readers and borrow, on average, 20 books each per year. Adults as well as children are intrigued by the Moominvalley section which has the original fantasy characters, the Moomins, created by Tove Jansson.

In the 1990s, Tampere's pride is the new **Tampere Hall**, a spectacular blue-white building. Light streaming in picks out the main lobby's fountains, which commemorate the Tammerkoski rapids as the source of prosperity. The main hall holds 2,000, a small auditorium 500 and, if you arrive on a festival morning,

from the stage comes the sound of one of the choirs or orchestras at rehearsal. Lit for an opera such as *Parsifal*, the large hall is magnificent, and Tampere people are happy to tell you that their hall is bigger than Helsinki's Finlandia, and the acoustics are much better. The hall is used for conferences and congresses and there is a whole beehive of meeting rooms, with a restaurant, Fuuga, and Café Soolo.

A little earlier in this rich architectural century, Lars Sonck was only 30 when he won a national competition with his design for what was then St John's church, now the **Cathedral**, completed in 1907 at the height of the national romantic movement. It stands in its own park, a few blocks east of the river, and has some of the best of Finnish art, including Magnus Enckell's altar fresco of the Resurrection and his circular window that forms a cross and wreath of thorns. Hugo Simberg painted *The Wounded Angel*, a shattered form carried by two boys, who may have caused the wounding; and

The Garden of Death, despite its name, not a gloomy picture – his note on the back of a working sketch reads: "A place where souls go before entering heaven." Around the gallery, his *Garland of Life* shows 12 boys carrying a green garland of roses, symbolising humanity's burden of life. This great church seats 2,000 and, softly lit, makes a beautiful setting for a Sunday evening concert, with every seat taken.

The **Kaleva Church**, east on the Kaleva road, stands solid in the centre of a sloping green park, like a silo rising out of a farm field. No wonder it's nicknamed "the silo of souls". Inside, the stark appearance changes to dramatic, with a white soaring light that pulls your face upwards. One striking feature of this remarkable church, another Pietilä-Paatelainen design from 1966, is the organ, its 3,000 pipes shaped like a "sail". Behind the altar the wooden statue is intended to be a reed – "a bruised reed He shall not break" – but it seems more like a tree destroyed.

Oldest church: Of course, Tampere has older churches, the oldest of all being a rare example from the 15th century, **St Michael's** at **Messukylä**, around two miles (5 km) east along the Iidesjärvi (lake) on the Lahti road. The oldest and coldest part is the vestry which once stood beside an even earlier wooden church. A moment of high excitement in 1959 revealed extensive wall paintings, now restored, from the 1630s. The church's most valuable wooden sculpture is believed to be the Royal saint King Olav of Norway, whose tomb in Trondheim became a place of pilgrimage during the Middle Ages.

Having come this far, it is well worth looking in at the **Haihara Doll Museum** nearby, in a manor owned by the Haihara family as far back as 1554. The last owner, Gunvor Ekroos, built up a huge private collection of some 1,000 dolls including one from 12th-century Peru, also puppets and puppet theatres, and many exhibits that illustrate the history of play and the old magic skills. On her death, the collection became the Haihara Museum Foundation with

The spectacular interior of Tampere Hall.

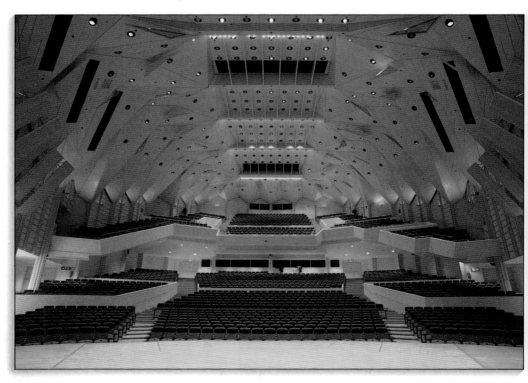

3,000 dolls, and many more items that illustrate the life of the upper classes from the rococo era to modern times.

Tampere's industrial history is also rich and, as though to prove how international the city was nearly two centuries ago, one of the most important industries, textiles, was founded by a Scotsman, James Finlayson. He arrived in 1820 from Russia to build a heavy engineering works at the north end of the Tammerkoski, with the first water-powered spinning mill. When he sold to Rauch and Nottbeck in 1836, it grew to become one of the biggest textile factories in the Nordic countries but in those early days, Mrs. Finlayson was not too proud to sell the mill's products in the market. James Finlayson was an industrialist in the Quaker mould and Finlaysons became almost a town within a city, with its own police, health programme and hospital, factory school, and a church: the yellow building with a wooden door near the factory complex. Visitors can look inside some of these old buildings and those of the

Kaleva Church, showing the 'Bruised Reed" statue behind the altar.

other main company, Tampella, on the eastern side of the river, which started as a foundry in 1850.

Czarist grandeur: After Finlayson returned to Scotland, the new owners continued the traditions and the name, and lived in a mansion house nearby, known as the **Finlayson Palatsi** (Finlayson Palace) and built by Alexander von Nottbeck. It became a famous house, visited by Czar Alexander II and his court, and there are portraits of both Alexander I and II on the central staircase, grand enough to feel you should be sweeping down it in full evening dress. At present, Finlayson's Palace is a restaurant, popular for functions and art exhibitions. There are plans to turn the stable block into a children's cultural centre, something Finlayson would have approved of, and the city hopes to form a new museum in the workshops.

The greater part of **Tampella** has moved further out of town but, as many of its old buildings deserve preservation, the aim is to convert them to apartments, offices and similar uses. One

former Tampella factory on a peninsula above Lake Näsijärvi is now the Lapinniemi Spa Hotel, the first of a style of hotels which concentrate on health, with massage and other treatments in an atmosphere of good food and comfort.

Another Nottbeck home was Näsilinna, a lovely old mansion on a hill in Näsinpuisto Park, also overlooking the lake, an easy walk from the Finlayson buildings. Be sure not to miss Emil Wikström's **Pohjanneito Fountain** on your way through. To illustrate how knowledge and skill are passed from generation to generation, on one side a grandmother explains handwork to a little girl, on the other a boy shows an old man how water power has made work easier. On top is the Maid of the North from the Kalevala sitting on a rainbow, spinning golden thread.

The Nottbeck house is now Häme Museum, a collection of items from the the old province of Häme around the city. There are often exhibitions of traditional arts, such as ryijy rug-making, an ancient Scandinavian technique which probably arrived through Sweden. These old rugs were not only warm and beautiful, they were practical too, even doing duty as money to meet the tax collectors' demands.

High point: From Näsilinna, across the northern harbour entrance is an even higher viewpoint, the **Näsinneula Observation Tower** at the centre of the **Särkänniemi Park**, with its Aquarium, Planetarium and Children's Zoo. There is no better way to get an overview of Tampere than from the open-air platform over 400 ft (120 metres) up and, looking immediately below, the funfair's scenic railways, roundabouts and ferris wheels look like a child's toys whirling and climbing on their metal girders. The tower has a good, medium-priced, revolving restaurant, which takes 50 minutes to complete a circle and is open until midnight.

If your tastes run to modern art rather than funfairs, or if you like both, don't miss the **Sara Hildén Art Gallery** in a beautiful building close by, which claims to have Tampere's best lake

The 16th-century Messykylä Church.

view. Sara Hildén was a business-woman and art collector who specialised in Finnish and foreign art of the 1960s and 1970s, and there are also visiting exhibitions and concerts.

Between the lakes, the western part of the isthmus rises in a raised beach to a tree-clad ridge which joins the lakes in a series of steps down through the woods. This is the Pyynikki Ridge, born 10,000 years ago during the last Ice Age round the old bowl of an ancient sea. It was once the home of the Bishop, and its old viewing tower is a popular place for looking over both lakes and towards the **Pyynikki's Open Air Theatre** down near Lake Pyhäjärvi. In a remarkable example of lateral thinking, the theatre auditorium revolves rather than the stage – truly theatre in the round as the audience turns to face each new scene, with *A Midsummer Night's Dream* fairies perched high in the trees. The theatre, open from mid-June to mid-August, is especially beautiful when the bird cherries are drenched in white blossom. There are also a restaurant and café.

Full circle: Further west is Pispala (Bishop's village), now considered a very prestigious place to live. In fact, it was built two generations ago by factory workers. As a sign of progress, their children left and went to live in central Tampere but now the grandchildren of the original builders are eager to return and restore. On the way back, the **Amuri Workers' Museum**, on Makasiininkatu, shows how these houses would have looked between 1910 and 1970. There are 25 houses and two shops, all giving the impression that the owners might return at any moment.

Whatever else you miss in this water city, do not miss a boat journey. If the Silverline or the Poet's Way take up too much time, try an excursion (City Information Office has details) or hop on a boat to Viikinsaari or another island. In half an hour you are on one of the beaches, you can birdwatch or botanise under cool forest trees, and picnic away from everyone else. Hard to believe that, strictly speaking, you are still in Finland's leading industrial city.

The Workers' Museum.

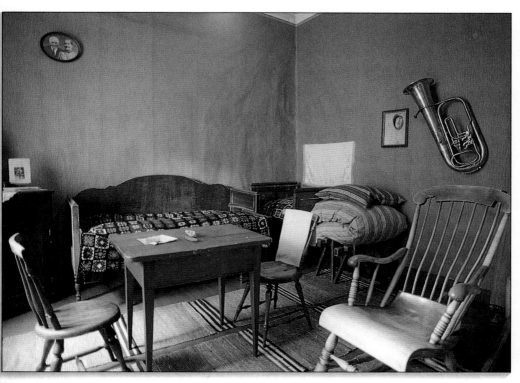

BACK TO HELSINKI

Many of the elements that make up Finland – history, industry, agriculture, lakeland, hill and forest, design and the arts – follow you along road 3 from Tampere to Helsinki. The first stop is **Valkeakoski** and **Sääksmäki**, yet another of those Finnish industrial centres that contrive to place themselves in beautiful surroundings between two lakes, where water and islands seem to thread their way through the town. In the Middle Ages, Valkeakoski was no more than a hamlet, later a mining village in the important parish of Sääksmäki; but, even then, it had the rapids that meant water power, first to grind corn and then to make paper. In contrast, the 19th-century national romantic movement also brought artists to Sääksmäki, and these two ingredients still combine today.

For a feeling of Valkeakoski's industrial history, go to the wooden outdoor museum of **Kauppilanmäki**, typical of the early paper-mill workers' homes up to 1920. The hurriedly-built driftwood home of a young couple contrasts with the comfortable house of mill foreman Esaias Ax but both still show traces of a recent farming past. The workers' hall, with its union flags, was the centre of political thought as well as community entertainment.

Before the bridge leading to Sääksmäki, the old **Voipaala Manor** on Rapola Hill has become an art centre. The museum was once the studio of the sculptor Elias Ilkka, who owned the manor and the farmyard where Valkeakoski Summer Theatre performs. On the hill above is the site of an ancient hill fort and a view of **Sääksmäki Church**, a short walk away. This early parish had an even older church but the present greystone building goes back to the 15th century. An accident in 1929 brought fire and, worse, the fire struck on April Fools' Day and, at first, everyone thought the alarm was a joke. The church was restored and reconsecrated in 1932 but some wall paintings by the windows remain from the old church, as do the altarpiece and two wooden statues from the Middle Ages.

Just over the bridge, detour right towards Toijala and then right again to **Visavuori**, the studio home of one of Finland's best known sculptors, Emil Wikström (1864–1942). Aged 29, he had just won a competition to design the frieze for Helsinki's House of Estates, when he designed his house, "Curly-Birch Hill" (**Visavuori**) on the beautiful peninsula overlooking the lake. Here he worked, in the dark wood-lined studio, spending his nights observing the stars in his rooftop observatory.

Do not touch!: Of all Finland's well-known glassmakers, **Iittala** is probably the most famous, with austere designs, beautiful functional glassware, and objets d'art such as glass birds and fruit shapes so perfect that you immediately want to hold them – a practice not recommended in the museum which houses past and present designs by such eminent people as Alvar Aalto and Timo Sarpaneva, designer of the i-collection which became Iittala's trademark. Helped by an expert glass-blower who does most of the work, you can try your talents on a misshapen paperweight. Even better is the Iittala shop where seconds are often indistinguishable to the inexpert eye and less than half the price of perfect work.

There is no escape from modern history at the **Parola Tank Museum** (Panssarimuseo*)*, set up by the Association of Armoured Troops and Veterans, survivors of the Finnish campaigns during World War II. There the tanks sit, inside and outside on three terraces. Some Winter War tanks go back to 1910, and the Continuation War terrace has some captured Soviet tanks, their hammer and sickle replaced by the still-sinister swastika, after Finland found itself fighting on the same side as the Germans.

Mighty machine: For military historians this little known museum is fascinating, a tribute to the Finnish tank operators, but even the most casual visitor is fascinated by the armoured train in the woods above. The Finns had two of these mighty trains, adapted and armed with 76mm guns and machine-guns. Parola is not the easiest place to find. Take road 57, marked Hattula, off the main road, and then, just past the next crossroads, branch left again to Parola. Ask in the museum itself for directions to the old army camping-ground nearby with the **Lion of Parola** statue. This commemorates Czar Alexander II's signing of the Language Charter in 1863, in nearby Hämeenlinna, to give Finnish equal status with Swedish.

Continue back on road 57 to Hattula Church, one of Finland's best-known and oldest churches. It was built in 1320 beside the lake of Hattula when Roman Catholicism had not long come to this part of Finland after the Swedes built Häme Castle, about 4 miles (6 km) further south. Inside, your eyes are immediately drawn upwards by the delicate colours of the intricate 16th-century frescoes which cover ceilings and walls and which later suffered the fate of being lime-washed and not re-discovered and restored until the mid-19th

century. Today, Hattula has regained the atmosphere of a medieval church and its oldest and most valuable statue is a wooden St Olav, the 15th-century Norwegian royal saint.

Aulanko Forest Park, just off road 3 on the short drive to the centre of Hämeenlinna is ideal for a break. The forest had a fortress long before the days of Christianity but the man who made Aulanko what it is today was Colonel Hugo Standertskjöld, in the 1930s the governor of Häme province. He had made his fortune as an arms dealer in Russia and returned to build a new manor and beautify the forest park with ornamental lakes, follies such as the Rose Valley Pavilion, and the **Observation Tower** overlooking Aulankojärvi (lake).

From the top, the view is superb and a café below provides a welcome restorative after the 332 steps up and down. The **Bear Cave** nearby has an appealing family group of bears carved by Robert Stigell.

When he again saw Aulanko's trees

Altar detail in one of Finland's oldest churches, Hattula, built in 1320.

and water in the 1930s, the composer Sibelius, who was born in Hämeenlinna, is said to have commented: "I was thinking of these scenes from my childhood when I composed *Finlandia*." Aulanko is a stopping place for the Silverline boats and the modern hotel, with golf courses and tennis courts, outdoor theatre, a Silk Museum, and numerous lake excursions attracts a quarter of a million visitors a year.

Castle and composer: Hämeenlinna's two claims to fame are **Häme Castle** itself and the fact that it is the birthplace of the composer Jean Sibelius. In the early 13th century, when Earl Birger led the first Swedish foray into this ancient countryside, Swedish governors were ever-conscious of the closeness of Russia and obsessed with the need for defence. His first task was to build a square, walled defensive "camp" with towers at its corners, which still form the heart of the castle. Over the next 700 years, Häme has been remodelled or renovated to suit the mood of kings and politicians and Swedish, Finnish and

Russian history is intertwined in the old red-brick walls.

Hämeenlinna itself was granted town status in 1639 by another famous Governor, Count Per Brahe, but it was already an important settlement on the Oxen Trail between Turku in the Aura river valley and Häme Castle. This well-worn centuries-old route has served soldier, merchant and traveller alike, though pack animals and carts have given way to motor cars and the track has become a modern road. With its busy centre and shady park between the old market square and church, Hämeenlinna makes an excellent base for touring this area between Tampere and Helsinki, and is the southern terminal of the Silverline boats.

Sibelius was born on a freezing December day in 1865 in the little grey timberboard house of the town physician, Christian Gustaf Sibelius. The three Sibelius children were musical and one room in the house shows Sibelius's upright piano from some 20 years later and an old photograph of the

Sibelius's home, Ainola.

young family trio performing at the Loviisa Spa Casino, where they gave summer concerts. The big dining room is now used for occasional recitals, and the house is full of memorabilia of the composer's childhood

The **Finnish Glass Museum** is the most popular place to visit in **Riihimäki**, just off road 3 some 26 miles (35 km) south of Hämeenlinna. The building is an authentic glassworks from 1914, still active in the 1930s. The ground-floor exhibition traces the history of glass-making and some of its most interesting exhibits are photographs of glassmaking in the early days of Finnish independence when the industry concentrated on mundane items such as window panes. The 1930s saw both the beginning of glass-making as a fine art and, at the opposite end of the scale, more mass production. Recently, there has again been a partial return to individual glass-blowing and handmade glass, all shown in the upstairs collection of glass of every sort.

Next door is the **Finnish Hunting Museum**, and a short walk away the **Hyttikortteli Art and Handicraft Village**, from an old glassworks converted by a group of artist-craftworkers as workshops and display areas.

Lake dwellers: Heading on south through Hyvinkää, to **Järvenpää**, you are only some 30 miles (45 km) from the centre of Helsinki. Like many others near the capital, the area's **Lake Tuusulanjärvi** attracted late 19th-century artists away from their city haunts, to build studio-villas on the eastern (Rantatie) side of Lake Tuusulanjärvi, just beyond Järvenpää. But before you leave the town, have a look at the Market Square with the modern statue, **Pikku Kalle** (Little Charlie), and at Finland's biggest statue, the gigantic yellow arches of the **Triad Monument**, in Rantapuisto Park.

The first of the artist-intellectuals were writer, Juhani Aho and his artist wife, Jenny Soldan-Brofelt. Within the year they were followed by the artist Pekka Halonen, whose painting had already been inspired by the beautiful

Strawberry picking.

Lake Tuusula, the centre of his skiing and walking trips, and by the ordinary farming life around him, as was another incomer, the portrait painter Eero Järnefelt, famous for his rural and folk scenes. When Sibelius and his wife Aino moved to the lake shores, as well as Järnefelt who was Aino's brother, the Halonens' home, **Halosenniemi**, became a meeting point for convivial saunas, recitals, and the drinking of Halonen's homemade white rhubarb wine. Today the house, on its beautiful rocky peninsula, is open every day except Monday from May to September.

Ainola was the Sibelius home for 53 years. Designed by Lars Sonck, another friend, it is still furnished as it was in Sibelius's time. The drawing room holds the composer's piano and, if you are lucky, sometimes one of the many musicians who visit Ainola will ask to play it. In the composer's time, Ainola was a place of stillness because Sibelius never used an instrument for composition and, when he was at work, there was absolute silence. His daughters visited friends and the servants were not allowed to hum, even in the kitchen.

Outside, in summer the tall trees and garden are quiet and peaceful though the trees round the lake have now grown high enough to hide the view. Sibelius died at Ainola in 1957 at the age of 91, and his wife lingered until 1969 when she was 97. Underneath the apple trees, their grave is a square flat stone, with always a few tributes of flowers close by. Sibelius's home is also open all summer but these two houses are the only survivors of an artists' colony that was not so different from the self-sufficiency communities of today.

Driving from Järvepnää, you come first to Ainola and then less than a mile further south on the lakeside road, Halosenniemi. Roughly the same distance further on, a sign to the right leads to the cottage where the writer Aleksis Kivi died. The next town is Hyrylä, with only some 15 miles (27 km) to go to Helsinki, thus completing a 300-mile (500-km) triangle that encompasses the essential Finland.

In summer and autumn, the markets are full of brilliant berries.

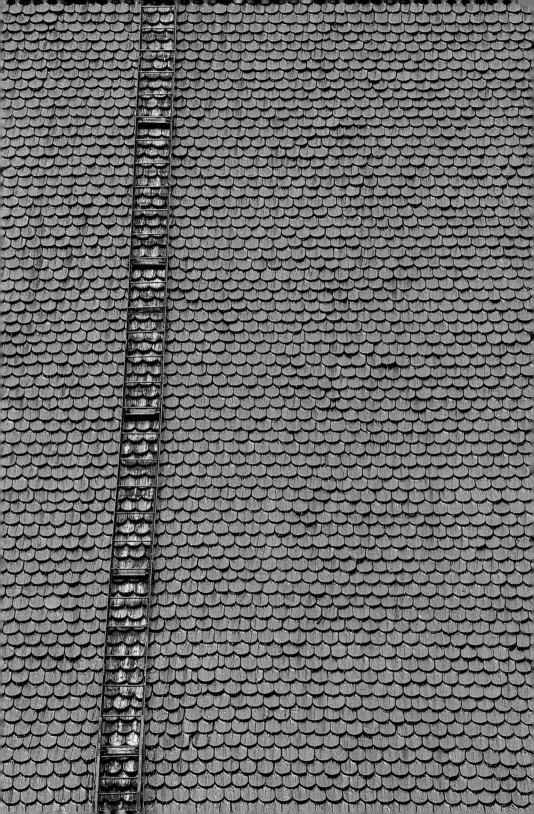

THE SOUTHERN COAST

To follow the south coast of Finland from west to east is to follow a route once travelled by Nordic kings and princes to St Petersburg. It is mainly flat, coastal country covered with farmland and densely grown forest. Because proximity to the sea has always given extra value to land – in addition to the beneficent, warming effects of the Gulf of Finland – this area is heavily settled.

It is also heavily Swedish-speaking. From Pargas (Parainen) south of Turku at the head of the Turunmaa island chain through Ekenäs (Tammisaari), Karis (Karjaa), and further east through a cluster of small villages on the approach to Kotka, you will hear a great deal of Swedish, and read it as the first language on signposts. This is all part of the democracy of bilingualism in Finland: in any town with a majority of Swedish speakers, the Swedish name normally takes precedence.

The landscape changes only very subtly from west to east. As most of Finland is above the 60th parallel, its southernmost reaches are the heavily farmed areas. The land is low, and tends to be misty in the early morning and late evening. Although it is not as rich in lakes as the country north of here, it is well irrigated by meandering rivers and streams.

The green of new wheat and the yellow of rape seed dominate in late spring; then the wheat matures and the wildflowers burst into bloom. The grassy strips at the roadside are first overrun with cowslip and lupin, a midsummer flower with tall purple, pink, and white spindles. When the lupin fades, *maitohorsma* takes over; also a tall, spindly flower, the splash of its magenta petals fills not just the road edges but entire forests and fields.

Autumn is slightly more colourful in the west, where the linden adds its colour to the gold of the birches. The west is also hillier than the east. Set against this backdrop are clusters of old farm buildings, stained dark red; most larger coastal towns have old sections whose buildings are painted in an array of pastels. Manor houses in the region are painted a rich ochre or brilliant yellow.

The eastern portion of the coast, past Helsinki, is riddled with fortifications. For the Swedes, then the Russians, and finally the independent Finns, the Russian border has been a crucial dividing line. From 1944 to 1956, the Soviets had a military base at Porkkala, an elbow-shaped peninsula west of Helsinki.

The Finnish-Soviet borders still have a heavily guarded no-man's land running between them, and although travel between the two countries has become easier since the break-up of the USSR, there is no mistaking the sterner attitude of the Soviet customs guards and immediate deterioration of road conditions as soon as one crosses east.

Exploring the islands: Richly vegetated but sparsely populated, the **Turunmaa Islands** are quieter than the Ålands in terms of tourism, and are reached more quickly from the mainland. They are linked by a series of bridges and then

ferries. Ferries also service some of the smaller islands that spin off south from the main chain. Local buses connect the larger towns.

Turunmaa's finest harbour is on the northeast spur of **Nagu**. An old wooden house overlooking the marina has been made into a guesthouse-style hotel, with a French brasserie and restaurant next door. Also in Nagu are the **Borstö Folk Museum** and the 14th-century **St Olof's Church**.

As you approach **Pargas** (**Parainen**) from west or south you come to **Sattmark**, on Stortervolandet. This tiny log cabin was once a sailor's quarters. It now serves light meals in its prettily furnished rooms and down on the dock that runs below and behind it.

Pargas has one of the most stunning churches in Finland, **Harmaa Kivikirkko**, dedicated to St Simon. Built in the 1320s, it is unusual for the spreading brick columns that support the interior and contrast with the light blue trim of the pews. Notice, too, the panel paintings of Old Testament figures running

around the porch where the organ player sits. Pargas has a good marina, and a charming series of wooden buildings scattered around the church which together form a kind of extended folklore museum; some active weaving still goes on here.

Salo is the first large market town to the east on the mainland. Set off by a triad of churches – the **Lutheran Uskela** (1832), the **Greek Orthodox Tsasouna** at its foot, and the stunningly modern **Helisnummen** about 3 miles (4 km) outside the town – Salo still has a very lively market (except Sundays). Along the Uskela river are some beautiful residential garden districts.

Gingerbread houses: Due south of Salo is **Hanko**, Finland's southernmost town. Known not only for its annual July regatta and its long beaches, Hanko has some of the most jocular architecture to be found in Finland. A long parade of turreted and deeply-eaved houses follows the beach – in varying states of repair.

Hanko's **Frontline Museum** (Hin-

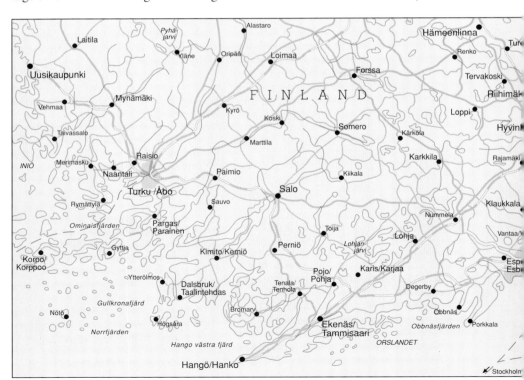

noitusmuseo) outlines the town's strategic history, such as the decimation of the fortifications during the Crimean War. Hanko was also the port from which 300,000 Finns emigrated between 1880 and 1930 to escape raging epidemics, and famine. It is still a large customs port.

Hanko's lively summer milieu centres around its large marina, which hosts boats from dozens of foreign ports. On land, there is a parachute jumping school, public tennis courts, and a tall watchtower from which to view the busy sea lanes. Information on archipelago boat tours from tourist information, Bulevardi 15, (tel: 911-803 411) or on the marina (summer only).

Ekenäs (Tammisaari) is the next main coastal stop along the route of kings. Its finely laid-out old town with cobbled streets, named after different crafts trades, is a great place for a stroll; some artisans still set up shop here in summer. Just south is **Ramsholmen Nature Park**, resplendent with marshes, forests, and water birds.

There is an extremely active boating life in and around Ekenäs (Tammisaari), and numerous outdoor concerts in summer. The **Knippan** boardwalk restaurant and the steeple of the old granite church (1680) are the town's main landmarks. There's also a pretty camping ground within walking distance. For historical background on the town, visit the **Ekenäs Museum** on Gustav Vasa Gatan 13 (tel: 911-712 111) (summer only).

A few kilometres eastward is **Snappertuna** (no connection with fish), a farming village of Swedish-speaking Finns, and the town closest to the splendid 13th-century **Raseborg Castle**, enfolded in a wooded valley. Most of the fortification is in good condition and you can freely tour its ramparts and impressive interior spaces, refurbished in wood.

The **Outdoor Theatre** in the Raseborg dale stages dramatic and musical evenings, and if you visit in July, you may catch a re-enacted medieval duel. (These tend to be comic rather than

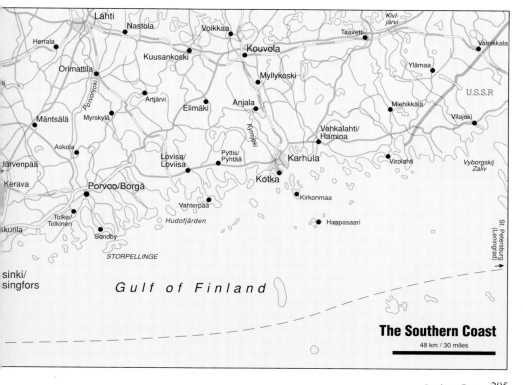

The Southern Coast

48 km / 30 miles

grave historic events; British groups are often featured.)

Further east beyond Snappertuna is **Fagervik**, the site of a tremendous old manor overlooking a protected sea inlet. Its granite and wood buildings make a fine backdrop for a picnic or horse ride. There are also good walking paths here; the so-called King's Road signposts point out landmarks.

Garden "city": Passing through Inkoo and Kirkkonummi, the next city of any size you'll come to is **Espoo**. You may not notice at first that you are in a "city" because it is a huge, spread out municipality. A bastion of wealthier Finns who work in Helsinki, Espoo is a mix of rural farm areas and genteel, leafy suburbs that give you, when taken in total, a large and colourful palette of Finnish residential architectural styles.

Espoo's **Tapiola** section is renowned as a planned garden suburb of the 1970s. Despite all the sleek newness, the area has been settled since 3500 BC, and Espoo parish dates from the 15th century. In addition, many artists and architects have made their homes in the area.

North and east of Helsinki is **Vantaa**, another city with endless open space. The Vantaa rivermouth, a wide wash of water just east of the capital, is the home of the "Vanhakaupunki" or old city upon which Helsinki was founded in the 16th century. Only a handful of wooden houses and scenic rapids now mark the spot; however, the river paths are beautifully tended and lead to some surprisingly rural countryside only moments away from Helsinki's centre. Eight kilometres from the mouth is **Tuomarinkylä Manor** with a museum and café. Across the river is a swimming beach.

Porvoo (Borgå) is one of Finland's most important towns of the past. For scenery, it has few rivals: its trim riverbanks are lined with fishing cottages and the pastel-coloured houses of the old town provide a backdrop. Swedish King Magnus Eriksson gave Porvoo a Royal Charter in 1346; it became a busy trading post and, ultimately, the place where the Diet of Porvoo (1809)

The Alikanto Museum, near Porvoo, dedicated to the explorer (shown centre).

convened to transfer Finland from Swedish to Russian hands.

While these rich historic facts make the town important, it is Porvoo's artistic side that gives it real character. The **Albert Edelfelt Atelier** shows the work of one of Finland's finest 19th-century painters, but the town is also alive with the work of current artists and writers.

East of Porvoo, the landscape becomes rural and empty, with only the occasional village to break up the spread of wheat-fields and forests. In summer, the grassy hillocks bristle with wildflowers.

East of Porvoo are just two more towns and one city of any size, all in fortification country. **Loviisa**, a pretty, provincial town with an esplanade headed by the **New Gothic Church**, is the smallest of these. A town museum tells the local history, including the role of the **Rosen and Ungern bastions**.

The frequency of rivers (originating in the great lake area immediately to the north) and Orthodox churches increases. After the old towns of Ruotsin-pyhtää and Pyhtää is the broad **Kotka Delta**. A first look at Kotka can be deceiving if you approach it through its industrial side. Yet it is one of the most beautifully situated cities in Finland.

Delta fishing: It is around Kotka that the Kymi river breaks up into five branches before rushing off into the sea, making for perfect salmon and trout fishing. There is a delicate spray of islands from the coast. The closer ones can be reached by bridges, the rest by ferry. Kotka centre is based around an esplanade. One street to the northwest, at Kirkkokatu and Koulukatu, is the main **Lutheran church**, with tremendous brick buttresses; the imposing **Orthodox church** complex and park runs along Papinkatu. Apart from the Kotka islands, the **Kymenlaakso** (Kymi river valley) extends for miles inland, where there are endless opportunities to explore calm and rapid flowing rivers and gorgeous forest paths.

One of the most famous fishing lodges of all times, that of Czar Alexander III, is at **Langinkoski** (signposted

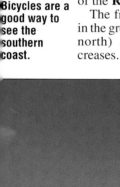

Bicycles are a good way to see the southern coast.

from Langin koskentie), Kotka. The tremendous log building was crafted by the Finns for the Czar; its furnishings are preserved as a museum.

Several nature paths begin from Langinkoski; if you walk north for 5 km, you'll pass **Kyminlinna fortification**, over Hovinkoski river through **Kyminkartano** (manor) to **Keisarin Kosket**. These "Czar's rapids" course around Munkkisaari island, with its Orthodox chapel or **Tsasouna**. A pilgrimage of the faithful is made here every 14 August. The spot is also ideal for fishing and rapids shooting. On the bank is **Keisarin Kosket Lodge** (Orthodox monastery site from 1650 to 1850) with café, boats, and cabins for hire; fishing licences sold (tel. 952-609 301).

In summer, Kotka's island youth hostel, **Kärkisaari**, makes for a lovely excursion. Even if you don't want to put up at this spacious, waterbound villa, have a sauna here. The long swimming dock leads into the island-filled inlet of the Gulf of Finland.

On the adjacent peninsula is **Santa-lahti**, with caravan and cabin facilities; the crescent-shaped beach has grassy knolls at the edge of a sandy bay. You can ignore the powerlines at the beach if you face the water.

The Kotka Tourist Board can point out nature-protected paths and rivers, as well as arrange other trips and activities (with guides, if needed). Kotka is 45 miles (70 km) from the nearest Soviet city, Viipuri (Vyborg) and 170 miles (270 km) to Leningrad; all varieties of Finland-USSR trips can be arranged, but remember to plan overnight trips in advance so your visa will be ready.

Hamina is the last of the large Finnish towns you'll see before crossing the border. Its concentric plan is part of a huge fortification, and its military nature is also preserved by the presence of thousands of young Finnish men based here for their year in national service. Pastel-coloured wooden houses contrast prettily with red brick barracks and magazines; for a closer look at the military history here, visit the **RUK-Museo** on Mannerheimintie.

Left, Hamina, a military town built with fortifications in mind. *Right*, rehearsal for *Aïda* at the Savonlinna Festival.

FESTIVALS

The most dramatic setting for any music festival must be the 500-year-old castle at Savonlinna. The audience sits tightly-packed into a courtyard, and the arc lights pick out the towering walls rising high over the lake and the brilliant costumes of operas such as *Boris Godunov* or *Aïda*. The superb accoustics can also do justice to a modern opera such as *The Knife* by Finnish composer Paavo Heininen, which had its première in 1989. In all, Savonlinna has seen the world premières of five operas by Finnish composers in a country where the composing and playing of classical music flourishes as never before.

The soprano Aino Acte founded Savonlinna in 1912 as the first Finnish classical music festival, when Finland was still a Russian Grand Duchy. Next came Jyväskylä, opened in 1955 by the composer Seppo Nummi, who also founded the Helsinki event 10 years later.

In common with the other Nordic countries, Finland has a long tradition of folk festivals, which made the most of the summer nights to play music, sing and dance. These continue in rural areas and have expanded to draw in farflung audiences. The biggest is Kaustinen Folk Music Festival which attracts 92,000 enthusiasts who come not only to watch

but to take part, and to learn in special teaching workshops. Throughout the nine days, impromptu groups of folk musicians from many countries play together in cafés and parks, handing on old, and developing new, traditions of folk music.

Another source of traditional festivals was the old-time fire brigades, once all volunteers, who got together to play music and dance at annual festivals and, in Finland's early days as an independent state, a strong Labour movement celebrated the 1st of May each year. The Festival of Workers' Music at Valkeakoski to the southeast of Tampere, includes marching band music and exhibitions of workers' art, as well as concerts. Some festivals have their roots in a more sinister past. In 1643, the Ruovesi Witch Trials were carried out in earnest when the unfortunate Antti Lieronen was tried and condemned "as a witch most obvious and potent" and burned at the stake. Today's trials include four days of drama, exhibitions, concerts, and traditional events but no-one gets burned.

Turku holds its classical musical festival in August but in June the island of Ruissalo, some 4 miles (6 km) from the centre, is the home of Ruisrock, which claims to be the world's oldest rock festival (*see page 182*). One of the most remote festivals, the Kuhmo Chamber Music Festival close to the Soviet border, was founded in 1970 by another Finnish musician, the cellist Seppo Kimanen. During his studies in Paris, Kimanen dreamed of a festival where musicians and audiences would listen to music in a very silent place with no voice to disturb them. He put his idea to the Kuhmo Music Association and, each year since, some 150 international musicians have gathered in Kuhmo in late July to play together and provide their audience with over 60 concerts of chamber music.

Being close to the border, Kuhmo has always attracted Soviet musicians. But, in the mid-l980s, the Festival made international headlines when the violinist Viktoria Mulova defected during the event. Soviet musicians such as the violinist Dimitry Sitkovestsky, who heads the Korsholm Festival, have also become artistic directors of Finnish festivals. From Estonia, with a strong tradition of music festivals, came Kalle Randula, a fine concert pianist who is also artistic director of the Jyväskylä Festival in partnership with Heikki Rauasalo.

Other festivals concentrate on different arts: Tampere has a Theatre Festival, Kupio has dance and Pori jazz; there are big bands at Imatra and a Brass Week at Lieksa as well as the Midnight Sun Film Festival at Sodankylä in Lapland.

In 1968, many of these festivals came together to form Finland Festivals. The organisation monitors festivals, proposes new ideas and, according to its director Tuomo Tirkkonen, makes sure the high artistic level of the festivals is guaranteed. Their audience of around 1.2 million is 90 percent Finnish. "The tradition of listening to music is stronger in Finland than in any of the Nordic countries," Tirkkonen said. Considering that the population is only 5 million, he must be right.

AROUND THE GULF OF BOTHNIA

The island-dotted west coast of Finland is a fascinating mixture of past and present. There are plenty of reminders of days gone by: old wooden houses; museums that focus on the great days of sail and the export of tar; and monuments to fierce battles when Sweden and Russia tussled over the body of Finland, caught fast between its powerful neighbours.

The present is represented by modern industry which, fortunately, is usually well clear of historic town centres. The hinterland is either flat or gently undulating, largely an area of farm and forest with a sprinkling of lakes – in other words, typically Finnish.

As this is the part of Finland closest to Sweden, Swedish was the language of many small communities on the southern part of this coast during the centuries when Finland was dominated by the Swedes. Even today, many here still speak Swedish as a first language and some towns have both a Swedish and Finnish name, shown on the map with the Swedish title first if that is the main language of the community.

The first main town north of Turku on road 8 is **Uusikaupunki** (**Nystad**), typical of this coast. At the end of the 19th century, it boasted Finland's second biggest sailing ship fleet. An earlier high point came on 30 August 1721, when the Peace Treaty of Nystad ended the Great Hate, a particularly bloody period in Russo-Swedish hostilities. The town's fortunes declined with the arrival of the steamship but revived with the coming of new industries in the 1960s. The Saab-Valmet car assembly plant offers tours and a motor museum which includes rally-winning vehicles. The small harbour is now used only by those who sail for pleasure around the beautiful archipelago, and the old salt warehouses have become antique shops and restaurants.

Nevertheless, maritime memories remain. The **Cultural Museum** is in the house of F.W. Wahlberg, a former ship-owner and tobacco manufacturer; **Vallimäki Hill** has a pilot's cottage, in use from 1857 to 1967, which is now a very small museum. The old church, completed in 1629, received a vaulted roof in the 1730s and the 1775 steeple also served as a fire watchtower. The town's **Windmill Park** (Myllymäki) is a reminder that many retired sailors became millers and the countryside was once dotted with windmills.

Rauma is one of six Finnish towns founded in the Middle Ages and today the old town is the largest of its kind in Scandinavia but no museum. The 600 or so wooden buildings, painted in traditional pastel shades, are home to some 1,000 people and, although the dwellings and shops are 18th and 19th-century, the pattern of narrow streets dates back to the 16th century.

Like most west coast towns, Rauma expanded and prospered in the days of sail and the **Marela Museum** is the home of a former merchant and master shipper, Abraham Marelin. Much of the interior – panelling, stoves and doors –

is original and the museum has an interesting display of period costumes. Kirsti's, a turn-of-the-century sailor's home, provides another maritime connection, continued by Rauma Museum in the Old Town Hall.

Fine lace: The museum's other main attraction is lace, for bobbin lace-making has been associated with Rauma since the mid-18th century. Nobody knows how lace came to the town: with seamen, by Franciscan monks or nuns from Vadstena in Sweden, or via a Dutch noblewoman are some of the suggested sources. However it arrived, by the 1850s lace was a major industry and almost every woman in the town a skilled lace-maker. The bubble burst when lace bonnets went out of fashion but the past 40 years have seen a steady lace revival, with a lace week in summer, and many Rauma ladies have acquired the old skill. Lace is sold in several specialist shops but none is so fine as that on display in the museum.

Pori some 37 miles (47 km) north owes its life to Duke Johan of Sweden. Attracted by its position at the mouth of the Kokemäenjoke (river), he founded the port in 1558. Since then the sea has receded and the land has risen, a phenomenon common to the Gulf of Bothnia coastline, and today Pori is 6 miles (10 km) from the sea. During the intervening years, the town burnt down nine times – something of a record even for Finland. The last conflagration in 1852 led to the stylish rebuilding of the present centre. Today, with a population of 77,000, it is, above all, an industrial centre and port.

Post-1852 buildings include the **Jennélius Palace**, now the Town Hall, built in the style of a Venetian Palace. The Pori Theatre, completed in 1884, has been completely restored and is now looked on as one of the most beautiful in Finland. More off-beat is the strange **Jusélius Mausoleum** built by a Pori businessman in memory of his daughter, its interior one of Akseli Gallen-Kallela's masterpieces. The Satakunta Regional Museum, from 1888, is a major attraction and the biggest Finnish cultural history museum

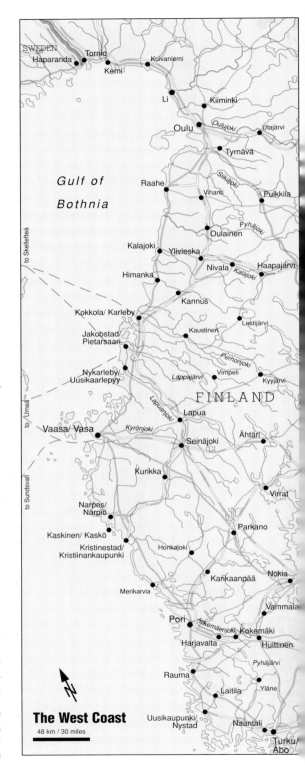

The West Coast

48 km / 30 miles

with over 60,000 items on display, plus an archive of 110,000 photographs and 10,000 books. The museum is comprehensive in scope with a particularly fascinating section on Pori itself. The Pori Art Museum, in a skilfully converted warehouse, is worth a visit.

Jazz in July: Kirjuinluoto island in the river has a natural park with a summer theatre on which centres the great annual **Pori Jazz Festival**. Of all Finland's famous summer festivals, Pori Jazz is both one of the best known and one of the earliest, with modest beginnings in 1966. It now lures in jazz musicians from many parts of Europe and beyond and, for a hectic week in July, this old town is alive with jazz day and night, out on the streets as well as in the festival theatre. Every town corner that can squeeze in a bed or two is crammed with visitors, and an annual audience of between 40 and 60,000 bumps up the town's population by more than a half.

The 12-mile (20-km) peninsula leading from Pori to Reposaari (island) has a long curving sandy beach on the side away from the port and shipyard. It is one of Finland's best, with a big hotel and congress centre. A new golf course has been laid out in response to a surge of interest in the game in Finland.

Kristinestad (Kristiinankaupunki) was founded by a familiar historical Finnish figure, Count Per Brahe, in 1649. A master of diplomacy, he gave the town the name of both his wife and Queen Kristina of Sweden-Finland. This Swedish influence is still noticeable and even today around 58 percent of the population is Swedish-speaking, and uses the town's Swedish rather than its Finnish name.

Despite its illustrious beginnings, Kristinestad remained quiet until the 19th century when it became the home port of one of the country's largest merchant fleets and a ship-building centre, an importance shown clearly in the **Maritime Museum** in the house of former shipowner, S.A. Wendelin. But, as elsewhere, the shipowners were caught out by the switch from sail to steam. The building of a railway in 1912

The old and new on the riverbank at Pori.

failed to halt the decline and many citizens emigrated to America, nothing uncommon along this western coast.

Kristinestad is now a modest sort of place beside the water with an interesting townscape, including an impressive Town Hall by E.B. Lohrmann dated 1856. During Swedish rule every traveller into the town paid customs duty and the wooden customs house built in 1720 is now the tourist information office. Another customs house, at the northern end, is even older – built in 1680 – and the oldest street is the quaintly-named Catwhipper's Lane. **Ulrika Eleonora's Church** (1700), named after another Queen of Sweden-Finland, was restored and reconsecrated in 1965. It is typical of a coastal church with votive ships, donated by sailors, hanging from the ceiling.

The museum in **Labell House** is worth seeing. Labell was a Polish aristocrat and soldier of fortune who married the mayor's daughter and took her name. He lived in the old Labell family home which had been gradually extended, with the result that its 10 rooms now represent a variety of styles spanning the 18th and early 19th centuries. From Kristinestad, the best way north by car is to take the secondary coastal road which clings to the coast to the northwest with splendid seascapes.

Vaasa (**Vasa**) is something of a marker along the coast and an obvious division between north and south. Its origins lie in Old Vaasa, established in the 14th century when the present site of the town was below sea level. It has had a chequered career of devastation by wars and fire, the last of which in 1852 left little but smouldering ruins.

In the Civil War of 1918, all the area around Vaasa was a "White" stronghold and **Lapua**, on road 16 inland from Vaasa, was the birthplace of the anti-communist Lapua Movement which reached its zenith in 1930, when 12,000 from all over Finland poured into Helsinki on the "Peasants' March", and forced the Finnish Government to ban communism. Today, Vaasa (population 55,000) is a handsome town with wide

<u>Left</u> **and** <u>right</u>**, the west coast has the best beaches in Finland.**

and attractively laid-out streets and a large market square, a mixture of Jugendstil and modern architecture. Axel Setterberg designed the Orthodox church, which is surrounded by the century-old buildings of the Russian Grand Duchy, and also the Court of Appeal in 1862. The Town Hall, which dates from 1883, is the work of Magnus Isaeus and equally as imposing. But for the best view of the town, clamber up the 200 steps in the tower behind the police station headquarters.

Vaasa is well endowed with museums reflecting the region's life, the most important being the **Museum of Ostrobothnia** and the **Hedman Collection**, which cover history and art. The Brage Open Air Museum shows how Ostrobothnian farmers lived at the end of the 19th century, and a strong culture is clear in several art museums and three professional theatres. A different note is struck by the **Car and Engine Museum**, not easy to find but with a collection of vintage vehicles all individually owned and lovingly restored, such as the glossy black 1939 American Pontiac.

Art and theatre: From an adjoining island linked by causeway, ferries leave on three routes to Sweden, and there is **Wasalandia**, the town's major children's attraction with the usual range of exciting rides; it is colourful and clean. A few hundred yards away is an enclosed tropical "water world".

Offshore islands which necessitate a short ferry crossing add to the charms of Vasa, as does the collection of old farm buildings and two windmills at **Stundars** a few miles from the town. North of Vaasa, the flat, farming country recalls certain parts of Sweden, with the Swedish influence being especially clear in the buildings.

St Birgitta's Church at Nykarleby (Uusikaarlepy), built in 1708, is one of the most beautiful in Ostrobothnia. Its ceiling paintings are by Daniel Hjulström and Johan Alm, while the windows behind the altar are much more recent, painted by Lennart Segerstråhle in 1940. The 1876 Thelin organ

is another prized possession. The town, founded in 1620 by Sweden's great warrior king, Gustav II Adolf, faces a beautiful archipelago.

Nykarleby also has its place in history. On 13 September 1808, a Swedo-Finnish force beat off an attack by a Russian army at the battle of Jutas just outside the town. The event is commemorated by a monument to Major General G.C. von Döbeln and in a poem by J.L. Runeberg, Finland's national poet. After this brief fame, Nykarleby did not develop to the same extent as some other coastal towns (today the population is 8,000). Though a narrow-gauge railway line opened at the turn of the century, it did little to promote trade and industry and closed in 1916. Today a museum society has re-opened just over a mile (2 km) off the track from Kovjoki, and the 55-year-old steam engine *Emma* puffs along on summer weekends.

Pushing further north, **Jakobstad (Pietarsaari)** is named after one of Finland's most famous military command-ers, Jacob de la Gardie, and founded by his widow in the mid-17th century. The history of the town is familiar, much of it being destroyed in the Russo-Swedish war of the early 18th century. Nevertheless, Jakobstad became the pre-eminent Finnish shipbuilidng centre, producing ships that opened new trade routes around the world. In the 18th century, no family of merchants and shipowners was more powerful in the town than the Malms. One of its members was reputedly Finland's richest man, who, on his death, left 6½ million gold marks – a vast fortune in those days – and the Malm house is now the museum.

One of the town's best known sailing ships *Jakobstads Wapen*, a 1767 galle-ass, was designed by Fredrik Henrik af Chapman, one of the most famous naval architects of the 18th century. (A sailing ship named after him is now a floating youth hostel in Stockholm.) An exact copy of *Jakobstads Wapen* has recently been completed from the original drawings. Jakobstad also has Europe's oldest tobacco factory, its office block sur-

The fun park Wasalandia.

mounted by what is claimed to be Finland's largest clock. There are also chicory and tobacco museums and one devoted to motorcycles. In the older part of the town, proud owners have carefully restored some 300 or so wooden houses. From Jakobstad to Kokkola (Karleby), take the attractive route called the "road of seven bridges", which runs from island to island across the archipelago.

Kokkola's famous son: Like Nykarleby, **Karleby** (or **Kokkola**) was founded by King Gustav II Adolf in 1620, and went through the familiar cycle of growth, prosperity, decline and a second period of expansion from the 1960s with new industries and a new port, established at Ykspihlaja (Yxpila) away from the town centre. One man, Anders Chydenius (1729–1803), had a decisive effect on Kokkola's development. He was a clergyman, Member of Parliament, economist, and one of Finland's first exponents of economic liberalism. At that time, the tar which should have brought prosperity to his town and coast had to be sold abroad through Stockholm, the then Sweden-Finland capital, which made most of the profits. Largely due to Chydenius's efforts, Stockholm's monopoly was broken and from 1765, one after another, the towns gained "staple" rights – the all-important freedom to sell and ship tar directly to foreign customers.

Kokkola's Town Hall was designed by C.L. Engel, who has left his mark on so many Finnish towns, but the town's most unusual trophy is to be found in a small building in the English Park. It relates to a somewhat bizarre episode in 1854 during the Crimean War. The boat is described as an English long boat but the inscription beside it explains all: "In 1854 in connection with the Crimean War, the British Fleet conducted raids along the coast of the Gulf of Bothnia. Two English frigates sent nine boats on a raid at Kokkola. Each was equipped with a cannon and a crew of about 30. After one hour's battle the enemy had to retreat. One boat ran ashore and was captured. Nine members of the crew

Finns get their sea legs early.

were killed and 22 taken prisoner. In all, English casualties numbered between 100 and 150 men dead and wounded.

"This was the only war trophy ever taken from the Royal British Fleet. This was the skirmish of Halkokari."

Behind the old harbour and a bathing beach is a memorial to the battle.

On the long road, some 140 miles (230 km) between Kokkola and the northern town of Oulu, there are only two places of any consequence. The sand dunes around the mouth of the river **Kalajoki** have made the town of the same name into something of a holiday area with fishing, bathing and sailing. Further on is **Raahe** (**Brahestad**) which, as its Swedish name implies, was founded by Count Per Brahe in 1649. Shipping used to be its dominant industry; today it is the Rautaruukki Steelworks, fortunately outside the centre. In summer, guided works tours are popular and there are also summer boat trips around the offshore islands.

Oulu, with a population of more than 100,000, is the largest city in Northern Finland. It owes its existence to the Oulu river and King Karl IX of Sweden and its early fortunes to tar, essential for wooden sailing ships. After excessive Central European tar-burning in the 18th century led to a decline in the coniferous forests, the industry moved to the Baltic. Ostrobothnia was soon one of the most important areas for tar.

Tar villages: Making tar was a long-winded business which occupied the whole northern area, ending in the burning of the logs in turf-covered pits, so that the tar ran through a wooden trough into barrels. Every village east of Oulu had its smouldering tar pits, and barrels of tar by the thousand came down to the coast in long narrow boats, some 40 ft (12 metres) long, each carrying 12 to 14. In 1781, the merchants of Oulu set up a Tar Exchange (in the style of a Stock Exchange) and in the 19th century the town was the leading tar exporter in the world. Prosperity ended abruptly in 1901 when the Tar Exchange went up in flames. The demand for tar declined and disappeared with the sailing ships.

You can find tar pits and tar boats at the **Turkansaari Open Air Museum** (Turkansaaren Ulkomuseo), over a footbridge to a small island in the Oulujoki (river) 8 miles (14 km) east of Oulu, off road 22. Established in 1922, the museum has an interesting collection of 19 Ostrobothnian buildings, including a church, farm buildings and windmills. It is well worth a visit.

After the era of tar and sail, Oulu languished in the doldrums but the establishment of a university in the 1960s was a turning point. It attracted hi-tech companies to the area and led to the creation of the Finnish Technical Research Centre. This emphasis on the latest technology has been responsible for one of Oulu's notable attractions, the **Tietomaa Science Centre**, opened in 1988. The wealth of exhibits on three floors is not so much for looking at as for trying out. This hands-on approach appeals to both adults and children alike. Exhibits range from an aircraft simulator to a means of checking on the world's weather and population. In all, Oulu has seven museums, from those

It's almost impossible *not* to catch a fish in Finland.

concentrating on geology and zoology to the oldest surviving wooden house in the city (1737). The new and elegant **Art Gallery** has a permanent exhibition of Finnish contemporary art plus temporary exhibitions.

The obligatory fire – this one was in 1822 – led to a new city centre and cathedral, designed by that indefatigable architect C.L. Engel and the buildings bear the stamp of his style. Mingling with these are typically modern Finnish buildings. The city benefits from a number of islands, linked by bridges, the Oulu river and some pleasant green oases, such as Hupisaaret Park. **Linnansaari** (island) has castle ruins; the sailor's home museum is on Pikisaari; there are leisure facilities on Raatinsaari and a tropical recreation spa, leisure centre and amusement park on the larger Mustasaari.

Towards Sweden: From Oulu to Kemi on the Swedish frontier, road and railway cross numerous rivers draining into the Gulf of Bothnia and the scenery undergoes a subtle change. This is no longer the west coast but the approach to Lapland and the north. **Kemi** is called the seaport of Lapland or, rather optimistically, the "Pearl of the Gulf of Bothnia". Largely destroyed in World War II, the town is now a port and industrial centre. The local **History Museum** and the **Workers' Museum** show the 1920s and 1930s living conditions of Kemi's factory workers. The **Kemi Gemstone Gallery** has a collection of 3,000 gemstones, and copies of some of Europe's most famous Crown Jewels, including the Crown of the King of Finland – who never reigned. If you are this far north in winter, you can make an excursion on an 1961 icebreaker, *Sampo*, which displays its remarkable power to force a way through ice up to 6 ft (2 metres) thick.

Kemi lies at the mouth of the Kemijoki (river) and just on the border a little way north is **Tornio** (and the main airport of the area) near the mouth of the Tornionjoki. As Tornio ends, the Swedish town of Haparanda begins and, since its founding in 1621, this

border position has made Tornio the scene of much bitter fighting, the last time during World War II.

Fortunately, the town's three major churches have survived and **Tornio Church**, with its separate bell tower is one of the most beautiful in Finland. Completed in 1686, it is dedicated to the Swedish Queen Eleonora. **Alatornio Church** on the outskirts is a vast edifice, the largest in northern Finland and able to hold a congregation of 1,400. It is a splendid example of Jaakko Rijf's neoclassical style. Czar Alexander I ordered the building of an **Orthodox Church** in 1825. After Finnish Independence in 1917, the present small 1884 building lay empty until 1987 when, restored and reconsecrated, it reopened to serve the 150 Orthodox Christians who live locally.

There is a remarkably fine **Art Museum** housing the Aine Kuvataide foundation collection and a Historical Museum giving an idea of the history of western Lapland. On a fine day, the best place to get a sense of town and surroundings is the observation platform on the top of the water tower.

Tornio Golf Club is the oddest in Europe. During a round of 18 holes, you play nine in Sweden and nine in Finland – and there's a one-hour time difference between the two. It is a rare delight to play a night round in summer, thanks to the midnight sun.

Drive 9 miles (15 km) north of Tornio off road E78 and you come to the longest free-flowing rapids in Finland at **Kukkolankoski**. They are 3,827 yards (3,500 metres) in length and at the highest point, the fall is 45 ft (13.8 metres). They have been famous for fish since the Middle Ages. Today, as they balance precariously on a crude board walk out over the fast-flowing river, fishermen still use the old technique of a long-handled net. At the nearby **Café Myllypirtti** freshly grilled and skewered white fish is the main item on the menu, an authentic taste to end the 600-mile (1,000-km) drive north along a coast that has always depended for its living upon sea, ships, and river.

Left, picnic time. **Right**, in the sauna.

SECRETS OF THE SAUNA

There are certain things along the way which a traveller does not forget. A real Finnish sauna is one of them. Next to afternoon dancing, there isn't anything more uniquely Finnish than the sauna, and it is a rare Finn who admits to not liking one. Official statistics estimate that there are over 625,000 saunas in Finland, not counting those in private houses or in the summer houses that dot the shoreline of the country's 100,000-plus lakes or lie along its extensive sea coast. The actual figure could easily be over 1 million in a country of about 5 million people. But that is not too surprising as the sauna is a national institution.

Although its origin is obscure, the sauna came to Finland over 2,000 years ago. A Finnish proverb says: "First you build the sauna and then the house." This was common practice in rural Finland since the sauna was not just the place in which to get clean but where babies were born and sausages smoked.

The sauna outgrew its rural roots long ago. Today, anywhere you go in the country, be it large city or small village, you will find public saunas for those who do not have access to a private one. Nowadays, it is safe to assume that every new apartment building has a sauna for its tenants, and it is only natural that many companies have saunas for their employees as well as to entertain guests.

There is no "right way" to take a sauna. Individual preferences prevail with regard to temperature and style. The ideal temperature is between 80 and 100°C although it can be a cooler 30°C nearer the floor on the bottom platform, reserved for children. Water is thrown over the hot stones in the sauna stove to create a dry steam, called *löyly* in Finnish, which makes the high heat more tolerable and stimulates perspiration. Another common practice is to brush oneself with a wet birch switch called the *vihta*. This not only gives off a fresh fragrance but, more important, it increases the blood circulation and perspiration.

How long you sit in the sauna is entirely up to you. It is not a competition to see who can stick it out the longest. When you have had enough, you move on to stage two: cooling off. This is just as important as the heating up. A cold shower is the most common way but, if the sauna is by a lake or the sea, a quick plunge into the cool water is stimulating. During the winter, brave or foolhardy souls even jump through a hole in the ice or roll around in the snow. Neither method is recommended for people with high blood pressure.

You can repeat the heating up and cooling off as many times as you like, although most people stop after the third. You then move on to the final stage which is to dry off and this should be done naturally without hurry, to avoid further perspiration. It is also time for something to drink and eat. A beer or, if you prefer, a soft drink or coffee and a snack are essential to complete the ritual.

A real Finnish sauna is not a meeting place for sex, as it is in some countries. Codes of behaviour are strict and, despite the nudity, a Finnish sauna is a very moral place. Generally, men sauna in the company of men and women in the company of women. A mixed sauna is a family affair and even that depends on the ages of the children.

A proper sauna leaves you relaxed, refreshed and even more alert. Nevertheless, there is more to the sauna than just getting clean. It is a happening, a time to meet friends or opponents, to talk and socialise. Titles and position are, they say, left hanging in the changing room alongside the clothes. It is is not unusual in Finland for board meetings and the government's cabinet meetings to be held in a sauna. Inviting one's business rival or political opponent to a sauna is also common. But it's not done to consume hard spirits during a sauna, or to swear or raise one's voice.

For visitors to Helsinki: Even if your hotel has a sauna, why not try a traditional smoke or wood-fired sauna? You can at the Finnish Sauna Society situated on the island called Lauttasaari, a short taxi or bus ride west of the city centre. After the sauna, you can swim in the sea in summer and even jump through a hole in the ice in the winter. There is also a woman in white waiting to scrub you clean. The facilities are closed to the public on Sundays and Mondays, with Thursdays reserved for women. (Check opening hours: tel: 67-86-77.)

THE ÅLAND ISLANDS

The Åland Islands (Ahvenanmaa in Finnish) are a collection of granite-bound skerries spraying out to the west of the Finnish coast. Most people outside Scandinavia have never heard of them, though they are a part of a unique, semi-autonomous political set up that gives the 25,000 Swedish speakers here much more self-determination than the Québécois in Canada or the Scots in Britain.

In 1917, when the Russians began sending reinforcements to the islands, the Ålands were the western limit of the Grand Duchy of Russia that Finland then was. While Finland was celebrating independence from the Soviet Union, Ålanders were petitioning (1918–19) to become part of Sweden.

Although the League of Nations assigned the islands as a demilitarised, semi-autonomous entity to Finland (with Swedish as the official language), today's Ålanders hold no grudge. Like mainland Finns, Ålanders take tremendous pride in a Finnish athlete or team beating the Swedish competition.

But don't assume, either, that the Ålanders think of themselves as ordinary Finns. Far from it. Ålanders have inhabited their islands since the dawn of the ages, giving them a good long time to build up a strong ethnic culture and a formidable pride in their identity as Ålanders. The fact that they did not become associated with Sweden seems if anything to have nurtured this pride in their uniqueness. So never call an Ålander a Swede; you can call an Ålander a Finn, but the preferred title is, simply, Ålander.

For most of June, July, and August, the archipelago is a place of breeze-ruffled inlets edged with tiny, sunkissed bathing beaches of glacier-worn granite. Some are shaded by the spindly shadows of umbrella pines. Old fishing villages huddle at the edges of rocky promontories, dwarfed to child-size when one of the larger Sweden-Finland ferries, or even one of the grander private yachts, sails past. Winters here are sodden and windy, and rarely cold enough for any real snow.

Although the islands attract fleets of oversize sailing and motor yachts, and with them, crowds of well-to-do boat owners, the feeling here is never clubby or elitist, merely restful.

Old-time trade: The Ålanders have scraped a living from the soil and floated it off the sea for centuries. With rare exceptions, theirs has not been the privileged world of the titled, landed Swede-Finn gentry on the mainland. "This is why," says one young Ålander, "that despite our language differences, we Ålanders often feel more akin to the mainland Finn than the Swedish-speakers there. We have had the same simple livelihoods – farming, fishing, forestry, and shipping. There are no old dukes here."

In the days before motorised sailing, it took about six weeks to sail to Helsinki where Ålanders traded sealskins and oil, and sold apples and herring and loaves of sweet black bread known as *limpa*, which goes especially well with herring.

Today, Ålanders earn their living in a slightly less gruelling fashion. Fifteen percent are directly employed in tourism while a total of 30 percent are employed in tourist-related services. Seal hunting has dropped out of the picture, but farming, fishing, and construction are still the other major professions. One unique Åland product you'll see, apart from *limpa*, is the Finnish potato crisp, made from Åland-grown spuds.

On a rotating biannual schedule, the Ålands host the international **Island Olympics**. Participants are mainly from British islands such as the Isle of Man, Shetland and Orkney, and from further afield, the Falklands. However, recent years have had added excitement, as when the Estonian coaches from the Baltic isle Saaremaa arrived penniless, and demanded money to feed their athletes – in US dollars. (They got food coupons.)

Sea traditions: The grand-scale shipbuilding that once went on here has mostly died out, but a large part of

Finland's merchant navy is still owned by Åland shippers, and Ålanders have recently revived their traditional boat-building skills with two ocean-going, wooden sailing ships that you may be lucky enough to see in Mariehamn. The Finland-Sweden ferries provide hundreds of jobs, but some Ålanders still work on merchant and freight ships, following the shining trails of the old Åland grain ships that plied worldwide routes as far as the Antipodes.

Mariehamn is the capital of the main island, Åland, and has 10,000 inhabitants; the original town on this site was called Långnäs, and some of its old buildings can still be seen in south Mariehamn. Mariehamn is the only town-sized settlement, but there are dozens of villages, many dating back centuries, such as **Önningby**, at Jomala. The smallest islands are either wholly uninhabited, or inhabited perhaps only by a single family.

The main ring of islands – connected by free ferry service – includes Åland, Föglö, Kökar, Sottunga, Kumlinge, and Brändö. A splendid way to tour the islands is by bicycle and ferry. You'll find many Finnish and Swedish families doing so, too, particularly in July. From Åland, there is a daily bike ferry to **Prästö**; bikes you can hire from the Mariehamn harbours.

Only Mariehamn has real hotels; it also has a summer boat hotel, great for budget travellers (tel: 928-13 755). On the smaller islands accommodation is in camping-grounds, rented cottages, or guesthouses. Ålandsresor (tel: 928-28 040) and Viking Line (tel: 928-26 211) arrange rented accommodation.

In Mariehamn west harbour is the **four-masted museum ship** *Pommern* – built in Glasgow in 1904 – which together with a visit to the nearby **Åland Maritime Museum** will give you a full complement of the archipelago's sea-going history.

On the cultural side, too, is the **Åland Museum** at Storagatan 9 with beautifully assembled exhibitions on prehistoric and Ice and Bronze Age Åland. (English-language brochure, 1 Finn-

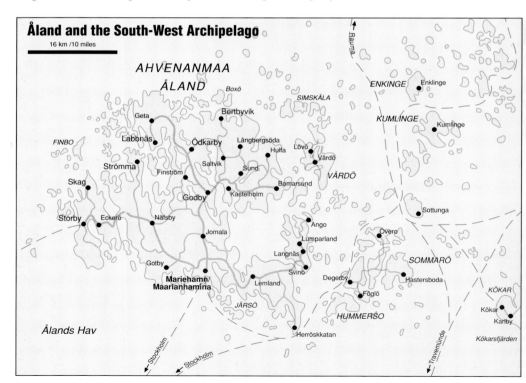

Åland and the South-West Archipelago

16 km / 10 miles

AHVENANMAA
ÅLAND

Boxö

SIMSKÅLA

ENKINGE   Enklinge

KUMLINGE

Kumlinge

Geta

Bertbyvik

FINBO

Labbnäs

Ödkarby

Långbergsöda

Hulfa

Lövö

Vårdö

Strömma

Finström

Saltvik

Sund

VÅRDÖ

Skag

Bomarsund

Godby

Kastelholm

Sottunga

Storby

Eckerö

Näsby

Ango

Övero

Jomala

Lumparland

Langnäs

SOMMARÖ

Gotby

Svinö

Degerby

Hastersboda

Mariehamn/
Maarianhamina

Lemland

Föglö

KÖKAR

JÄRSÖ

Kökar

HUMMERSÖ

Karlby

Ålands Hav

Herröskkatan

Kökarsfjärden

Stockholm

Stockholm

Travemünde

Rauma

mark.) From slightly more recent times are displays on folk customs and archaeological finds from digs at the islands' many medieval churches.

Wedding customs: In fact some of the more extraordinary Åland customs centre around weddings; until very recently, brides from certain islands wore black. A few brides still wear the traditional high crown of birch leaves and wildflowers. One tradition has held – a real Åland wedding can go on for days.

Lilla Holmen Bird Reserve (free admission) below the east harbour is an island park filled with roving peacocks and roosters. Mixed in with these are several Angora rabbits and guinea pigs (caged). There's a café and short strip of beach – far enough from the pushier birds to save you from sharing your picnic with them.

On the main island, the countryside stretches out for dozens of miles in all directions from Mariehamn, alternating between wide open fields and sea vistas to dense, pungent forests crowded with pines and birches. The scenery is particularly beautiful along the straits that cut into Eckerö, straits which resemble rivers at their narrower points. **Eckerö Harbour** is set off by the cherry-red boathouses clustered along its bays and promontories. Due to its western exposure, you can watch the midnight sun in Eckerö from its evening dip towards the sea till its early dawn rising.

Eckerö is closest to the Swedish mainland (Grisslehamn) and so is a popular car ferry departure point. The journey is two hours.

Post-boat race: Also leaving from Eckerö is the **Postrodden** or mailboat race in mid-June, a re-enactment of the once arduous journey to Stockholm to deliver post. Participants sail over in period costume, and stay at the old postal workers' hotel at Storby.

Moving across the north to **Geta**, you'll find tremendous shelves of granite laced with natural grottoes dug out aeons ago by glaciers and then the sea. There is a small café at the end of the Geta road. The grotto path is to the right. The teetering piles of stones that edge

Boats at Mariehamn.

the path are said to be remains from old bread ovens.

Saltvik, Sund, Lumparland, and Lemland on the east side of the island are farming areas. With its numerous, forest-fringed inlets and natural protection from the open sea, **Lumparland Sound** is a fine spot to fish or picnic, or arrange a cottage stay.

In Åland's northeast are the historic **Kastelholm and Bomarsund fortresses**. **Kastelholm** in Tosarby Sund was once the administrative centre of the islands, and dates from the 1300s. The Russians began fortifying it in 1829; ultimately the site was destroyed by fire, but it is now under extensive restoration. Adjacent are the Cultural History Museum and Jan Karlsgården Open Air Museum. Three miles (5 km) to the north of Kastelholm is the 13th-century granite church of Sund.

East of Kastelholm (about 8 miles/13 km) is the **Bomarsund** fortification, built as a huge fortified area, surrounded by a great stone wall, by the Russians and knocked out by British and French firepower during the Crimean War. The 1856 Peace of Paris that followed included Russian Czar Alexander's declaration that henceforth the islands would have no fortifications or military reinforcements. The declaration set the precedent for Åland de-militarisation; Ålanders are, even today, exempt from national service in Finland.

Bird Island: To the southeast of Åland lies the second-most-populated island, **Föglö**. The ferry (duration of trip about 30 minutes from Svinö, Åland, bus from Mariehamn to Svinö takes about 40 minutes) lands at the enchanting port town of **Degerby**, once an important vodka smugglers' destination, and also an important customs post. In the eastern part of the island is a natural bird reserve, inspiration for the three golden birds on Föglö's coat of arms.

Degerby's cross-shaped **Maria Magdalena Church** was once a key landmark for sailors crossing the north Baltic. Set in north Degerby, it dates from the 12th century. An 1859 renova-

The Ålanders continue the Swedish dancing traditions.

tion was carried out at the cost of 10,000 roubles. On the altar is a precious silver crucifix from the 1500s (excavated in the 1960s), preserved in a lucite casing. The church's sacristy holds an extraordinary collection of priests' robes.

The Maria Magdalena cemetery also holds something extraordinary. Several headstones carry the name Peron; any Föglö resident named Peron is related to the family of the late Argentine president. One version of the story explaining this link holds that an Argentine seaman became involved in work at the Degerby customs station, found a Degerby wife, and never left.

The tiny **Föglömuseet** by Degerby harbour and the handcrafts shop there are the only other diversions of the cultural sort. Föglö has wonderful possibilities for touring by bike, with its empty roads and lack of any really steep terrain. The roads are bound by low meadows and long, narrow strips of moss-floored forest.

From Degerby you can ride to **Överö**, the northernmost island in the Föglö group, in just over an hour, using a series of car bridges that stretches to the last strait before Överö. To cross this, you must go on board the cable ferry, which, like the inter-island ferries, is considered an extension of the road system, and so is free.

Unless you decide to rent a private cottage along the Föglö straits, the only choice for accommodation will be the charming **Enigheten Guesthouse** at Degerby, a preserved farmhouse manor run by volunteers (tel: 928-50310).

Archaeological treasures: Kökar is a bare island, and so most of its vistas look towards the open sea. By the rocky coast at **Hamnö** is a fascinating **medieval church**, founded by Franciscan fathers. The soil around the church has yielded up rich archaeological treasures including a medieval graveyard, Estonian coins, and the church's original baptismal font, now located near the altar. Other finds are displayed in the stone chapel in the churchyard, also the site of informal prayer sessions during the week.

Near the font is the memorial stone of the Franciscan-trained native son **Stephanus Laurentii**, who in 1496 was made Finland's first Doctor of Theology. At the churchyard entrance is a stone catafalque, where relatives still lay out their dead before the formal funeral inside the church. This fine old church was renovated to its present form in 1784.

The **Kökar Museum** has a superb collection of old photos whose written commentary has been hand-corrected by locals who recognise a wrongly identified grandparent. There are also farm tools and costumes, as well as narratives about the Germans' failed attempts to shoot down Kökar's beacon tower during World War II.

The amenities here include only two food shops, one café, one bank, and two taxis. There is a handsome old guesthouse, **Anton's**, (tel: 928-55 729) on a family estate with its own beach, camping-ground, and bike hire. A new complex of seaside cabins, somewhat resembling a Norwegian fishing village, opened in 1991 at **Karleby**.

The Museum ship Pommern.

THE GREAT LAKES

If you could flood the whole of Scotland and dot it with some 33,000 islands and peninsulas, you would have the equivalent of the Saimaa Lake area alone. Add on the Paijanne system and you could cover Wales as well.

The Great Lakes of Saimaa and Paijanne in Central Finland are among the best known and most popular places to visit in the country and are the target for thousands of visitors who long only to be in, on, or beside them. But people do nothing to make this watery landscape crowded because there is so much of it – lakes and lakelets, smooth curving bays with yellow-grey beaches or ragged and broken shores, rushing torrents squeezed between high banks or flooding over hidden rocks, and rivers linking the different waters.

Where the land intervenes, Finnish engineers turned their skills as long ago as the 19th century to building canals to connect the stretches of water. Today, boats big and small can journey the length and breadth of both lake systems, calling at the small, strategically placed towns, where people have lived for centuries, and the even smaller villages, or stopping along the lakesides where no-one lives.

Sometimes, the land is flat beside the water or crunched up into ridges where rocks and trees point upwards. This varied landscape owes its beauty to the Ice Age when glaciers carved out the shape of lake and ridges, the most famous being at Punkaharju, a 5-mile (8-km) chain of ridges which winds between the lakes. Far inland, Saimaa nevertheless has its own seal, the Saimaa marble seal, whose ancestors were trapped in the lake system long ago when the glaciers cut off its route to the sea.

There are two perfect ways to get to know the Great Lakes: from the water by passenger steamer or smaller craft, or by doing as the Finns do and renting a lakeside cabin, to fish, swim, canoe or simply to sit in the sun.

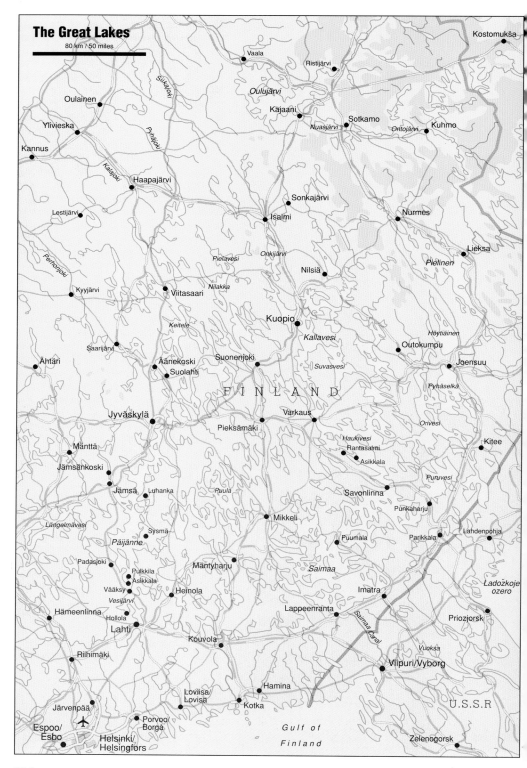

The Great Lakes

80 km / 50 miles

Kostomukša

Vaala

Ristijärvi

Oulujärvi

Oulainen

Kajaani

Sotkamo

Nuasjärvi

Ontojärvi

Kuhmo

Ylivieska

Siikajoki

Pyhäjoki

Kannus

Kalajoki

Haapajärvi

Sonkajärvi

Nurmes

Lestijärvi

Isalmi

Lieksa

Perhonjoki

Pielavesi

Onkijärvi

Nilsiä

Pielinen

Kyyjärvi

Nilakka

Viitasaari

Kuopio

Kallavesi

Höytiäinen

Outokumpu

Keitele

Joensuu

Ähtäri

Saarijärvi

Äänekoski

Suonenjoki

Suvasvesi

Pyhäselkä

Suolahti

F I N L A N D

Orivesi

Jyväskylä

Varkaus

Pieksämäki

Kitee

Mänttä

Haukivesi

Rantasalmi

Asikkala

Jämsänkoski

Puruvesi

Jämsä

Luhanka

Puula

Savonlinna

Punkaharju

Längelmävesi

Sysmä

Mikkeli

Päijänne

Puumala

Parikkala

Lahdenpohja

Padasjoki

Mäntyharju

Saimaa

Ladožkoje
ozero

Pulkkila

Asikkala

Vääksy

Heinola

Imatra

Vesijärvi

Hämeenlinna

Hollola

Lappeenranta

Priozjorsk

Lahti

Saimaa Canal

Riihimäki

Kouvola

Vuoksa

Viipuri/Vyborg

Järvenpää

Hamina

U.S.S.R

Espoo/
Esbo

Loviisa/
Lovisa

Kotka

Porvoo/
Borgå

Gulf of

Zelenogorsk

Helsinki/
Helsingfors

Finland

THE SAIMAA SYSTEM: The great Saimaa waterway was the historic buffer zone between the kingdom of Sweden-Finland and Czarist Russia, at times changing hands with dizzying frequency. Subsequently it became part of the longest of any western nation's frontier with the Soviet Empire. The effects of these shifting borders are recurring themes as you travel the area.

It would be hard to visualise landscapes more fragmented or more liquid than the Saimaa waterway. A series of large and lesser lakes are linked by rivers, straits and canals, and framed by an amazing complexity of headlands, ridges, bays, islands and skerries, to form Europe's largest inland waterway system. Up to a quarter of the Saimaa region's total area of 27,000 sq. miles (70,000 sq. km) is covered by water.

Saimaa's waters provided natural highways for goods and people long before railways and, especially, roads probed into its remoter reaches. To a large extent, they still do. No lakeside home is without its rowing boat, usually with outboard engine. Tugboats hauling their floating timber trains, up to a mile long, from forest to factory are common sights.

Embryonic tourism dates from the 19th century as the well-to-do of Czarist St Petersburg boarded the then newfangled railway to explore the Grand Duchy of Finland on the neighbouring fringes of their empire. They went to take the waters in the handful of newly created spas, to marvel at such natural wonders as the foaming cascades of Imatra and to hunt and fish the richly stocked forests and waters.

The best approach is via industrial **Kouvola**, about 86 miles (140 km) northeast of Helsinki and a junction of road and rail routes into Saimaa. There are much shorter ways to your destination of **Kuopio** but, to capture the spirit of Saimaa, ignore these and first head east on road 6. About 50 miles (80 km) on, you reach **Lappeenranta**, South Karelia's main town.

Like almost every Finnish community, Lappeenranta combines work and

Preceding pages: sunset at Aurinko; the Great Lakes. Below, a boat is essential.

play. There is a great deal of industry and some excellent holiday facilities – for most kinds of water sports, for example. Its spa amenities have undergone a recent renaissance too, though their origins lie in the Czarist 1820s. The town is the southern terminus for Saimaa's venerable lake fleet.

Historically this was also a major military town, heavily fortified by the Swedes in the 18th century, only to be rebuilt by the Russians after they destroyed it. Linnoitus (fortress) remains the oldest and most interesting part, where you will find Finland's oldest Orthodox Church (1785), the South Karelian (Etelä-Karjalan) and Cavalry (Ratsuväkiomuseo) Museums, a number of handicrafts workshops and quite a lot of military hardware.

Lappeenranta is only a few miles from the border with its large eastern neighbour; but it was not so in the days when Vyborg (Viipuri) and substantial portions of huge Lake Ladoga formed part of the Grand Duchy and (during its first decades) of the Republic of Fin-

land. It was certainly not so in 1856 when the **Saimaa Canal** was completed, thus linking Saimaa with the Gulf of Finland through entirely Finnish territory and encouraging the development of a string of inland ports, Lappeenranta among them.

Victorian travellers hailed the canal as one of the greatest engineering feats of the 19th century and, soon after leaving Lappeenranta, road 6 crosses its watery slit or, rather, that of its successor. Post-World War II reparations transferred over half the canal into Soviet domains, after which it lay disused and in growing disrepair until the 1960s. After lengthy negotiations and the privilege of paying for its restoration, the Finns regained use of the canal, which reopened in 1968. It now handles around a million tons of cargo and 30,000 passengers a year, providing an interesting "side door" into the Soviet Union; Western visitors need visas except on day cruises from Lappeenranta.

Despite the overwhelming predominance of lake and forest, parts of

Lappeenranta, close to the border and a favourite with 19th-century Russian travellers.

Saimaa's southern shores are undeniably industrial. Perhaps the most concentrated industrial area of Finland lies a few miles ahead, centred on **Imatra**. This also has some claim as a famed beauty spot and was described by one turn-of-the-century British visitor, with shameless exaggeration, as the "Niagara of Finland". Nevertheless, the very fine rapids of **Imatrankoski** were responsible for the presence of the grand old (now much-restored) **Imatran Valtionhotelli** built to cater for the sightseers who flocked here, including many distinguished and high-born.

It was the eventual taming of the rapids, of course, which triggered off the industrial boom. Happily their full power and splendour can still be seen on certain days in summer; check with the local tourist office for there is no other good reason to linger here.

About 30 miles (50 km) on from Imatra, road 6 passes within a few hundred yards of the Soviet border; multilingual frontier-zone notices and watch towers did not quickly succumb to the best efforts of *glasnost*. Soon after, around **Parikkala**, the road turns north away from the border. Switching to road 14, you soon come to one of Finland's best loved beauty spots.

Punkaharju is one of countless ridges bequeathed to Finland by the last Ice Age. In places it is just wide enough to carry the road; elsewhere it widens to carry magnificent pine and birch woods framing the ever-changing permutations of lake and sky, island and skerry, bedrock granite and the forests' "green gold". The light is ever-changing too, to combine all the main scenic elements of essential Finnishness.

Tucked away amongst it are well-equipped holiday centres, the **Kesämaa** (**Summerland**) **Leisure Centre** (family fun) and – on no account miss this – the quite startling Art Centre of **Retretti**. Part of this is housed in caverns literally blasted out of the living rock. Artificial pools and waterfalls provide stunning settings for changing exhibitions of Finnish art and design. An underground concert hall can cater

Saima, Sulkavan Soutu, boat race.

for over 1,000 spectators. Olavi Lanu is the sculptor responsible for the striking human and other shapes that populate Retretti's surrounding pinewoods.

In summer, a regular lake steamer sails between Punkaharju/Retretti and Savonlinna: the trip is a delightful mini-odyssey through the islands, taking over 2 hours compared with a 20-minute spin along the highway. Road travellers should make the short deviation on road 71 to **Kerimäki**, a typically scattered Finnish rural community harbouring the world's largest wooden church (1848) – capacity 3,500 people. Concerts are held here in summer.

Savonlinna – the name means "the castle of Savo" – sprawls over a series of interlinked islands. It is the most charming of Finland's main lakeland towns and the best base in Saimaa for making trips. It has the medieval castle of Olavinlinna, as well as spa facilities, excellent lake sports amenities, varied sightseeing, and a lot of culture. Castle and culture combine very happily in the annual **International Opera Festival**, one of Finland's leading events, which takes place throughout July. Tickets for, and accommodation during, the Festival should be booked well ahead.

Olavinlinna occupies an islet a short walk from the centre. With its massive granite walls, ramparts and shooting galleries topped by three great round towers (surviving from the original five), its Knights Hall and grim dungeon, it has everything you might expect from a medieval castle. Originally built by the Danish-born nobleman Erik Axelsson Tott in 1475, it was intended to be a main defence against the Russians but so frequently did the eastern border shift that Olavinlinna often lay far from the battlefield.

As an operatic setting the castle is simply splendid, whether it's for *Aïda* in Italian, *Rusalka* in Czech, or *The Bartered Bride* in Finnish. Experiencing an opera here begins not when the curtain rises, but as you join the rest of the audience heading for the massive bulk of the castle. Many are in their best finery and most are wisely armed with

Savonlinna, with the castle of Olavinlinna, home of the Savonlinna Opera Festival.

blankets, for Finnish summer nights are predictably cool. After the performance, with daylight fading at last, Olavinlinna is softly illuminated to provide a memorably romantic backdrop as you stroll back past boutiques and coffee shops open and welcoming.

Savonlinna itself developed from a small trading centre by the castle, its growth greatly hampered by wars and fires. The coming of steam and the opening of the Saimaa Canal gave the necessary stimulus, for the town's situation made it a natural junction for lake traffic that in due course spread to the four points of the Saimaa compass.

The days have long gone when the venerable Saimaa fleet was powered by wood-burning engines but, converted to diesel, a number of the attractive double-decked wooden vessels continue to ply Saimaa's waters as they have for three score years and more. One of the sights of Savonlinna is the morning departure and evening return of these romantic vessels to and from the passenger harbour, right by the open-air market on **Kauppatori** in the centre of town. Another, near the castle, is the museum ship *Salama*, a steam schooner built in 1874, shipwrecked in 1898 and raised from the lake in 1971. It forms part of the **Museum of Inland Navigation** which, in a neighbouring building, gives an excellent picture of the history of Saimaa's floating traffic.

From Savonlinna to Kuopio by lake steamer is a full day's journey. This could be your opportunity to get the true feel of these lakescapes, for it is only by travelling on them that you can fully experience that slowly unfolding scene of forest and meadow, of reed bed or granite shore, of timber-built farm and summer cottage, of islands emerging from headlands that might or might not be islands after all; and watch the reflections tossed from huge sky to broad lake and back again in endlessly varying light and colour tones.

Road travellers have a choice of continuing west from Savonlinna on roads 14 and 5 to Mikkeli and thence further west still into the Päijänne lake system (*see page 244*); or staying with Saimaa

to its northern limits beyond Kuopio. **Mikkeli** is a pleasant market community and also an historic army town in which Mannerheim's Headquarters in World War II is now a museum (*Päämajamuseo*); exhibits include a copy of London's *Daily Telegraph* from 18 December 1939, headlining "Finns smash two Soviet Divisions". Just outside town, the **Visulahti Family Leisure Centre** is in a park populated by life-size model dinosaurs.

The recommended way to Kuopio is to leave road 14 about 20 miles (35 km) west of Savonlinna and follow road 464 via **Rantasalmi**, a particularly attractive and watery route. This joins road 5 a little south of Varkaus. **Varkaus** itself is industrial (specialists should note its **Museum of Mechanical Music**, unique in the Nordic countries), but the little town of **Joroinen** 10 miles (15 km) to the south is very typical of a smaller Finnish community. In contrast with its own modernity are the fine old farms and manor houses dotted about these fertile landscapes, some used as settings

for the music festival, which is arranged here each summer.

Road 5 is the direct way to Kuopio, 45 miles (75 km) north of Varkaus. West of Varkaus along road 23 the pleasant rural community of **Pieksämäki** lies on Saimaa's western fringes on another approach route to Päijänne. Northeastwards from Varkaus, road 23 leads to Joensuu in North Karelia (*see page 253*), passing within a few miles of two major religious houses: the Orthodox monastery of **Uusi Valamo** and the Convent of **Lintula**. On all three counts of history, culture and scenery these merit a visit, a recommended possibility being by special monastery cruises ex-Kuopio in summer.

The clue to the monastery's history lies in its name. Valamo is the large island on Lake Ladoga on which an Orthodox religious foundation was established in the Middle Ages, attracting a growing number of pilgrims over the centuries, though latterly its fortunes declined. During the Finno-Russian Winter War of 1939–40, the surviving handful of elderly monks was forced to leave, and eventually accorded the present site of **Uusi ("New") Valamo**, originally an old manor house and outbuildings. One of these was adapted as the monks' first place of worship, embellished by the precious 18th-century icons and other sacred objects which they had brought with them.

Uusi Valamo has since experienced something of a renaissance. An injection of younger blood ensures its continuance; there is a fine new church completed in 1977, a cafeteria, souvenir shop and a modern hotel to cater for the growing number of visitors and pilgrims. The Convent of Lintula, a few miles away has a similar but shorter history. The pious inhabitants of both contribute to their upkeep by working the land in these delightful lakeside settings, though you may find the rather humbler aspects of Lintula more conducive to spiritual thought.

Kuopio is a thoroughly nice town and one of Finland's liveliest, with a crowded summer calendar including **A cruise boat at Lahti.**

the **International Dance and Music Festival** in June. Its daily market is one of the most varied outside Helsinki, and hard to miss as it fills most of Kuopio's central Tori (Market Place). Here you can try freshly baked *kalakukko* (fish and pork in a rye crust), traditional local fare that is definitely an acquired taste; or in due season you may be tempted by the varied edible fungi or succulent mounds of berries straight from the forests or bogs. There is a smaller market on summer evenings at the passenger harbour (east side of the town).

Like many Finnish country towns that developed in the 18th and 19th centuries, central Kuopio follows the gridiron pattern, a chessboard of parallel streets more familiar to Americans than Europeans. This was designed to provide plenty of firebreaks between the then predominantly wooden buildings though, alas, it failed in its purpose all too often. Most of those that survived have been replaced by modern buildings but the **Open-Air Museum** at Kirkkokatu 22, a few blocks south of the

market place, preserves a number of original dwellings, warehouses and gardens – a quiet oasis showing how small-town Finland used to look.

A little east of the market place the **Kuopio Museum** at Kauppakatu 23 houses excellent regional collections of a cultural and natural history order in a castle-like building that is a typical example of Finnish turn-of-the-century national romantic style. Among several famous Finns associated with Kuopio, statesman Johan Vilhelm Snellman worked and married here in the 1840s. The conjugal home at **Snellmaninkatu 19** is also a museum.

On the edge of the town centre, the **Orthodox Church Museum** at Karjalankatu 1 is unique in western Europe, housing collections of icons (many from the 18th century) and sacred objects brought here from Valamo and Konevitsa in Karelia and a few from Petsamo in the far north, all territories ceded to the Soviet Union. A little further on is Puijo hill topped by **Puijo Tower** (over 240 ft/70 metres). The

ferry perator rings the amily too.

vistas from its viewing platforms and revolving restaurant are staggeringly beautiful with lakes and forests merging into purple distances. Try and time your visit for an hour or two before sundown; the colours are out of this world.

By the time you reach **Iisalmi**, 50 miles (80 km) north of Kuopio on road 5, you are almost exactly half way between Helsinki and the Arctic Circle, and you are still – just – in the Saimaa region. It's a pleasant small provincial town, birthplace of writer Juhani Aho in 1861 (the family home is a museum on the outskirts of town), and site of one of Finland's innumerable battles against the Russians (1808; the Finns won this one, even though they were outnumbered seven-to-one). A new **Karelian-Orthodox Cultural Centre** displays valuable relics recovered from territory now in the Soviet Union, along with 80 models of churches and chapels since destroyed there.

But perhaps oddest of all is the thought that should you launch a canoe from Iisalmi's lake shore, it would be either level paddling or gently downhill all the way to the Gulf of Finland – over 250 miles (400 km) away.

THE PÄIJÄNNE SYSTEM: Päijänne is Finland's longest and deepest lake – 74 miles (119 km) long as the crane flies, though many times that if you follow its wondrously intricate shoreline. At opposite ends of the lake system are two of Finland's more substantial towns, Lahti and Jyväskylä. The watery topography between the two defeated the railway engineers, but they are linked to the west of Päijänne by one of Europe's main highways, E4, and to the east of it by a network of slower more attractive ways. Alternatively in summer there is the leisurely 10½-hour waterborne route by lake boat.

Further removed from troublesome historical border areas than many regions of Finland, this central district has been less subjected to conflict and to change. Tourism also reached it later, though has made up for it since. Sports, education, industry, and architecture are among its major themes – perhaps

Lahti from the ski jump.

not the most magnetic components for a holiday area, but all in their way helping to shape today's Finland. In any case, in this forested heart of the country the well-watered, deeply wooded landscapes are as lovely as ever.

Lahti lies 64 miles (103 km) north of Helsinki on road 4 (E4). It straddles part of one of Finland's more distinctive topographical features, the extensive ridge system called Salpausselkä, which is regularly the setting for major world skiing championships. Here, too, is the **Lahti Sports Centre** with some of Finland's best winter sports facilities, including three ski jumps (50-, 70- and 90-metre).

Lively market: From the viewing platform on top of the highest ski jump, the town spreads at your feet. Beyond lie the gleaming sheets of **Vesijärvi** (lake) linked, by the **Vääksy Canal** a few miles to the north, to the much greater waters of Päijänne. Lahti is essentially a modern place, one of its few older buildings being the **Town Hall** (1912) designed, as were so many Finnish public buildings of the period, by Eliel Saarinen. Three blocks to the north is the market, a lively morning spot, and two blocks further north the highly individualistic **Church of the Cross** (1978). This was the last church in Finland designed by Alvar Aalto, powerful in its simplicity and a fine main venue for the Lahti Organ Festival every summer. Indeed a major feature is the great organ built into its "window" wall.

The **Lahti Historical Museum** in Lahti Manor, a rather exotic late 19th-century building at Lahdenkatu 4, has very good regional ethnographical and art collections. For living history, though, go a few miles northwest to the area known as **Tiirismaa**. Here is south Finland's highest hill (730 ft/223 metres), some of her oldest rocks and the tourist centre of **Messilä** combining an old manor house, crafts centre and Summerland fun park. A few miles further (and not actually *in* Hollola) the 15th-century greystone **church of Hollola** has some good wooden sculptures and is among the largest and finest

Hollola Church.

of about four score churches surviving from that period in Finland. Near it are a good rural museum and some excellent coffee houses.

From Lahti it's only 21 miles (35 km) northeast on road 5 to the pleasant little town of **Heinola** (*see Paddle Your Own Canoe, page 249*), on the way passing the top **Finnish Sports Institute** at Vierumäki. By the popular summer lake route, it's an astonishing – and lovely – 4½ hours by steamer, 3¾ hours by hydrofoil. A glance at the map reveals the contortions needed for lake traffic plying this route, first negotiating the Vääksy Canal north into Päijänne, and later squeezing southeast through narrow straits into the wider waters that lead to Heinola.

Fishing made easy: There are more narrow straits at Heinola, where the scurrying waters of **Jyrängönkoski** (rapids) provide good sport for local canoeists and for fishermen casting for lake and rainbow trout. You can also try for the latter, with rather more likelihood of success, from the teeming tanks of **Siltasaari Fishing Centre** by the rapids where, for a few Finnmarks, you can rent a rod and have your catch smoked to eat on the spot or take away.

Heinola blossomed into yet another spa town in Czarist times. There are a number of wooden buildings dating from that turn-of-the-century period, including a **Chinese pavilion** on the ridge top park, now a restaurant redolent of a more leisured age. Not far away, the pond of **Kirkkolampi** is a focal point of the well-arranged **Bird Sanctuary** (and bird hospital). The town's main church, an octagonal building from the early 19th century, has a separate bell tower designed by Engel, with whose neoclassical Helsinki you are probably already familiar.

From Heinola, road 5 continues northeast to Mikkeli in western Saimaa. From this you could branch north on to road 59 for Jyväskylä, but there is a slower and more attractive way. For this, leave Lahti north on road 4 (E4) and after 15 miles (25 km), soon after crossing the Vääksy canal at **Asikkala**, **Finland's short summer is full of flowers.**

branch right on to minor road 314. This soon carries you along the several miles of **Pulkkilanharju** (ridge), another relic from the last Ice Age which vies with that of Punkaharju for narrowness and magnificence of lake-and-forest views. You continue by a series of asphalted but lesser roads via **Sysmä** and **Luhanka**, twisting along or across the complex succession of headlands, bays, capes and interlinked islands that make up Päijänne's contorted eastern shore. At Luhanka, the **Peltola Cotters Museum** (*Mäkitupalaismuseo*) throws light on the unenviable lot of the 19th-century "cotters": smallholders who effectively mortgaged their working lives to wealthy landowners in return for a scrap of land whose lease could be revoked at the owner's will.

To rejoin road 4 (E4) at Korpilahti for the final leg to Jyväskylä you will need to take the car ferry across **Kärkistensalmi**, one of Päijänne's many narrow straits. Road 4, of course, provides a more direct main road link all the way from Lahti to Jyväskylä in 107 miles

(174 km). A particular beauty spot a little off this route is the long, slender island of **Kelvenne**, about 37 miles (60 km) north of Lahti, with its lakes, lagoons and curious geological formations. You reach it from Kullasvuori camping area at **Padasjoki**. Road 4 also bypasses **Jämsä** and passes near the industrial community of **Jämsänkoski**.

Finnish-language pioneer: Jyväskylä is a versatile sort of town, with industry, sport, art and architecture all major features. But it was as an educational centre that, historically, it contributed so much to the country's cultural development: at a time when the Finnish language was still regarded by the Swedish-speaking ruling classes as the language of the peasant majority, the first Finnish-language secondary school opened here in 1858 and a teachers' training college a few years later. It now also has a lively university whose campus is the work of Alvar Aalto. Indeed it was in Jyväskylä that this renowned architect embarked on his career, and there are no less than 30 major buildings by him around the

From the air, limitless lakes.

area, as well as the **Alvar Aalto Museum** at 7 Alvar Aallonkatu (yes, Alvar Aalto Street!).

Like so many Finnish towns whose older timber buildings have been destroyed by fire or replaced in the name of progress, Jyväskylä is predominantly modern. From the observation platform of the **Water Tower** on the ridge running through the town you can gaze across it to the lakes. There are sports facilities on the same ridge and even more out at **Laajavuori**, a winter and summer sports centre on the northwest outskirts of town. Jyväskylä caters for most sports but is internationally best known as the venue for the 1,000 Lakes Rally in August, which draws 400,000 spectators to Finland's premier motor racing event. In June, the **Jyväskylä Arts Festival** chooses a different theme each year, examining its every aspect in seminars, exhibitions, concerts and theatre performances.

For a glimpse into the region's past, go to the excellent **Museum of Central Finland**, next to the Alvar Aalto Museum. Or, with a little more time, head west on road 23 to **Petäjävesi** (20 miles, 32 km) and **Keuruu** (a further 17 miles, 28 km). Both have charming 18th-century wooden churches in typical central Finland rural settings. Road 23 continues west to Virrat at the northern end of the Poet's Way route (*see page 185*).

North of Jyväskylä, road 4 (E4) continues through yet more forested lake-strewn landscapes harbouring a growing scattering of holiday and leisure centres. After 21 miles (35 km) road 13 forks left to **Saarijärvi** (17 miles, 28 km), focal point of a pleasant holiday area. Just before it, turn south on road 630, then shortly east to **Summassaari** where a Stone Age village has been reconstructed. A little beyond Saarijärvi in **Kolkanlahti** is the elegant 19th-century house, now a museum, where Finland's national poet, J. L. Runeberg, worked as a tutor in the 1820s.

Back on road 4 (E4) you soon bypass **Äänekoski**, of no particular interest, as the highway leads ever northwards towards the Arctic Circle.

Below, Jyväskylä outdoor market. Right, the fish market at Jyväskylä.

PADDLE YOUR OWN CANOE

One of the more testing events on the European canoeing calendar is the Arctic Canoe Race which takes place every summer north of the Arctic Circle from Kilpisjärvi to Tornio along 334 miles (537 km) of the swift border rivers between Finland and Sweden. Another is the six-day 434-mile (700-km) Finlandia Canoe Relay each June, usually through the complex Saimaa system.

With 187,888 lakes (at the last count) and innumerable rivers to choose from, it's surprising that canoeing has only become popular in Finland in quite recent years. There is now, however, a growing range of usually rather loose packages whereby you can canoe well-tried routes of varying lengths, the cost based on whether you are in a group or alone, the hire of canoe, paddles, provision of map and/or guide, with the option of hiring camping equipment or pre-booking farmhouse accommodation.

A particularly well-tried series of routes forms an overall 217-mile (350-km) circuit beginning and ending at Heinola. This needs 10–15 days but can also be fragmented into more manageable two to five-day sections. Another, along 200 miles (320 km) of the Ounasjoki river in Finnish Lapland from Enontekiö to Rovaniemi, features sec-

tions of true Arctic wilderness; the rapids are mainly Grade Is with a couple of Grade IIIs, but it's possible to portage round the most daunting of these. Yet another follows the over 200-mile (285-km) traditional lake-and-river route taken by the old tar boats from Kuhmo through Kainuu to Oulu on the Gulf of Bothnia.

If you're attracted to the idea of pioneering your own route across the lakes the possibilities are legion and the challenges particular. Any of the 19 road maps which cover the entire country on a scale of 1:200 000 will be sufficient for general planning, but absolutely essential for more detail are the special inland waters charts, e.g. for Saimaa on a scale of 1:40 000/1:50 000.

It's not until you are actually in your canoe, however, facing the reality of those charts trans-

lated into land and water that the full extent of your navigation problems begins to be apparent. From the low level of a canoe one island of rock and pinewood looks extremely like another – even if you have managed to establish beyond doubt that it *is* an island and not a headland or a promontory. Across wide expanses of water the distant dark rim of forest presents few helpful landmarks. You will then appreciate those other vital aids to canoeing the Finnish lakes: a compass and a pair of binoculars (useful for birdwatching anyway).

The greatest inconvenience – at times amounting to hazard – you are likely to encounter is wind, which is almost invariably in the wrong direction, i.e. against you or, worse still, side-on. Squalls can blow up quickly and, across these majestic expanses, waters are soon whipped up into a dramatic turbulence. It's wise to head for shelter at the first sign.

Away from communities and official camp sites camping may prove more difficult than you might expect in such seemingly empty landscapes. Much of the shoreline is either rocky or fringed by broad swathes of reed beds. Once landed, finding space enough between the ever-present trees can be a problem even for a small tent and, where a clearing does exist, it has probably been created to accommodate a holiday cottage or farmland. "Everyman's Right" – the right to wander at will and pitch your tent anywhere other than unacceptably close to a private house – has been badly abused by some foreigners and is no longer so readily promoted. You may help redress the balance by respecting its generous spirit, seeking permission to camp whenever possible.

But, of course, there is often no one to ask. It is one of the huge joys of canoeing in Finland that you may travel all day, or longer, without sign of humanity other perhaps than a tugboat hauling its floating train of timber, or a distant fisherman; a second joy is that you can get in touch with the natural world and perhaps with yourself too.

You can obtain further details of canoeing packages and routes from the Finnish Tourist Board or local tourist organisations; or from the Finnish Canoe Association, Radiokatu 20, 00240 Helsinki. Local canoeing clubs exist in most lakeside communities and will make you most welcome.

KARELIA AND THE WILDERNESS WAY

Eastern Finland, which stretches broadly to the eastern frontier, is a changeover zone between the great Finnish Lake area and Lappi or Lapland. Few people live in its wild territory but the character of Karelia and the Orthodox churches add charm, tradition, and colour.

Finland's most famous and perhaps most photographed scenery stretches below the lofty summit of the Koli Heights above Lake Pielinen, which also has good winter skiing. The "Bard and Border Way" takes the traveller to the frontier sights, including battlegrounds from World War II. Hiking in the wild, shooting the rapids and winter sports are the specialties of this region.

Joensuu at the mouth of the river Piesjoki, is the "capital" of North Karelia. It has a relaxed and welcoming air which is largely due to the fact that the majority of the inhabitants are Karelians, a people with a well-earned reputation for good humour and ready wit, traits particularly in evidence at the bustling market place.

Festival centre: At the end of June each year, Joensuu plays host to the Festival of Song, centred on the **Joensuu Song Bowl**, which has a stage large enough for 11,000 singers. The **North Karelia Museum** (*Pohjois-Karjalarsmuseo*) exhibits articles from prehistory, history and the folk culture of this part of Karelia. There are also an Art Museum, with an icon collection and Finnish painting from the 19th and 20th centuries, and Botanical Gardens. In many places, you find restaurants with Karelian specialties. Joensuu's **Restaurant Puukello** offers Karelian pies with salted fish and Karelian roasts.

Before turning north, why not go as far east as you can in Finland to **Ilomantsi**? Take road 6 south out of Joensuu and then road 73 east for the 50-mile (70-km) drive. Ilomantsi was the scene of heavy fighting in World War II, and in the village of Hattuvaara to the northeast the **Warrior's House** marks

the spot where fighting ended in 1944. Since the 14th century, the town has been a stronghold of the Orthodox Church and the main church is dedicated to St Elias. Easter is the most impressive festival, but the area is full of old rites and rituals. For more music and colour, it would be hard to beat the village of **Rääkkylä**, a few miles south of Joensuu on a secondary road along the southern end of Lake Pyhäselkä. Its renowned folk band has won the national championship, and many other awards and some of the young musicians play that most Karelian of instruments, the *kantele*, a stringed instrument a bit like a zither.

Heading north from Joensuu, take route 18 out of the town towards Eno. Where the road divides, take the right fork eastward (route 73) which leads along the eastern shore of Lake Pielinen to Lieksa. The roads through this countryside are tarred and well maintained but they are neither broad highways nor motorways and sometimes seem little different from the minor roads and lanes

that lead off into the forest. But usually driving is simple, with main routes numbered and villages signed.

Shooting the rapids: The **Ruuankoski rapids** are a sight not to be missed from Lieksa. For some 21 miles (33 km) the Ruunaa plunges through six sets of foaming rapids and drops around 50 ft (15 metres) on the way. With lifejacket and waterproofs, shooting the rapids is safe under the careful supervision of a proficient guide. The **Pielinen Outdoor Museum** (Pielisen Museo) has numerous buildings from different ages, the oldest from the 17th century. At **Vuonisjärvi** (18 miles/29 km from the centre) is the studio of Eeva Ryynänen, a wood sculptor, and **Kaksinkantaja**, 24 miles (38 km) from the centre, has an exhibition of bear skulls and stuffed animals by Väinö Heikkinen, a famous bear hunter.

Lieksa, one of the many forest centres in Finland, is less than 20 years old and has a population of only 19,000 (and a few bears) in an area bigger than London. It may not be the most prepossessing of towns, but it is an important centre for visitors to this part of Finland's wilderness, which stretches as far as the Soviet border. Capercaillie, elk, bear, reindeer and even wolves roam these dense pine forests. The best way to get an idea of its sheer size is from the viewing platform of the town's 150-ft (47-metre) water tower.

"Never go hiking on your own," is the warning motto of this region, and inexperienced walkers in particular should take guided tours, which can be arranged for individuals or groups. Most walks involve camping and the local shops in Lieksa can provide all the equipment and maps. Expeditions and things to do include the "Bears' Walk" along the Soviet border, lake fishing in summer, and ice-fishing in winter.

Trout, landlocked salmon (a relic of the Ice Age), coarse fish, and bream all swim in these unpolluted waters. Join a guided fishing expedition if you would like to try your hand at catching them. A package will include the services of a guide, transport, accommodation, and

Wildflowers in the sauna.

Karelia and the East

licences. Otherwise, post offices supply fishing licences; and tourist offices, regional fishing licences.

From Lieksa, the same road 73 leads to **Nurmes** in about an hour, keeping close to the shores of Lake Pielinen. First mentioned in documents in 1556, Nurmes only became a city as recently as 1974. Nicknamed "the country of the birch", Nurmes sits on a ridge between two lakes at the northern end of the Pielinen lake system; it is a beautiful town, with wooden houses built in authentic early-Karelian style.

Bomba is a traditional Karelian house at Ritoniemi about a mile from the town, surrounded by a recently built "Karelian village" which provides visitors not only with comfortable accommodation but also with delicious meals of local specialities.

Bomba House's menu includes an assortment of local pies, the tiny fish vendace, cold smoked whitefish, warm smoked lamb, butter with chopped egg, venison meat balls, fried wild mushrooms, baked cheese with arctic bramble jam – all designed to get the taste buds working overtime.

It would be a pity to miss Finland's most gracious way to travel and Nurmes is the place to leave the car and take a leisurely steam boat ride down Lake Pielinen to that famous beauty spot, the **Koli Hills**. The lake scenery is wonderful, and you may meet Finland's largest inland waterway ferry as well as numerous other boats big and small.

The Koli Hills rise half way down the western side of the lake, the highest Ukko-Koli (Old Man Koli) reaching 1,100 ft (347 metres). Scramble up to the top (there are steps) and spread out below is a view that has inspired some of the greatest artists, including Albert Edelfelt and Eero Järnefelt, whose paintings immortalised Koli around the turn of the century and did much to stimulate the national awakening of the time. Sibelius, too, wove the Koli Hills into his symphonies and, looking down, it is not hard to understand why this countryside is always called Finland's "national landscape".

A typical Karelian house.

THE KARELIANS

If Finland has a soul, that soul lives in Karelia. When Finns have gone to war, the war has concerned Karelia. The muses favoured Karelia, for a Karelian theme runs through most of the music of Sibelius and his *Karelian Suite* reaches sublime heights of elegy and patriotism.

The Karelians were one of the earliest of the Finnish communities. They are evident in Bronze and Iron Age discoveries and their true origins are lost in myth and legend. Or perhaps not so lost, for the *Kalevala* , that great epic saga of ancient life in the far North, is really about the Karelians.

This long poem, which in the 18th and 19th centuries became the cornerstone of the struggle for national culture, tells how with magic and sword the Northern heroes fought for survival against the powers of evil. It recounts perilous journeys over land and sea, weddings, rituals, bear hunts and journeys into the mysterious Otherworld.

Finally it recounts the heroes' joy as they celebrate in song and music the salvation of the land of Kalevala from its enemies. And although the *Kalevala* depicts a pre-Christian period, this last poem predicts the decline of paganism, with the maid Marjatta giving birth to a son. The son is baptised and then becomes king of Karelia.

The saga is written in blank verse characterised by alliteration and repetition, and was an inspiration for the music of Sibelius, the paintings of Gallen-Kallela, and even, it is said, *The Song of Hiawatha* by Henry Longfellow.

The Karelians emerge into recorded history as a people living in the area of forest and lakes stretching from the present-day southeastern Finnish-Russian border to the White Sea. The Karelians came under Russian influences, although in no sense did they become russified. Slash and burn was their way of converting the impenetrable woodland into productive fields and they used the ash as as a fertiliser.

With slash and burn came the production of grain and the need to dry it. Steam heat was probably a Russian invention, but the Karelians adopted and adapted the process, first for grain drying and then for human relaxation and therapy. The sauna was born.

Orthodox religion is also a feature of the Karelian people, although it is accorded the title Greek Orthodox rather than Russian. There are 60,000 adherents of Greek Orthodoxy and many churches in southeast Finland today. Karelian as a dialect has more or less died out, though at one time originally there were two dialects.

The terrible Winter War of 1939–40 was fought to save Karelian land. It has become the Finns' great *causes célèbres* but it was only one war out of some 200 wars and battles which were fought to preserve the Karelians and it did not save much of Finnish Karelia.

As a result of the settlement forced on Finland at the end of the Continuation War, some 400,000 Karelians had to leave, to be re-settled and re-housed in the 1940s. The Karelian Isthmus was lost, along with all of East Karelia, which has now been settled by Russians and Byelorussians.

Since then, people of Karelian origin can be found in all parts of Finland. They tend to be lively and talkative, in contrast to the more taciturn nature of other Finns. Their Orthodox religion may distinguish them from their Lutheran neighbours but many have changed religion, or lost it in their marriage.

True Karelia today exists only as a fragment of its former self and of modern Finland. The border has all but cut it out of the Finnish body politic. Its people have been dispersed. Those that are left are either a remnant in the Soviet Union or living in forest dwellings and hamlets. A line roughly parallel to the border from Lieska down to the Isthmus approximately delineates modern Finnish Karelia.

Yet even in this small region something distinctive remains. Perhaps it is the particularly delicious way they prepare food. Salmon tastes better here than anywhere else in the country. Perhaps it is the almost cathedral-like grandeur of the forest, where the capercaillie flaps its wings like some great plane and the stately elk treads softly on the moss. But the Karelian legacy is more than a lost homeland. Sauna, saga and Sibelius – these are the Karelians' true memorials.

The Wilderness Way north: Finland's wilderness way north has three of the country's glories – sauna, salmon, and scenery, the last embodied in its National Parks although not confined to them. You will meet these three great assets at almost every turn in Finland but never so frequently as in the region that starts north of Nurmes, roughly along the line of the Oulu waterway – lake and river – that almost bisects Finland, and stretches north to Rovaniemi and Lapland proper.

There is one sauna for every four people in Finland and visitors will find them everywhere – in hotels, private homes, on board ships, at motels, vacation villages, and forest camps. Every Finn is proud of sauna, the one word which the Finnish language has offered to the rest of the world, and nothing better complements a long northern day in the open air.

On the stove or in the stream there is only one really classic fish and that is the Atlantic salmon. Though Finland has no sea border with the Atlantic,

thanks to the Ice Age, this area, like others, retains an Atlantic legacy in the salmon of the big natural landlocked lakes and from smaller stocked waters.

National parks are protected areas where nature is left as untouched as possible but some amenities are provided for visitors; marked trails, camp sites, and cabins are set in the larger parks, with hotel accommodation just outside the park proper. With so much unspoiled territory, it may hardly seem necessary for Finland to designate national parks but it has 25, some of the best along this wilderness way north.

From the eastern side of the country, the natural way in would be from Nurmes on road 75 to Kuhmo, or via road 18 north, either turning right on to road 76 just before Sotkamo to reach Kuhmo or continuing left on road 18 for Kajaani on Oulujärvi (lake) to the west. (From the west coast the natural route would be from Oulu along the waterway that connects the Oulu river, lake, Kajaani, and Kuhmo.)

A natural world: Even before you reach

the Olou area if your choice is road 18 north, you might like to detour to the remote **Tiilika National Park**, near Rautavaara. After Valtimo, some 16 miles (25 km) north of Nurmes, turn left on to road 585 towards Rautavaara, and some 32 miles (50 km) on you come to the park. It was established to conserve the uninhabited area of **Lake Tiilika** and the surrounding bogs. The centre of its village accommodation and restaurant services is the Kalevala Hotel which, like so many other designs in Finland, is based on the spirit of the *Kalevala*. Retrace your route back to road 18 and continue north.

The **Hiidenportti National Park** is southeast of Sotkamo and best reached also from road 18. Take road 584 right off road 18, and some 16 miles (25 km) on you come to the park on the left. This is a rugged untouched area, where the narrow Hiidenportti Gorge, a rift valley with rock sides dropping some 70 ft (20 metres) to the floor of the gorge. Both the park and the neighbouring Peurajärvi hiking and fishing area have marked trails with tent sites. Though you could wriggle through a complicated series of minor roads on the Sotkamo from here, unless you are feeling adventurous, it is probably easier to go back to road 18.

Both in and outside the parks, the further north you go, the more likely you are to find reindeer. These semi-domesticated animals are the main source of income for many people living in these parts and it is very important to take special care on roads when reindeer are around.

The frontier: Kuhmo is a frontier town surrounded by dense forests in the wilderness area of Kainuu. The largest municipal area in Finland, it covers 5,458 sq. km. Close to the Soviet border and remote and empty though the area is, Kuhmo has established an international reputation through the annual **Kuhmo Chamber Music Festival**, first held in 1970. Thirty miles (50 km) east in Saunajärvi is the **Winter War Memorial** marking Finland's desperate 100-day struggle in 1940 against overwhelming odds.

At one time this whole area was devoted to making tar, by a lengthy process of cutting, leaving, and then burning forest trees to extract the sticky liquid that formed the basic ingredient. Once it was in barrels, peasants loaded their small boats for the slow journey down through lake and river to the port of Oulu where, in a rare symbiosis, shipbuilders bought it for their own craft and entrepreneurs shipped it abroad. In the 19th century Finland was the biggest exporter of tar in the world.

A recreated **Kalevala Village** in a wooded park on the outskirts of Kuhmo displays folk traditions. The aim is to give modern-day visitors some idea of Finnish culture as it was immortalised by the folklorist Elias Lönnrot and artists such as Akseli Gallen-Kallela. The result is a living demonstration of the daily culture of ancient times as portrayed in Finland's epic, the *Kalevala*.

The village also serves as the scene for numerous events based on folk literature, including plays, celebrations and performances by theatre groups.

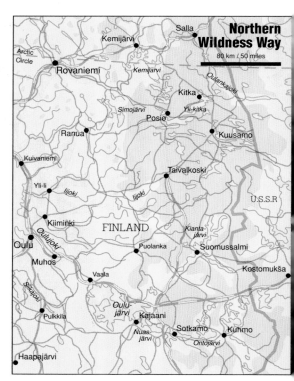

Guided tours teach visitors about primitive hunting and fishing and how tar was made in the Finnish wilds. The village has models of ingenious traps to catch birds and animals, including bears, and examples of how the old fishing families and peasants lived.

North of Kuhmo at Lentiira is the **Pine Peninsula Adventure Village**, one of the most welcoming and comfortable hut complexes by the lake. Smoke sauna and cold beer included, this is tourist hospitality at its very best.

Dark green forests: A long straight road through some of Finland's darkest forests leads west out of Kuhmo to Sotkamo and then onwards to Kajaani, the area's main town, on the eastern edge of Oulujärvi (lake) and once the collecting point for barrels of tar ready for their journey to the coast.

Kajaani was founded in 1651 by the Swedish governor-general Per Brahe in the shelter of an existing fortress designed as a bastion against Russia. But in 1716, the fortress fell and the whole town was razed during the disastrous war between Sweden and Russia. Elias Lönnrot at one time lived in Kajaani, and the town is also known as the home of Finland's longest-serving president, Urho Kekkonen. The town still has the ruins of the **1604 castle**. The **Town Hall** is yet another designed by the well-travelled German architect, C.L. Engel, who was responsible for so much of early Helsinki. The old tar boat canal and the lock keeper's house by the river Kajaani are still visible.

The **Czar's Stable** in **Paltaniemi** is a relic of a visit by Alexander I. Also in Paltaniemi is the birthplace of the poet Eino Leino, and the city has a **Cultural and Congress Centre**. Twelve miles (20 km) from the centre, **Ruuhijarvi Wilderness Village** has peaceful fishing grounds and old hunting lodges which are open all year.

The road from Kajaani to Oulu hugs the shores of Lake Oulu, plunging first into thickly wooded hill country. Before entering Oulu, the route goes through Muhos which has the second-oldest church in Finland, dating from

Lynx, as well as elk, bear, wolf and more live in the Finnish wilderness.

1634. Oulu continues the tradition of tar making and the town lights tar pits on midsummer's eve (*see the Gulf of Bothnia, pages 213–222*).

Distances are long in this scantily populated area where Finns come to walk and fish and look at nature and the only other main centre, Kuusamo, almost at the Soviet border, is some 225 miles (360 km) northeast across the breadth of the country along road 20. (If you feel like a detour, turn left at Pudasjärvi and take road 78, for 55 miles (90 km) to Ranua, which claims the world's northernmost zoo. Next to it is a piece of Santa Claus nonsense called the Murr-Murr Castle and featuring Santa's animal workshop.

Rushing water and wind: Kuusamo is marvellous wilderness country, with tundra as far as you can see in any direction, forest, racing rivers with water foaming through gorges and canyons, some bare, others a dense dark green. The main sound in these parts is a mixture of rushing water and wind high in the pines. There are dozens of

rapids, some suitable for canoeing, others for fishing. The Oulankajoki and Iijoki (rivers) are excellent for family canoeing trips, but the Kitkajoki calls for experienced canoeists only.

There are literally thousands of excellent fishing spots in both rivers and lakes. The "Russian" brown trout rise in the rivers from Lake Paanajärvi in greater numbers each year thanks to efficient tending of the fishing grounds. This is also berry country, with blueberries, raspberries, lingon, and cloudberries all growing in great profusion on the Arctic tundra. The only snag is the number of mosquitoes; they multiply rapidly in the northern summer.

In both summer and winter, this vast unspoiled area is given over to recreation. In the middle, **Karhuntassu Tourist Centre** has been specially built to provide information on every activity, accommodation, and most other aspects of the region, and there are other more distant centres. In winter, the area is fine for skiing and the skidoo or snowmobile comes into its own. Snowmobiling is both an exhilarating and a practical way to get around the snowbound country, though many consider this convenience outweighed by its noise and fumes.

There are two national parks near here. The largest, **Oulanka**, to the north stretches over an untouched region of 105 sq. miles (270 sq. km), bordering the Oulanka river. It is a landscape of ravines and rushing torrents, sandbanks and flowering meadows. **Karhunkierros**, the most famous walking route in Finland, stretches 60 miles (100 km) through the Oulanka canyon to the Rukatunturi fells. A few miles will give the flavour but to cover the whole route, staying at camp sites or forest cabins, takes several days. A smaller national park, **Riisitunturi**, lies to the northeast of Oulanka, an untouched wilderness of spruce dominated by hills and bogs.

Almost imperceptibly on the wilderness way north, the landscape and culture have changed from the old traditions of Karelia to the ancient ways of the Sami people. From here on, without doubt the land is Lappi.

Left, hunting and fishing often combine... right, waiting for the prey.

HUNTING

The great bull elk of Finland, standing 6 ft (1.8 metres) high at the shoulder, gazes through the northern forest. Crowned by massive horns, this great elk is not the sluggish, lumbering giant it looks. Silent as night, wary, elusive, nimble, fast, skilled in animal woodcraft and with highly developed senses, this titan of the tundra and one time cohabitant of the dinosaur tests modern man's hunting skills and fitness to the utmost.

The justification for shooting elk is the paramount need to protect both their food and the young timber that is so important to Finland's economy. The elk breeds so well in modern Finland that an annual cull of around 50,000 animals is necessary. But while a hunter is justified by the need to cull, he is no pest control officer. Justification is one thing; motivation is another. It is the thrill of the chase that brings the elk hunter with his .300 calibre rifle and his dogs to the forest in October for the short elk-hunting season.

The ridge and furrow, the boulders, the tangled bushes and the lichen of tree-covered, sub-Arctic tundra make pursuit of the elk arduous and competitive, modern arms notwithstanding. The trees are dense, the cover is thick; highly trained dogs aid the hunter.

An elk, male or female, is big enough to disregard a dog. Sometimes the elk will take off, but not out of fear. A dog can hold an elk at bay simply because it is disinclined to move, and the best Finnish hunting dogs will stand with an elk and bark for 24 hours.

If the quarry moves, the dogs will hunt it mute by scent. The signal for the hunter who is following up is the renewed barking of the dog, for this means the elk is standing still and the approach can begin. Now comes the most critical part of the day, for if an elk is tolerant of a dog, it is most decidedly not tolerant of a dog's best friend.

The ground is covered in material which, to quote an old advertising slogan, "snaps, crackles and pops". The hunter must proceed with light footsteps, and quite likely may have to crawl for the final approach. He must make sure the wind is in his favour, and be aware that the wind may suddenly change. At any moment the beast may smell or see him. It is sudden movement that attracts attention and a whole day's effort may be ruined by one false move.

If culling is the reason and justification behind elk hunting, it is also the *raison d'être* for wolf hunting. Wolves still prowl the border area of Finland and Russia though Finns insist that there are more wolves on the Russian side. In Russia, wolves are a pest, a nuisance and a threat, and so are bears.

A rare species of forest reindeer lives and roams on either side of the border in the east and in Russian Karelia and is prey for the wolves. Finns will tell you that wolves "come from Russia" and then go back. None stay and breed, unlike bears which, though scarce in Finland, do make their dens and rear their cubs in the Finnish forests.

Once in Finland, wolves are unprotected in Lapland, where they kill domestic reindeer, protected by a close season in eastern Finland, and in the south they are protected year round.

Hunting wolves is a hard and difficult affair but long understood by professional Finnish hunters, who use an ingenious method of encirclement which is also found in other parts of Eastern Europe. From large spools strapped to their backs, the men lay a line of string with red flashes through the woods. It can take up to two days to set the lines but some curious instinct tells a wolf not to cross them; it's the opposite of a red rag to a bull.

The helpers then drive the wolves to where the hunters are waiting. The guns now have some advantage, though the cunning and speed of the wolves may well still save them and only a few wolves are shot each year. Without the red string trick, it's fair to say very few hunters would get their wolf.

You can make hunting tours with guides in several parts of Finland, with elk hunting – lasting three or four days – the most popular. Hunting usually means living in a hut or cabin, invariably clean, bright and made of new wood. After hours in the open, nothing could be better than the ritual of the sauna to give a sense of total well-being.

LAPLAND

Two main roads bore their way northwards through the province of **Lapland** (Lappi). Road 4, sometimes called the Arctic Road, links Kemi with Rovaniemi before continuing northeastwards through ever more sparsely inhabited landscapes to cross into Norway at Karigasniemi. The other is road 21 (E78) which follows the Tornio valley upstream from Tornio, continuing beside various tributaries that form the border with Sweden, eventually to cross into Norway near Kilpisjärvi.

This is the river route of the Arctic Canoe Race (*page 249*) and the road that accompanies it is also sometimes known as the **Way of the Four Winds** after the four points of the Sami traditional male headgear. Bridges and ferries provide links with Sweden.

Respectively the two routes cover 336 miles (540 km) and 284 miles (457 km). Either will show you superficially a great deal of Arctic countryside, but from neither will you glean anything but the faintest hint of what Lapland is all about. For that you must leave the main roads – preferably the minor ones too – and take to your feet or a canoe or, in winter, a pair of skis. It's not even necessary to go very far for there are silences to be found within a few hundred yards of the most modern hotel that seem barely to have been touched since the last Ice Age. But of course the experience deepens with distance and duration. The vital need for proper clothing and equipment, however, can't be sufficiently stressed: climatic changes occur with ferocious suddenness and, for all its magnificence, the Arctic wilderness can be a totally ruthless place.

As you progress northwards the trees become spindlier, the forests sparser, the habitations fewer, the hills more numerous and gradually higher until you reach the sweeping undulations of the bare-topped fells of northern and northwestern Lapland. Beyond the tree line vegetation crouches and crawls – dwarf juniper and willow and miniature birch clinging to the fellsides among the mosses and the lichens, the minuscule campions and tiny saxifrages. In summer take plenty of mosquito repellent; every paradise must have its serpent.

In 1944 the German army followed a scorched-earth policy as it retreated north into Norway, so such old buildings as survive are mostly away from main roads. But despite the monumental changes wrought on the province by the second half of the 20th century (*see The Sami, page 95*) a way of life endures, at least some of whose elements pre-date any man-made constructions.

From Kemi, road 4 follows the valley of the Kemijoki in which a rash of timber-based industries has spawned a succession of communities. You reach **Rovaniemi** in 71 miles (115 km). This, the administrative capital of Lapland, all but nudges the Arctic Circle and is the launching point for most trips into the province. The town, well placed at the confluence of the Ounasjoki and Kemijoki (rivers), has been completely rebuilt since World War II, almost

quadrupling its population (now about 33,000) in the process. In early summer the Ounasjoki is still used for floating timber down from the forests of central Lapland, the logs jostling in their multi-thousands past Rovaniemi's skyline. Rising up from the confluence are the wooded slopes of **Ounasvaara**, now a well-developed skiing area and site of annual international winter games. It's also a favourite strolling area and gathering place on Midsummer Night to watch the non-setting sun.

The reconstruction plan for Rovaniemi was made by Alvar Aalto who also designed the fine complex of **Lappia-House** in Hallituskatu, containing the Provincial Museum, a theatre and congress facilities and, next to it, the Library. The Provincial Museum gives a good "instant" introduction to Lapland's flora and fauna, Sami traditions and Rovaniemi's history, but you'll get a better feel of bygone living from the 19th-century farm buildings at the **Pöykkölä Museum**, by the Kemi river 2 miles (3 km) to the south on road 78. Not far from Lappia-House the main **Lutheran Church** has a modern and mighty altar fresco, *The Source of Life*, by Lennart Segerstråle.

Five miles (8 km) northeast of the town on road 4, soon after the turn-off for Rovaniemi airport, the **Santa Claus Workshop Village** straddles the Arctic Circle. Its post office annually handles thousands of letters from children world wide and there are some rather good shops, a glass factory, a few reindeer and, of course, Santa Claus himself.

A number of fell areas east of road 4 in southern Lapland have been developed for winter and summer tourism. One of the best is centred on **Pyhätunturi**, about 84 miles (135 km) northeast of Rovaniemi. Another, just north of it, is **Luostotunturi**, south of **Sodankylä**.

You will have noticed the landscapes – predominantly forested – becoming progressively emptier. **Sodankylä**, 80 miles (130 km) from Rovaniemi, is the first substantial place, a long established community reputed to be the coldest in Finland. Next to its 19th-century stone church, you can visit its

wooden predecessor, Lapland's oldest church, dating from 1689. Road 5 comes in to Sodankylä from the southeast and minor roads wander off east and west to link tiny scattered communities. Northwards, there's little to detain you for the next 60 miles or so (100 km) until, a few miles beyond Vuotso, you reach **Tankavaara**.

Gold washing has been practised in various parts of Lapland for well over a century. Indeed, at **Kultala** (*kulta* means gold) in trackless wilderness to the northwest, on the banks of the Ivalojoki, you can still see a gold-washing station dating from 1870 at a time when almost 500 hopefuls were panning river dirt in search of the eternal dream. Much more accessible here at Tankavaara the **Gold Prospectors' Museum** (Kultamuseo) not only chronicles man's endeavours, but for a modest fee allows you to pan for gold yourself for an hour, a day, even several days, in an authentic wilderness setting and with expert tuition.

Tankavaara is one of many tiny Sami

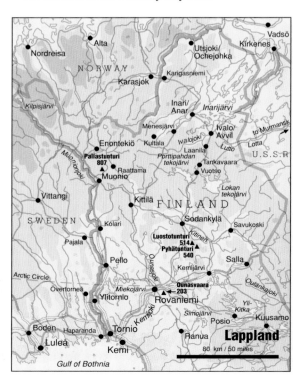

communities offering self-catering accommodation. About 25 miles (40 km) further north there is a great deal more, together with modern hotels and sports facilities, centred on **Laanila** and scattered about the forests and slopes of **Saariselkä**, a huge area of primeval fell and forest towards the Soviet border. Much of this is designated as a national park named after Urho Kekkonen, Finland's longest serving former president.

In another 14 miles (23 km) you pass the turn-off for Ivalo airport, Finland's northernmost, and in a few more miles **Ivalo** itself straggling along the east bank of Ivalojoki. It's the largest community in northern Lapland, with modern shops, hospital, first-class hotel and several schools, though in terms of Sami culture much less important than Inari. It does, however, have an attractive little wooden **Orthodox Church** tucked away in the woods, serving the Skolt Sami, a branch of the Sami people who formerly lived in territory ceded to the Soviet Union in 1944. They have different costumes, language and traditions and some have moved away from reindeer to sheep breeding, or sometimes combine the two. A number of Skolt Sami families live in Nellim, about 29 miles (45 km) northeast of Ivalo towards the Soviet border.

Ivalo's **Lutheran Church** stands near the bridge which carries road 4 over Ivalojoki; then it's another 27 miles (39 km) to **Inari** – much of it a delightful route along parts of the contorted shores of Lake Inari. **Inari** village itself is an excellent base for wilderness exploration. Though smaller and far more scattered than Ivalo, it is nevertheless the administrative centre for a vast if sparsely populated area and a traditional meeting place for Sami people from far and wide for weddings and other festivities, especially during the church festival times of Lady Day and Easter.

Focus of much of such festivities is the simple modern church near the lake shore. **Lake Inari** is Finland's third largest, covering 808 sq. miles (1,300 sq. km) and dotted with about 3,000

Snow sculpture competitions are popular.

islands, some of them considered holy according to Sami tradition. It is a wild, lonely beautiful lake, the theme of haunting songs and many legends. Boat trips and sightseeing flights are available in summer.

Inari's excellent open-air **Sami Museum** (Saamelaismuseo) comprises old buildings and equipment showing the earlier nomadic way of life of the reindeer and fishing Sami, with some exhibits concerning early Skolt Sami culture. From the museum a marked trail (9 miles/15 km return) leads to a remote 18th-century wooden church at **Pielppajärvi**, one of Lapland's oldest surviving buildings. It's a lovely spot and the walk gives a small taste of Lapland's silences. It's also accessible by boat.

Minor road 955 from Inari leads southwest to **Menesjärvi** (25 miles/40 km), a Sami settlement from which it is possible to continue by road then river boat or on foot up the wild and beautiful Lemmenjoki ("river of love") valley to a remote gold prospectors' camp. Gold fever here dates only from 1945 but still

infects a hardy few. The river gives its name to another extensive national park area; though less isolated than it was a couple of decades ago, this is still a very lonely area of rocky canyon and primeval forest where you are wise to hire a guide unless you are experienced in wilderness travel. (From Menesjärvi, road 955 continues across Lapland to join road 79 at Kittilä.)

Around Inari and north of it, the road passes a number of attractive holiday centres, mostly of the self-catering variety. After 16 miles (26 km) you come to **Kaamanen** from which a minor road branches northeast to **Sevettijärvi** (60 miles/100 km), the modern new main settlement for the Skolt Sami. An interesting time to go there is during the Easter Orthodox festival. Just a couple of miles north of Kaamanen there is a further parting of the ways: due north by minor road to Utsjoki 58 miles (94 km) away on the border with Norway; or bearing northwest along road 4 to the Norwegian border 41 miles (66 km) away at Karigasniemi.

When roads are few, people take to the water, Nurmes.

Either way, the landscapes become progressively hillier, wilder and emptier of human presence. You will also pass the coniferous tree line, beyond which only the hardier dwarf birch survive on the lower fell slopes, their gnarled and weathered forms looking curiously biblical in this barren Arctic countryside. The more beautiful route is the minor one to **Utsjoki**, passing a series of lakes and close to the eastern fringes of the **Kevo Nature Park** where Turku University runs an experimental station recording all aspects of Lapland's natural elements.

Utsjoki is an important Sami community and fine for fishing and hiking close to Finland's northernmost point. Its church (1860) is one of the few pre-World War II churches still standing in Lapland. The village straggles along the road for several miles as it follows the Utsjoki downstream to join with the Tenojoki, a famed salmon river.

Both Utsjoki and **Karigasniemi** are dominated by fells called Ailigas, once considered holy by the Sami people, the one dominating Karigasniemi reaching over 2,000 ft (620 metres). From these border points you can also join the Norwegian road system for a variety of routes eventually returning into western Lapland at Kilpisjärvi or Enontekiö.

Your route through western Lapland is likely to begin at Tornio about 50 miles (80 km) south of the Arctic Circle. The earlier stretches of the Way of the Four Winds or road 21 (E78) present a very different face of Lapland from the Arctic Road, for the lower section of the Tornio valley is, relatively speaking, quite heavily populated. It is also served by Finland's northernmost railway branch to just beyond Kolari, about 115 miles (186 km) north of Tornio.

In its southern stages the road passes through a string of small communities mainly based, in these marginally milder and more fertile conditions, on agriculture and dairy farming. The Tornionjoki is also a good salmon river; at **Kukkola** look out for the Kukkolankoski (rapids), the biggest on the river where traditional fishing methods,

using landing nets, are still practised. About 43 miles (70 km) north of Tornio, beyond Ylitornio, the hill of **Aavasaksa**, 794 ft (242 metres) is the most southerly point from which the midnight sun can be seen, attracting considerable throngs for Midsummer Eve festivities. A few miles further, near Juoksenki, you cross the Arctic Circle. The scenery now becomes wilder as you pass between the main communities of **Pello** and **Kolari**. A little south of the latter Tornionjoki is replaced by one of its tributaries, the Muonionjoki, at the Fenno-Swedish border.

About 7 miles (10 km) north of Kolari a worthwhile detour by minor road 939 to the right leads to **Äkäslompolo** in about 18 miles (30 km). This well-equipped tourist centre is scattered about the shores of a small lake set amongst magnificent forested hills and bare-topped fells; the highest is Ylläs, 2,355 ft (718 metres) served by chair lift. A marked trail follows the chain of fells stretching northwards from here, eventually leading in about 90 miles

(150 km) to the Pallastunturi fell group. It's a glorious trail for those properly equipped, with overnight shelter in untended wilderness huts, marked even on the 1:200 000 road maps.

From Äkäslompolo you can continue north along minor roads and in 19 miles (31 km) turn left on to road 79. This is the main road from Rovaniemi providing an alternative approach to western Lapland. After a further 7 miles (10 km) minor road 957 to the right is highly recommended as the best approach to Enontekiö. A further branch left off this leads in a total of 13 miles (21 km) from road 79 to the lonely hotel complex of **Pallastunturi**, magnificently cradled in the lap of five of the 14 fells which make up the Pallastunturi group (highest, Taivaskero at 2,647 ft (807 metres).

From here there is a fine choice of fell walks including the long-distance trail from Yllästunturi and north across the fells to Enontekiö, 37 miles (60 km). Road 957 brings you in due course to the upper Ounasjoki valley and via the small community of **Raattama** to **Ketomella** where there's a car ferry across the river. Until fairly recent times this part of the valley was accessible only on foot or by boat or sledge, so a number of venerable farm buildings have survived wartime destruction, highly photogenic as they lean, tipsy with age, among the meadows. All the way, you are accompanied by lovely views of first the Pallas, then the Ounas fells. At the junction at **Peltovuoma** you turn west for Enontekiö and, eventually, Palojoensuu, back on road 21.

Enontekiö, sometimes known by its older name of Hetta, is one of the most attractively sited villages in the province. The administrative centre of yet another extensive and sparsely populated area, it's widely scattered amongst meadows along the northern shore of Ounasjärvi (lake) looking across to the great rounded shoulders of the Ounastunturi fells (highest Outtakka, 2,372 ft/ 723 metres). Not so long ago, it was rather an isolated place; now it's accessible by air and road from all directions, with a road link north into Norway.

Most of Enontekiö's buildings are

Drying reindeer meat.

modern, including the pretty wooden church which has an altar mosaic depicting Sami people and reindeer. There's a good range of accommodation, from camp sites to top-class hotel, for the fishermen, hikers and canoeists for whom this is an excellent centre. It's also a main centre for the Sami of western Lapland, most of whom live in lone farmsteads or tiny communities widely scattered about the area. Here, too, there are major Sami gatherings at times of the year such as Lady Day or Easter.

From Palo Joensuu, road 21 continues northwest along the Muonionjoki and Könkämäeno valleys, the scenery becoming ever wilder and more barren. A few miles north of **Kaaresuvanto** you cross the coniferous tree line and pass the last spindly pines. A little south and north of **Ropinsalmi** there are good views respectively of Pättikkäkoski and Saukkokoski, two of the more testing rapids of the Arctic Canoe Race. By now, too, the mountains reach to ever greater heights, eventually topping well over 3,200 (1,000 metres). The highest of all, Haltia, soars up to 4,357 ft (1,328 metres) out of an uninhabited nowhere on the Norwegian border at Finland's northwesternmost point. More accessible and more distinctive is Saana, lifting to 3,376 ft (1,029 metres) above the village and resort of **Kilpisjärvi**.

Saana, another once-holy Sami eminence, is a handsome fell, and Kilpisjärvi an excellent launching pad for wilderness enthusiasts. There is a lake of the same name whose western short forms the border with Sweden, and a marked trail leads in a few miles to the **boundary stone** marking the triple junction of Finland-Sweden-Norway. The **Malla Nature Reserve** to the north of the lake needs a permit for entry.

The rest of these immense, empty, rugged, grandiose acres are as free to all comers as the elements – and as unpredictable. *Never* set off without proper equipment and provisions and, unless you are experienced, a guide; *always* inform someone where you are heading and when you expect to return. It cannot be said often enough.

Northern flat bread has a distinctive taste.

THE NOBLE TIME

JUVENIA

— 1860 —

Golden Age ®
COLLECTION

STEEL - STEEL/GOLD - 18KT GOLD AND WITH PRECIOUS STONES

Worldwide list of JUVENIA Agents available on request

JUVENIA MONTRES SA - 2304 LA CHAUX-DE-FONDS - SWITZERLAND
Tel. 41/39 26 04 65 Fax 41/39 26 68 00

So, you're getting away from it all.

Just make sure you can get back.

AT&T Access Numbers
Dial the number of the country you're in to reach AT&T.

*ANDORRA	19◊-0011	GERMANY**	0130-0010	*NETHERLANDS	06-022-9111
*AUSTRIA	022-903-011	*GREECE	00-800-1311	*NORWAY	050-12011
*BELGIUM	078-11-0010	*HUNGARY	00◊-800-01111	POLAND†◆²	0◊010-480-0111
BULGARIA	00-1800-0010	*ICELAND	999-001	PORTUGAL†	05017-1-288
CROATIA†◆	99-38-0011	IRELAND	1-800-550-000	ROMANIA	01-800-4288
*CYPRUS	080-90010	ISRAEL	177-100-2727	*RUSSIA† (MOSCOW)	155-5042
CZECH REPUBLIC	00-420-00101	*ITALY	172-1011	SLOVAKIA	00-420-00101
*DENMARK	8001-0010	KENYA†	0800-10	SPAIN	900-99-00-11
*EGYPT† (CAIRO)	510-0200	*LIECHTENSTEIN	155-00-11	*SWEDEN	020-795-611
*FINLAND	9800-100-10	LITHUANIA◆	8◊196	*SWITZERLAND	155-00-11
FRANCE	19◊-0011	LUXEMBOURG	0-800-0111	*TURKEY	9◊9-8001-2277
*GAMBIA	00111	*MALTA	0800-890-110	UK	0800-89-0011

Countries in bold face permit country-to-country calling in addition to calls to the U.S. *Public phones require deposit of coin or phone card. **Western portion. Includes Berlin and Leipzig. ◊Await second dial tone. †May not be available from every phone. ◆ Not available from public phones. ¹Dial "02" first, outside Cairo. ²Dial 010-480-0111 from major Warsaw hotels. © 1993 AT&T.

Here's a travel tip that will make it easy to call back to the States. Dial the access number for the country you're visiting and connect right to AT&T **USADirect**® Service. It's the quick way to get English-speaking operators and can minimize hotel surcharges.

If all the countries you're visiting aren't listed above, call **1 800 241-5555** before you leave for a free wallet card with all AT&T access numbers. International calling made easy—it's all part of **The i Plan.**℠

THE *i* PLAN™

AT&T

TRAVEL TIPS

GETTING THERE

BY AIR

Finnair is the national carrier of Finland and operates international and national routes. Both Finnair and British Airways connect London and Helsinki with daily flights. Finnair (and many other airlines including Lufthansa) fly direct between Helsinki and most European capitals, and Finnair also links several North American cities including New York. You may be able to find cheaper package fares and charter flights from New York or London, but they are rare; watch newspaper advertisements for offers.

From Helsinki, Finnair also flies numerous domestic routes, including several to North Finland airports, and has cross-country flights between some of them.

BY SEA

The best routes to Finland by boat are from Sweden and Germany. Silja Line, tel: (9)0-18 041 and Viking Line, tel: (9)0-12 351 have daily routes between Stockholm and Helsinki. These ferries are new, luxuriously-fitted ships with restaurants, saunas, swimming pools, tax-free shops, and children's playrooms. Silja's refurbished Finnjet boat makes the trip to and from Germany (Travemünde/Helsinki) in 24 hours.

It's slightly cheaper to travel by ferry from Stockholm to Turku or Naantali in western Finland and then overland to Helsinki rather than by direct ship to Helsinki. For example, Viking provides free, or very cheap, train or bus tickets for the overland trip; the ferry ticket is also cheaper as the voyage is shorter. One can also travel to Finland's Åland islands by boat from Stockholm or Turku; and Viking Line has a daily service to the Åland capital, Mariehamn. Other lines, such as Vasa Line (c/o Sally Lines tel: [9]0-173 321) run services between Finland and Sweden to points further north than the Stockholm and Turku areas.

East of the Baltic: Visas have usually been required for travel to the former Soviet Union though, in the light of events, this may change. You can get visas in Finland from Finnish travel agents but it is safer to allow 10 working days for processing.

Sally Lines, tel: (9)0-173 321, sell a summer St Petersburg/Baltic Express trip, lasting three to four days, with accommodation on the boat and guides available for St Petersburg. Passengers without visas may go on this trip but, once in St Petersburg, are supposed to stay with the guided tours.

Boat journeys to Tallinn in Estonia are via passenger ferry such as the *Georg Ots* or hydrofoil (summer only, by *m/s Tallink*).

For information on sea or other options for travel to the former Soviet Union – bus, train, or 'plane – contact any larger Helsinki travel agent: Area Travel, tel: (9)0-18 551; FinnSov, tel: (9)0-694 2011; Finland Travel Bureau, tel: (9)0-18 261. Travela, tel: (9)0-624 101 is a good agency for student and budget travellers.

BY RAIL

It's a long haul to Finland from just about anywhere by rail, because you inevitably finish the long rail trip north with a 15-hour journey by boat and train from Stockholm to Helsinki. From Britain, the handiest route is Sealink from Harwich to the Hook of Holland, overland to Copenhagen, then connecting train to Stockholm and boat or boat and train to Helsinki. Total travel time about 45 hours. Cheaper than Apex flights only if you get a special fare rail ticket (e.g. youth ticket); note that residents of Nordic countries now qualify for Interrail tickets regardless of age.

Rail travel to north Finland requires completion by bus as Finnish rail lines only come as far as Rovaniemi and Kemimjärvi (in winter to Kolari). Buses from the north link into this rail system.

BY ROAD

By bus to Finland from anywhere on the Continent would be a real trek but it can be done. Enquire at the Finnish Tourist Board in your home country to see if it is possible.

If you want to take your own car, the most likely route from Northern Europe is via Germany (ferry: Travemünde/Helsinki), or from Britain, across Sweden (ferry: Harwich/Gothenburg) then also by ferry over the Baltic.

TRAVEL ESSENTIALS

VISAS & PASSPORTS

Citizens of most western countries do not need visas to travel to Finland; a valid passport will suffice. The Nordic countries only stamp you in once for a three month tourist stay, so if you arrive via, say Sweden, you won't need to be stamped at the Finnish border. It is difficult for non-Nordics to work in Finland; if you want to try and work, though, contact a Finnish Embassy or Consulate outside Finland well before you go. Normally, some kind of an employer's letter is needed in advance of the work permit being granted.

MONEY MATTERS

Finland's unit of currency is the Finnmark (FIM) always referred to as a mark. There are 100 pennies in the mark. At less than a mark are the 50, 20, 10, and 5 penny coins. The one penny coin, and almost all the 20 and 50 penny coins, have gone out of circulation, but there are still prices of between 0 and 5 pennies, which has led to a rounding off system; if the cash register rings up 50 marks 72 pennies, you pay 50 marks 70 pennies. If it rings up 50 marks 73 pennies, you pay 50 marks 75 pennies. The largest coin is five marks, then come banknotes of 10, 50, 100, 500, and 1,000 marks. There is no limit to how much foreign currency you bring in to Finland, but foreigners carrying more than 10,000 FIM must make a currency declaration.

You cannot take out more than 10,000 FIM without proof of having brought that amount in on arrival.

Credit cards are very widely accepted in Finland; MasterCard/Access, Visa, and Diner's Club and American Express are accepted in all but the most humble establishments.

Traveller's cheques can be exchanged easily in banks (opening hours: 9.15am–4.15pm Monday–Friday) and so can most major currencies. In addition, boats and many harbour points and airports have exchange bureaus open well outside banking hours.

At time of writing, exchange rates were one pound sterling = 7 FIM and one US dollar = 4.2 FIM.

CUSTOMS

Cigarettes/tobacco: Non-Europeans over 16 years of age may bring in 400 cigarettes or 500 gm (1 lb) of tobacco products duty free. Europeans aged 16 or over can bring in 200 cigarettes or 250 gm (½ lb) manufactured tobacco products.

Alcohol: Any visitor aged 20 or over can bring in 2 litres of beer, 1 litre of other mild alcohol (drinks containing not more than 22 percent by volume of ethyl alcohol) and 1 litre of strong alcohol (spirits). For visitors 18 or 19 years of age, the quantity limit is the same, but must not include strong alcohol.

In addition, visitors can bring in up to 1,500 marks worth of gift items or items intended for one's own use. And in case you are tempted, don't think of bringing in more than 2.5 kg (around 5 lbs) of butter because that is the limit. Also, limit your food weight on entering to 15 kg (33 lbs); no more than one third this amount may be edible fats.

Pets vaccinated against rabies are in most cases allowed into Finland (pets must have been vaccinated at least 30 days and less than 12 months before entry). Be sure to double check these requirements and your vaccination certificates if bringing your pet is crucial because Finland is sometimes rabies-free and sometimes not, and these rules cjange from year to year.

HEALTH

You'll have little to worry about healthwise in Finland. However, you may have an uncomfortable time if you coincide with the mosquito season, which descends on the northern and central parts of the country in July and into August. Enquire in Finland about the most effective mosquito repellants from chemists, who know their own brand of insect.

If you need medical treatment in Finland, it is generally free or dispensed at a nominal charge (60 marks general charge at most outpatient clinics, 80 marks per day for a stay in a hospital ward). Almost any Terveysasema (health clinic) or Sairaala (hospital) will treat you for less and more serious problems; you can also schedule regular appointments at a Terveysasema (listed as such in phone books). The Emergency section is generally called *Ensiapu*. Visitors needing hospital care are recommended to contact (for surgery and medicine) Meilahti Hospital in Helsinki, Haartmaninkatu 4, tel: (9)0-4711 or Helsinki University Hospitals' Töölö Hospital, Topeliuskatu 5, tel: (9)0-40 261 (orthopaedics specialisation). In other cities, consult hotels for hospital emergency numbers.

A pharmacy is called Apteekki, and charges for prescriptions, but not outrageously. There is usually at least one pharmacy open in larger towns on a late night basis. In Helsinki, Yliopiston Apteekki is open daily 7am–midnight, tel: (9)0-179 092, at Mannerheimintie 5; tel: (9)0-415 778 for the around-the-clock on-call pharmacy number.

The best advice on packing for Finland is to bring layers of clothes, no matter what the season. While it is famous for frigid winters – when gloves, long underwear, hats, woollen tights and socks, and several layers of cotton topped by wool and something waterproof are recommended – Finland is less known for its very temperate summers.

In winter, bring heavy-duty footgear not only to keep out damp but to avoid the heartbreak of good shoes ruined by salt and gravel put down to melt the ice on the pavements. Spring and autumn are rainy, and summers are usually pleasantly dry and sunny, but occasionally wet.

GETTING ACQUAINTED

GOVERNMENT & ECONOMY

Finland is a parliamentary democracy, with a president and a prime minister. The president is elected directly while the prime minister is chosen by a conference of parties participating in the current government.

Coalition governments led by Social Democrats dominated Finland's short history as an independent republic until the current government. Assembled after parliamentary elections in early 1991, this government is exceptional in that it is led by the once agrarian Centre Party. Also in the government are the Conservatives, the Swedish People's Party, and the Christian League. The Social Democrats, now the third most popular party, are in opposition.

The Swedish-speaking Åland Islands, off the west coast, have an MP in the national Parliament or Eduskunta in Helsinki. However the Ålands are semi-autonomous, following a post-World War I ruling by the League of Nations, and so have their own Parliament or Landsting, which administers regional matters and budgets. There are 461 Finnish municipalities. The municipalities look after social services and welfare, as well as education.

Finland is a country that had very little but modest agricultural and textile trades before the end of World War II. A few older companies founded in the 19th century, like the family-owned Ahlstrom Oy, which began as metalworks and has now diversified into the paper and boiler industries, have survived into the 20th century.

Finland's obligation to pay war damages to the Soviet Union after World War II gave it the impetus to develop its modern industry because it was able to pay off much of its debt in manufactured goods. Pulp and paper products and machinery, the forestry industry, and a few electronics and engineering giants, like Nokia (mobile telephones) and Neste (oil refining), are the lords of Finnish industry.

The rest of the economy is made up of service industries and agriculture. Although Finnish farmers are the most protected in the world when it comes to government subsidies and overproduction payments, farming is rapidly losing its appeal to the younger generations and, as a result, less than one third of the population is now involved in the farming industry.

GEOGRAPHY & POPULATION

Finland is set on the Baltic Sea between Sweden to the west and Russia to the east. A tiny arm of Norway is flung over the top of Finland to join with Russia. About one-third of Finland's land mass is above the Arctic Circle, which defines the area known as Lapland or Lappi.

Shaped like a drumstick heavy-end down, Finland is 338,000 sq. km, the sixth biggest land area in Europe. The population is sparse, however, with only 15 inhabitants per sq. km; in total there are five million inhabitants, about 40 percent of whom live in rural areas. Approximately 500,000 Finns live in greater Helsinki. The other cities – Espoo, Tampere, Turku, Vantaa, Oulu, and Lahti – have populations of under 200,000.

Finland is 65 percent covered by forest, 10 percent by lakes, and 8 percent by cultivated land (17 percent conurbations, industrial use, etc.). The last Ice Age left a lot of flat land but, towards the north, glaciers pushed ridged mountains into the landscape, creating the famous rolling hills or *tunturi* of Lapland. The highest is Haltiatunturi, at just over 4,000 ft (1,400 metres) above sea level. The lakes are concentrated in south central Finland.

The languages of Finland are Finnish (a non-Scandinavian language), spoken by 93.6 percent of Finns; Swedish, spoken by 6.1 percent, and Sami, spoken by the less than 2,000 Finnish Sami or Lapps. There are approximately 25,000 foreign residents of Finland. The two "official" religions are Lutheran and Greek Orthodox.

TIME ZONES

Finland is two hours ahead of Greenwich Mean Time, one hour ahead of Central European Time, and seven hours ahead of North America's Eastern Standard Time. Clocks are set ahead one hour on the last Saturday/Sunday in March, and set back again on the last Saturday/Sunday in September.

swatch+
automatic

swatch+
SCUBA 200

POP
swatch

swatch+
C·H·R·O·N·O

swatch+

PART OF
THE ART

SWISS
made

THE WORLD IS FLAT

MCI
123 456 7890 1111
A.R. SMITH

Its configuration may not be to Columbus' liking but to every other traveller the MCI Card is an easier, more convenient, more cost-efficient route to circle the globe.

The MCI Card offers two international services—MCI World Reach and MCI CALL USA—which let you call from country-to-country as well as back to the States, all via an English-speaking operator.

There are no delays. No hassles with foreign languages and foreign currencies. No foreign exchange rates to figure out. And no outrageous hotel surcharges.

If you don't possess the MCI Card, please call the access number of the country you're in and ask for customer service.

The MCI Card. It makes a world of difference. **MCI**

CLIMATE

No one knows what is going on with the greenhouse effect, but in recent years in Finland the winters have been slightly milder than the old average (which was about minus 4° C (20° F) in February in Helsinki, and average minus 9° C (15° F) at Ivalo in north Lapland). Finland is not as cold in winter as North American places on the same latitude, and the cold is usually a dry one.

Spring comes so late that it almost bumps into summer, and autumn can be gone in a gasp, too. Spring and autumn are generally rainy. Summer, though it comes late, finds daytime highs averaging in the mid-20s Celsius (70s Fahrenheit) in Helsinki and around 20° C (67° F) in Lapland.

CUSTOMS & CULTURE

In general Finns are courteous, particularly to foreign guests. However, they do not squeak "Sorry!" any time they brush past you on the street, not even if they tread on your toes. This is because the Finns have failed to come up with a normal word for "Sorry" or "Excuse Me". For graver offences or extreme politesse, there is the word *Anteeksi*. But for minor offences, a simple "Oops" – in recognition at least that you have jostled someone – is usually enough.

If you are going to a Finn's house for dinner, a plant or flowers for the host or hostess is the norm. Also, if you go to someone's home and expect to drink a lot, a bottle of wine is an appreciated gift. However, if you bring spirits to a casual gathering, it is *not* considered rude to bring an already opened bottle. This is in homage to the very high cost of booze.

Tipping: Situations where one must tip are few. Hotels and restaurants include a service charge, so employees are not disgruntled if they don't get a tip. If you want to tip anyway, 5–10 percent is a good guideline. The same goes for taxi drivers (although if the driver helps with heavy baggage, a small tip is appreciated). One does not normally tip hairdressers but it is essential for cloakroom attendants where there is no cloakroom fee; 4 or 5 marks is a suitable tip.

ELECTRICITY

Voltage is 220 AC in Finland, as in the other Nordic countries. Plugs have two small pins, similar to Continental (German) plugs; UK appliances will need plug adaptors and North American appliances will need plug and currency adaptors.

BUSINESS HOURS

In larger cities, stores are generally open from 9am–5pm Monday–Friday, with Thursday a traditional late shopping night in Helsinki when many stores are open until 8pm. Saturday hours are 9am–1pm or 9am–2pm. Larger foodstores will usually be open 9am–8pm weekdays and 9am–4pm Saturdays. The only really late-opening places are in the tunnel under the Helsinki railway station, open weekdays 10am–10pm and weekends noon–10pm. For basic needs outside shop hours, there are kiosks dotted across urban and rural areas which stay open until about 11pm to sell basics like milk and juice, cigarettes, toilet paper, newspapers, and so on.

Larger shopping outlets, like Stockmann's department store and the shops in the Forum shopping mall diagonally across from it on Mannerheimintie, Helsinki, are open weekdays 9am–8pm, Saturdays 9am–5pm.

Banking hours are 9.15am–4.15pm, Monday–Friday. Some exchange bureaux open later, particularly at travel points such as the airport and major harbours, as well as on international ferries.

HOLIDAYS

Public holidays in Finland begin with New Year's Day, followed by Epiphany on 6 January. Good Friday and Easter are the next holidays, then there is the secular May Day Eve and May Day, which fall on 30 April and 1 May. This is the traditional labourers' and students' holiday; April 30th is usually a half-working day. Ascension Day in May and Whitsun in late May or early June are next, and then comes the consummate holiday of the warm season, Midsummer, or Juhannus, in late June. This includes lighting of bonfires, odysseys to the countryside, and a fair amount of drinking as everyone watches over the lightest night of the year. The holiday officially takes up two days, but you'll find things shutting up early the afternoon before Midsummer's Eve.

No more holidays then until All Saints', at the end of October. Finnish Independence Day is celebrated on 6 December (independence dates from 1917), then come Christmas Eve and Christmas (24 and 25 December) and Boxing Day (26 December).

RELIGIOUS SERVICES

The Lutheran Church is the state church of Finland, with over 90 percent of Finns counted as Lutherans. There is a small Greek Orthodox population, and there are two Catholic churches in Finland. In Helsinki, services in English are held at the Temppeliaukio church, the church in the rock on Lutherinkatu; there are both Lutheran and ecumenical services here. There is one synagogue and one mosque in Helsinki.

COMMUNICATIONS

MEDIA

No one has yet been able to come up with a good explanation as to why papers published on the Continent cannot arrive in Finland on their day of publication. But, with the exception of the *International Herald Tribune*, which arrives on the afternoon of its publication date, you'll have to wait a day and a half for British newspapers to get to Helsinki. The papers are sold at the railway station, at least two bookstores (Suomalainen Kirjakauppa at Aleksanterinaktu 23, and Akateeminen Kirjakauppa at Pohjoisesplanadi 39) and at the larger hotels in cities, as well as at the main airport.

For news in English, you can tune in once a day to 103.7 FM in Helsinki. Transmission time changes with the season; ask the Tourist Board for an updated schedule or dial Radio Finland, tel: (9)0-1480-4321 for up-to-date information. You can also get information on broadcasts in other parts of Finland.

You can also get *News in English* by dialling 040 in Helsinki. Some hotels subscribe to British or American cable news networks. For books in English, try the two bookstores mentioned above.

POSTAL SERVICES

Post offices Monday–Friday are open daily 9am–5pm. Services include stamp sales, registered mail, insured mail, and *poste restante*. The address of the Poste Restante is Mannerheimintie 11, 00100 Helsinki. It's on the railway square side of the post office, and is open Monday–Saturday 8am–10pm, Sunday 11am–10pm. At time of writing, stamps cost 2.10 marks for domestic and Nordic country post, 2.90 marks for Europe, and 3.40 marks for North America.

When post offices are closed, there are stamp machines outside and in the railway station. Insert a five-mark coin and you get the equivalent in stamps. The machines are orange and mounted on the walls, as are the post boxes.

TELEPHONE SERVICES

The best way to call overseas cheaply is at the post and telegraph office in a main city. Look for the "Lennätin" section, which is for telecommunica-

tions. Finland's main post office is at Mannerheimintie 11B, Helsinki, and its Lennätin section is open weekdays 8am–8pm, weekends 9am–9pm. They will also send telegrams, faxes, and telexes.

Calls to Europe are 3.50 marks/minute during weekdays from 8am to 10pm; to North America and Australia, 5.40 marks/minute, New Zealand, 9.10 marks/min. If you want to reach an operator in your own country to make a billed or collect call, ask for the Finland Direct pamphlet, which lists the numbers. For the UK operator, dial (9)800 1 0440, US (9)800 1 0010/ATT or (9)800 1 0280/MCI, Canada (9)800 1 0011.

To make a regular direct call at Lennätin, use any booth with a green light and pay the cashier after your call. You must dial 990 to get out of Finland, then country code and number (e.g. 990 44 precedes UK numbers and 990 1 precedes North American numbers). Dial 92020 for overseas call assistance from a Finnish (English-speaking) operator. As well, the front of the white pages home numbers phone book has calling directions for foreigners; see the index (pages usually marked by purple tabs).

Don't forget that hotels usually add surcharges for calls made from your room.

EMERGENCIES

SECURITY & CRIME

Vandalism is the only noticeable sign of crime in this generally safe country, but that doesn't mean that more serious crime does not exist. Occasional pickpocketing is known in the Helsinki metro and main railway stations; it appears that alcoholics, on the hunt for money to pay for their next drinking bout, are often the perpetrators. Be on your guard in these places.

The main **national emergency number** in Finland is 000; no coins are needed to make this call. In Helsinki, you can also dial 002 to contact the **police**.

GETTING AROUND

FROM THE AIRPORT

Finland's main international airport, Helsinki-Vantaa, is connected by Finnair bus and local bus to Helsinki. Bus fare is 18 marks on the Finnair bus, 13.50 on the local bus. There is also a taxi stand at the airport; fare is usually 100 to 160 marks to get to the centre of the city, depending on time of day and traffic (usually not a serious problem).

DOMESTIC TRAVEL

BY AIR

Finnair operates most domestic flight services. Fares are relatively inexpensive; in July, fares are supercheap. It is a good idea to fly if, for example, you want to get to Lapland from the south without spending days on the road (distance from Helsinki to Ivalo, 1,125 km). Supersaver return fare about 575 marks. The Finnair Holiday Pass costs US$300 and is good for 15 days on an unlimited number of flights; not valid on "Blue Flights", usually the most popular business travel times. The pass is available to anyone who flies to Finland, and can be obtained from Finnair and some travel agents in Britain and North America; check with the Finnish Tourist Board nearest you. Finnair Holiday Youth Passes, to which roughly the same conditions apply, cost around US$250.

BY RAIL

The Finnish rail network is limited, but service is adequate in most cases, very good between major points like Turku and Helsinki. Finnrail passes are available for 8-day, 15-day, and 22-day periods, and cost 470, 730, and 920 marks respectively; first-class passes also available. Rail information from Finnish State Railways, Vilhonkatu 13, PB 488, 00101 Helsinki, tel: (9)0-7071, telex: 1230 1151 VR SF.

WATER TRANSPORT

Ferries and passenger boats in Finland play a strong role where international destinations are concerned (*see Getting There*) but there are some lakeland ferry routes worth pursuing. There are the Silverline and Poet's Way, which begin in Tampere tel: (9)31-124 803, and cover much of the western lakelands. There are also tours in the Päijänne region (central lakelands; contact Lake Päijänne Cruises, tel: (9)41-618 885, Haapaniemi, and over Finland's largest lake, Saimaa, in eastern Finland (contact Roll Ships Ltd, tel: [9]71-126 744). Many other operators run trips on the lakes; for more information, contact the central or regional tourist boards.

Coastal passenger traffic is organised by the Finnish Association of Coastal Passenger Shipping/Suomen Rannikon Matkustajalaiayhdistys, telefax: (9)0-879 5217 (no phone), who deal with boat traffic between major coastal points like Kotka, Porvoo, Helsinki, Turku, Naantali, Rauma, Pori, Vaasa, Pietarsaari, on up to Kalajoki.

Helsinki's only real commuter island is Suomenlinna, with ferries travelling back and forth roughly every hour (schedule depends on season). Most of these ferries are part of the public transport network of Helsinki. Other Helsinki islands closer to the coast are connected by road.

PUBLIC TRANSPORT

Finland is greatly dependent on buses for transporting the bulk of its passenger traffic. There are coach services on 90 percent of Finland's public roads (40,000 long-distance departures a day) which also cover the areas that trains don't, particularly in the north and in smaller places throughout the country. The head office for long-distance bus traffic is Matkahuolto, Lauttasaarentie 8, 00200 Helsinki, tel: (9)0-692 2088.

There is no penalty for buying a ticket on the coach but you cannot get group discounts (for 3 adults or more on trips over 75 km/47 miles) from the coach ticketseller. Over 65s and full-time students (university and lower) are also eligible for discounts. Both over 65s and university students must purchase, for 30 marks, a coach card entitling them to a discount, which is at least 30 percent on journeys of over 75 km; bring photo and ID. Children 4–11 years old travel at 50 percent of full fare (ticket available on coach) and accompanied children under 4 travel free.

One can reserve long distance coach places (fee 10 marks) by calling Matkahuolto or stopping in at the main bus station, situated at the corner of Mannerheimintie and Simonkatu, Helsinki.

UNDERGROUND, BUS, TRAM

Helsinki has a single metro line that runs east-west. It is fast and clean, but unfortunately it shuts down at 11.20pm, so is no good for late night travel. Services resume at around 6am. Tickets, which are good for one hour including transfers to bus and tram, should be cancelled at the special machines at stations before the journey begins. Trains run at either 5- or 10-minute intervals.

Local buses dominate the public transport network and will probably get you closest to your destination, although they are subject to more traffic conditions than trams and metros. The 3T tram doubles as a sightseeing route; it describes a figure 8 around most of Helsinki and there is a short recorded commentary in English. Catch it in front of the railway station, for example, between 6am and 1.15am. For buses and trams cancel your ticket the same way. Machines are on vehicles.

Bus and tram routes are usually not shown at the stops, only end destinations, so try to get journey advice before you go. Most run from 6am until near midnight, but ask the Tourist Board about night bus routes in Helsinki and to Espoo and Vantaa.

PRIVATE TRANSPORT

Finland's roads are not too plagued by traffic although they do get very busy between the capital and the countryside on Fridays and Sundays during the summer. There are very few multi-lane motorways. Most are just two-lane.

Driving is on the right, overtaking on the left. All cars must use their lights when driving outside built-up areas (indicated by a picture symbol depicting a town). Elsewhere, lights must be used at dusk or at night or in bad weather (UK cars must sweep their lights right).

For winter driving, studded tyres may be used from November to March, and winter tyres are strongly recommended for December–January. Use of safety belts is compulsory.

Don't risk driving while drunk in Finland. The limit is low (0.5 percent blood alcohol) and the fines very steep; imprisonment is also possible in some cases. Taxis are available throughout the country, even in the backwaters; do as the Finns do and use them if you've been drinking.

Other rules of the road: Traffic coming from the right has right of way. Exceptions are on roads marked by a triangle sign; if this is facing you, you must give right of way; similarly if you are on a very major thoroughfare it is likely that the feed-in streets will have triangles, giving you the right of way. Another exception is the roundabout (rotary); traffic already on the roundabout has right of way. Speed limits are posted, and range from 30 kph in school zones on up to 100 kph on motorways.

The number to call for foreign cars involved in accidents is (9)0-19 251 (Finnish Motor Insurers' Bureau). Foreign cars entering Finland should have a nationality sticker. In most cases, your own insurance with a green card will suffice in Finland, but check ahead to be sure.

CAR HIRE

The airport has rows of car hire desks, including most major European and North American outfits. Central Helsinki hire offices follow:
Ansa (Lacara International), Hämeentie 12, tel: (9)0-719 062.

Avis, Fredrikinkatu 67, tel: (9)0-441 155.
Budget, at airport, tel: (9)0-870 1606, in Vantaa (municipality that includes airport) at Äyrikuja 3, tel: (9)0-508 0805.
Hertz, Hernesaarenranta 11, tel: (9)0-622 1100; central reservation number (Helsinki), tel: (9)0-9800 2012.
Interrent/Europcar, Hitsaajankatu 7C, tel: (9)0-755 6133.

Most of the above have agents in other major Finnish cities and airports.

TAXIS

Finnish taxis run throughout the country, with fares starting at around 12 marks. Helsinki and other large cities as well as most major airports, bus, and railway stations have taxi stands. Otherwise local phone books list the number of the nearest dispatcher (under Taksi in white pages), and finding the closest one is worthwhile as the taxis charge from embarkation point (plus an order fee). One can hail a cab, but this is a rarer way of getting a taxi ride in Finland than those above.

BICYCLES

Finland is a good cycling country with its well-engineered cycle paths and gently rolling landscape. The number of outfits renting bikes has grown. Two major hire points are the youth hostel at Helsinki's Olympic Stadium and Ro-No rentals on both harbours of Mariehamn in the Åland islands (a popular summer cycling destination). The Finnish Youth Hostel Association also offers planned route tours at decent prices (can include accommodation); contact them at Yrjönkatu 38B, 00100 Helsinki, tel: (9)0-694 0377. Ask the Finnish Tourist Board about other firms that run planned cycling tours.

ON FOOT

Helsinki, the largest of Finnish cities, is an extremely pleasant walking city. It's fairly compact, and there is an increasing number of pedestrian-only streets. The same goes for the old "capital" of Turku and many other smaller cities and towns. Some offer guided tours on foot.

There are limitless possibilities for walks in the countryside, both of short and long duration. Even inside Helsinki proper, there are beautifully-tended forest paths, as in Keskuspuisto (with occasional work-out stations alongside), and once in the countryside, one can find paths that wind on for days. Lapland is one of the more popular hiking areas, where the elevation is slightly more dramatic, and where there are fewer and smaller trees than elsewhere, allowing more sweeping views. You might be lucky and see elk, reindeer, and the more exotic breeds like the hazel grouse and snow grouse. There are lynx and bears but both are rare. Two good hiking contacts are Suomen Ladun Matkapalvelu, Fabianinkatu 7, 00130 Helsinki, tel: (9)0-170 101, or in Lapland, Tunturikeskus Kiilopää, 99800 Ivalo, tel: (9)697-87 101.

HITCH HIKING

Thumbing is still a time-honoured way to get a cheap ride in Finland, but you may have to wait a long time to get picked up.

WHERE TO STAY

You can pretty much depend on Finnish accommodation being clean and in good shape, but prices are high. There are bargains to be hunted out, however. Big discounts (up to 60 percent) are available at most hotels on weekends, and in summer when they lose their business and conference trade. Budget accommodation includes youth and family hostels, farmhouses, *gasthaus* accommodation, family villages, camping, various forms of self-catering, and so on. During the summer vacation, some student residences become Summer Hotels, open 1 June–31 August; contact Summer Hotels, Yrjönkatu 38, 00100 Helsinki, tel: (9)0-693 1347.

General information on the above is available from the Finnish Tourist Board in your home country, or from the head office in Helsinki: Finnish Tourist Board, PB249, 00131 Helsinki, tel: (9)0403-011; international tel: 358-0-403011, as well as individual addresses given below. Helsinki has its own booking centre at the Railway Station: Hotel Booking Centre, Asemaaukio 3, 00100 Helsinki, tel: (9)0-171 133.

HOTELS

Finland has many large hotel chains of its own, as well as Scandinavian and foreign chains. Among the most prominent are:
Arctia Hotel Partners, Annankatu 42D, 00100 Helsinki. Tel: (9)0-694 8022.
Best Western Finland, Annankatu 29A, 00100 Helsinki. Tel: (9)0-680 1680.
Cumulus Hotels, Kaivokatu 8, 00100 Helsinki. Tel: (9)0-73 377.
Rantasipi Hotels, Takamaantie 4, 01510 Vantaa. Tel: (9)0-87 051.
Sokos Hotels (SOK), Kluuvikatu 8, 00101 Helsinki. Tel: (9)0-738 360.

Summer Hotels, Yrjönkatu 38, 00100 Helsinki. Tel: (9)0-693 1347.

A systematic way to get discounts is to enrol in the Finncheque scheme, in which some 250 hotels participate. By spending around 165 marks (1991 price) on a Finncheque, you get a night's accommodation in these hotels. The system is a co-operation between several hotel chains; details from Vesama Tours Ltd, Fredrikinkatu 48A, 00100 Helsinki, tel: (9)0-694 8877. The Scandinavia Bonus Pass gives 15–40 percent off room prices; information from Arctia Hotel Partners, Annankatu 42D, 00100 Helsinki, tel: (9)0-694 8022.

The following is a list of hotels in different price ranges in the three main cities of Helsinki, Turku and Tampere. The Tourist Boards and booking centres will provide accurate up-to-date prices and particularly weekend and summer discounts.

HELSINKI

Academica, Hietaniemenkatu 14, 00180 Helsinki. Tel: (9)0-402 0206. This is a basic summer hotel which is a student quarter during the university term. Small modern rooms have their own kitchen. Family rooms and extra beds also available. Residential but central location. Inexpensive.
Kalastajatorppa, Kalastajantorppatie 1, 00330 Helsinki. Tel: (9)0-45 811. Set near the sea in a handsome suburban district about 4 miles west of the centre, Kalastajatorppa has the feeling of a country-side resort. Expensive.
Klaus Kurki, Bulevardi 2–4, 00120 Helsinki. Tel: (9)0-618911. Located on a handsome street just a few steps away from Esplanadi. Early-20th-century carved granite exterior, cosy, recently-redecorated rooms in Continental style. Bar, restaurant, and terrace. Expensive (group discounts).
Lord Hotel, Lönnrotinkatu 29, 00180 Helsinki. Tel: (9)0-680 1680. Splendid, castle-like exterior with art deco conference and dining rooms; most guest rooms in modern wing in quiet courtyard; one tower suite in older section. One conference room with sauna and tower meeting room-in-the-round. Centrally located. Moderate.
MetroCity (Best Western), Kaisaniemenkatu 7, 00100 Helsinki. Tel: (9)0-171 146. Convenient to station and shops, this hotel has good service, pleasant Continental style decor, and also has rooms for the allergic. Moderate.
Omapohja Teatterimajatalo, ItäTeatterikuja 3, 00100 Helsinki. Tel: (9)0-666 211. This 1906 inn, once a boarding house for actors performing at the National Theatre around the corner, oozes with character in its old, large-windowed rooms. It is superbly located, too, just a few steps from the central railway station and botanical gardens. Inexpensive.
Royal SAS, Runeberginkatu 2, 00100 Helsinki. Tel: (9)0-69 580. A brand new (1991) addition to this

famed Scandinavian chain, the Helsinki SAS has sunny, open dining and bar areas and the usual good service. About a 10-minute walk from the centre, with a metro stop immediately in front. Moderate–Expensive.

Seurahuone, Kaivokatu 12, 00100 Helsinki. Tel: (9)0-170 441. Some of the rooms have Victorian antiques, others are Scandinavian modern. The Socis bar downstairs is a popular Helsinki meeting place, and the conditori-café is open until late. Located right on the railway square. Expensive (group rates available).

Strand Intercontinental, John Stenberginranta 4, 00530 Helsinki. Tel: (9)0-39 351. Located on the south shore of the lively Hakaniemi market area less than a mile north of the Esplanade, this branch of the internationally known hotel chain opened in 1990 with elegant public spaces, and views toward Kruunuhaka, the university district. Expensive.

Torni, Yrjönkatu 26, 00100 Helsinki. Tel: (9)0-131 131. Known as the tallest building in town at 13 storeys, Torni is a gracious hotel with an older and newer section. The older section is in art deco style, and the rooms have original features. Try for rooms overlooking the courtyard. The "newer" section, with bar-lookout tower, has a Finnish functional decor outside; its interior was renovated to a high standard of comfort in 1991. Moderate–Expensive.

Youth Hostel, Olympic Stadium, Pohjoinen Stadiontie 3B. Tel: (9)0-96 071. There are several other summer hostels, but this one is open all year. About 2 miles north of centre, with easy access by bus and tram. (35 marks for members, 50 marks for non-member, sheet rental 20 marks.) Accommodation in smaller rooms (2-, 3-, or 4-bed) 15 marks more. Inexpensive.

TURKU

Cumulus, Eerikinkatu 28, 20100 Turku. Tel: (9)21-638 211. A handsome contemporary hotel, geared toward business travellers and well-heeled tourists, Cumulus also has its own lively night spot, the Casablanca. Single rooms on inner courtyard. Moderate.

Domus Aboenisis, 10 Piispankatu, Turku. Tel: (9)21-320 421. This student-owned summer hotel has spacious, cheerfully modern bedrooms; each room has private bath or shower and WC. Its restaurant is open for all meals. Inexpensive.

Hamburger Bors, Kauppiaskatu 6, 20100 Turku. Tel: (9)21-637 381. Atmospheric old hotel, right on Market Place; excellent restaurants including rustic-French Fransmanni and German-style Hamburger Hof. Moderate–Expensive.

City Bors, Eerikinkatu 11 (across the market square). Tel: (9)21-637 381. Makes a slightly cheaper but excellent alternative.

Scandic Hotel Turku, Matkustajasatama, 20100 Turku. Tel: (9)21-302 600. One of the more imaginatively restored hotels in Finland, once a 19th-century warehouse. Its red-brick facade is rendered in original neo-Gothic style with beautiful wooden beams inside. Views of harbour or castle. Modern bathrooms. Inexpensive

TAMPERE

Cumulus Koskikatu, Koskikatu 5, 33100 Tampere. Tel: (9)31-242 4111. Built in 1979, the hotel's style is vibrantly modern throughout, and the bar and dining facilities are excellent. Moderate.

Grand Hotel Tammer, Satakunnankatu 13, 33100 Tampere. Tel: (9)31-228 111. The dramatically high entranceway leads into a later (1929) tribute to Finnish art deco. Set in a green, hilly district of the city. Moderate.

Ilves, Hatranpään Valtalie 1, 33100 Tampere. Tel: (9)31-121 212. An 18-storey high building with fine views over the harbour and Tammarkoski Rapids. Well furnished and stylish, swimming pool, saunas etc. Moderate–Expensive.

Victoria, Itsenäisyydenkatu 1, 33100 Tampere. Tel: (9)31-242 5111. This simple, hostel-style hotel has clean, woody, modern rooms and a lively bar and restaurant in the basement, the Tunneli. Inexpensive (group discounts).

YOUTH & FAMILY HOSTELS

Finland has a widespread network of some 160 youth and family hostels, which vary from small farmhouses, to manors, camping, and special centres. They usually have family rooms (2 to 4 visitors) or dormitories (5 to 10). Some 60 are open year-round, the remainder summer only. Details of hostels and the Finnish Youth Hostel Cheque system from: Finnish Youth Hostel Association, Yrjönkatu 38B, 00100 Helsinki, tel: (9)0-694 0377.

BUDGET ACCOMMODATION

Farmhouse, Bed and Breakfast, Family Villages, Student Rooms – Finland has all these categories of accommodation. In the farmhouse, the guest is treated as a member of the family though some farms have individual self-catering cottages; around 100 hosts offer bed and breakfast accommodation, and the holiday villages (mostly in the Great Lakes area, some along the west coast also) provide self-catering cottages, usually each with its own boat, and are often linked with camping sites. Many arrange holiday programmes such as fishing, canoeing and other sports, and evening barbecues. Details from: Lomarengas r.y., Malminkaari 23, 00700 Helsinki, tel: (9)0-3516 1321 or for farmhouses: Suomen 4H Liitto, Uudermaankatu 24, 00120 Helsinki, tel: (9)0-642 233.

CAMPING

There are numerous camping grounds across Finland, rated in a guide distributed by the Finnish

BERLIN MASTERPIECES

ROCAILLE,
Breslauer Stadtschloß
The unusual reliefs and
opulent embellishments
of this rococo design
places extremely high
demands on the artistic
abilities of the craftsmen.

SCHINKEL Basket
Design: app. 1820
by Karl Friedrich Schinkel.

KURLAND, *pattern 73*
The first classicistic service
made by KPM was created
around 1790 by order of
the Duke of Kurland.

KPM BERLIN · Wegelystraße 1 · Kurfürstendamm 26a · Postal address: Postfach 12 21 07, D-10591 Berlin · Phone
(030) 390 09 - 226 · Fax (030) 390 09 - 279 · U. K. AGENCY · Exclusif Presentations, Ltd. · 20 Vancouver Road
Edgware, Middx. HA8 5DA · Phone (081) 952 46 79 · Fax (081) 951 09 39 · JAPAN AGENCY · Hayashitok Co., Ltd.
Nakano-Cho. Ogawa. Marutamachi · Nakagyo-Ku. Kyoto 604 · Phone (075) 222 02 31 / 231 22 22 · Fax (075) 256 45 54

Our history could fill this book, but we prefer to fill glasses.

When you make a great beer, you don't have to make a great fuss.

Travel Association, Camping Department, Mikonkatu 25, PB 776, 00101 Helsinki, tel: (9)0-170 868. You can also buy the guide at R-kiosks throughout the country. Finncamping cheques (fixed, reduced price) are also available valid from 15 May–15 September.

FOOD DIGEST

WHAT TO EAT

It used to be said in Finland that the Finnish salad was a sausage. Pork and potatoes were once the mainstay of the inlanders' diet, with slightly more variety in coastal areas where fish was readily available.

Slowly, slowly, Finnish cuisine has broadened and improved as more foods are imported and farming and greenhouse methods are refined so that those items once unheard of above 60 degrees north latitude can now be seen in the markets, (e.g. Finnish-grown cucumbers, red tomatoes). You'll find that there are some excellent Finnish cooks who, given the right mix of fresh produce and good meats and fish can produce a superb meal. The wild game dishes are really a treat, and are usually served with exquisite mushroom and berry sauces. If you eat only in cafeteria-style restaurants, you'll go mad with the monotony of the offerings.

A lot of Finns eat a large hot lunch and then a smaller cold meal at dinner, although this is not to say that you can't have wonderful, fully-fledged evening meals in Helsinki and other cities. As well, international cuisines have crept in slowly over the years, and you'll now find Chinese, Italian, and French-style restaurants in almost all major towns.

In summer, you are strongly recommended to try Finnish crayfish, or *raput*. See the "Food and Drink" section (*pages 104–107*) for more details on Finnish gastronomy.

WHERE TO EAT

It is difficult to find a really cheap meal in Finland, but you can find places where you will definitely get value for money – in other words, where portions are generous and quality is high. Fixed-price lunches are often very good deals, and are usually advertised on signboards outside restaurants. Many restaurants have English translations on their menus.

For on-the-run, really cheap eats, go to a *nakki* (sausage) kiosk. Hot dogs and sausages are the main fare, and you can usually get French fries and drinks as well. Other slightly more expensive quick meals can be had at any one of the ubiquitous hamburger chains like McDonalds, Clock, or Carrolls. Pizza is also extremely popular in Finland.

Many of the hotels in the three main cities of Helsinki, Turku and Tampere, and elsewhere, have good restaurants, ranging from gourmet to wine bars and cafés, including restaurants that specialise in particular cuisines – Italian, French, etc. The Finnish Tourist Board divides categories into E for elite and G for general and added here, for ease, is INSIGHT's own category of I for inexpensive, signifying restaurants which serve an evening meal for below 75 marks, excluding wine.

Alexander Nevski, Pohjoisesplanadi 17. Tel: (9)0-639 610. Russian classics and delicacies served in elegant, Imperial-style dining room overlooking Market Square. E

Capitol and Cantina West, Kasarmikatu 23. Tel: (9)0-622 1500. The Capitol is one of Helsinki's best, with a cuisine based on good fresh fish and meat, vegetables and mushrooms and other produce from the forests. It is not cheap but in the same courtyard Cantina West is decorated with Americana and you can enjoy a Mexican buffet for a reasonable price. G

El Greco, Eteläesplanadi 22. Tel: (9)0-607 565. The lower section is a sleek, bustling café overlooking the park while upstairs is a Greek-style dining room with a varied menu of Hellenic-inspired dishes. G

Fatima, Eteläesplanadi 22. Tel: (9)0-611 001. The owner of this handsome Egyptian restaurant hails from Cairo, and the offerings include the Cairo Table set meal, featuring *falafel*, beef, *tahini*, and marinated vegetables. G

Hyvä Ystävä, Kaivokatu 8. Tel: (9)0-663 917. This centrally located branch of the very popular chain of tavern-style restaurants offers great value for money, especially on their steak dishes. Some locations have Karaoke nights – beware! I

Kaksi Kanaa, Kanavakatu 3. Tel: (9)0-669 260. This brasserie-style restaurant, with chicken dishes a specialty, also has cabaret-theatre and sometimes jazz. Performances usually Thursday–Saturday. Phone for events, or check local listings. G

Kynsilaukka Garlic Restaurant, Fredrikinkatu 22. Tel: (9)0-651 939. The three young chefs bring fresh market produce and high imagination to the garlic-centred dishes served here. Comfortable and friendly, with excellent food. Small and large portions. G

Lord Hotel, Lönnrotinkatu 29. Tel: (9)0-680 1680. The upstairs restaurant of this beautiful, quiet art deco period hotel serves extremely good fresh fish dishes with wonderful sauces. E but with a moderate fixed price menu at lunchtime.

Torni Salle de Chevalier, Hotel Torni's gourmet restaurant in this traditional hotel features the Knight's table buffet. E – but also try the Ateljee Bar on the 13th floor for light meals and drinks (outdoor seating in summer) and the best view in Helsinki. I

Walhalla, Suomenlinna. Tel: (9)0-668 552. Open to the public in summer and the rest of the year by arrangement, the restaurant is set in the archways of the old fortress on historic Suomenlinna island. It offers some of the finest Finnish cuisine to be found. Try the snow grouse or reindeer specialities. E

TURKU

Le Pirate Chez Claude, Borenpuisto. Tel: (9)021-511 443. Fresh seafood in an original boat restaurant. G

Pinella, Porthaninpuisto. Tel: (9)021-517 557. An archway-flanked building with a Victorian veranda greets you at this famous Turku restaurant that dates to 1848, when it was founded by a transplanted Italian. Two dining areas, one featuring seafood and meat, the other Italian fare. G

Samppalinna, It, Rantakatu, Sampalinnanpuisto. Tel: (9)21-311 165. Continental cuisine with roast mutton, and a host of Nordic specialities such as salmon soup, all served in a splendid Victorian building. G

Seaport, Matkustajasatama. Tel: (9)21-303 990 or 535 013. This spacious converted warehouse serves fine game dishes such as reindeer cutlets, and many fresh fish-based preparations. Dance floor. G

Trattoria Casa Felice, Linnankatu 3. Tel: (9)21-322 265. A handsome, Italian restaurant in a former Jugend villa. I

Villa Roma, Ruissalo 63. Tel: (9)21-589 025. This excellent period cafeteria is part of the Villa Roma Atelier (changing exhibitions and toy and home museums), on Turku's summer island, Ruissalo (reached by road). It is carefully presided over by the owner, Marjo Brunow-Ruola, (closes 6pm). I

TAMPERE

Bunkkeri, Kehräsaari, Laukontori 1. Tel: (9)31-142 696. A World War II look, decorated with pistols, rifles and wartime pictures. The food comes in mess tins, and drinks include "Molotov cocktails". Popular with young people. G

Fuuga, Yliopistonkatu 55. Tel: (9)31-2434 450. Restaurant in Tampere's magnificent concert hall. Ideal for combining a meal with a concert. G. Also **Café Soolo** with a conservatory atmosphere in the same building for lighter refreshment. I

Katupoika, Aleksanterinkatu 20. Tel: (9)31-122 204. Specialising in Cajun, Italian and Mexican food. I

Mona Lisa Wine Bar, Koskikatu 5. Tel: (9)31-242 4111. Conveniently set in Hotel Cumulus, this wine bar serves diverse, affordable dishes of international origins, from Indonesian to Mexican, to French, to local trout. Background rock music. I

Merirosvo, Näsinneula, Särkänniemi. Tel: (9)31-124 697. Handy for visits to Observation Tower and Funfair. Famed for its Baltic herring dishes. G

Alcohol is incredibly expensive in Finland due to high taxes, and beer and wine are no exceptions. The Finnish *tuoppi* is about 30 percent larger than the British pint and costs 20–26 marks. *Pieni tuoppi*, or about two-thirds that quantity, costs 16–19 marks. If you don't specify, you will be served a large, strong (number 4 = 4½ percent alcohol) beer. You must say if you want the 3½ percent beer, known as *keski-olut*, or medium beer. Number 1 beer is the weakest (*ykkös-olut*), at just over 1 percent alcohol.

Wines are imported, and very costly in restaurants. At least there is more choice in Alko (the state alcohol monopoly) these days, the range of prices begins with Eastern European wines at about 40 marks a bottle and goes up, precipitously.

Spirits and wine can be bought only from Alko, open Monday–Thursday 9am–5pm, Friday 9am–6pm, and Saturday 9am–2pm, but closed summer Saturdays, 1 May–30 September. (Stockmann's department store in Helsinki has a wine-only Alko unit on the ground floor.) Medium and lower alcohol beer can be bought in supermarkets. Most restaurants serve alcohol as long as they serve food. A restaurant marked *B-oikeudet* is licensed only to serve beer and wine. Most bars and taverns are open until at least midnight in Helsinki; some stay open until 3 or 4am.

THINGS TO DO

Finland is a country of smaller museums. The grandest in scale is the Ateneum national art museum in Helsinki, reopened in 1991 after 5 years of renovations, which could fit neatly into London's National Gallery at least three times. Art dominates the museum scene, with the greatest variety of venues in Helsinki. In total, there is probably more contemporary art to be seen than older art.

Admission prices are steepish, but Helsinki sells the Helsinki Card, which includes free entrance to many museums on presentation. At time of writing, a one-day Helsinki Card costs 70 marks, two days 100 marks, three days,120 marks. (Children's Card 40, 50, and 60 marks respectively.) The card is good for public transportation, for free entrance to many museums, and for discounts on hotel packages. Opening hours are almost always reduced in winter.

THE COLOUR OF LIFE.

A holiday may last just a week or so, but the memories of those happy, colourful days will last forever, because together you and Kodak Ektachrome films will capture, as large as life, the wondrous sights, the breathtaking scenery and the magical moments. For you to relive over and over again.

The Kodak Ektachrome range of slide films offers a choice of light source, speed and colour rendition and features extremely fine grain, very high sharpness and high resolving power.

Take home the real colour of life with Kodak Ektachrome films.

LIKE THIS?

OR LIKE THIS?

A KODAK FUN PANORAMIC CAMERA BROADENS YOUR VIEW

The holiday you and your camera have been looking forward to all year; and a stunning panoramic view appears. "Fabulous", you think to yourself, "must take that one".

Unfortunately, your lens is just not wide enough. And three-in-a-row is a poor substitute.

That's when you take out your pocket-size, 'single use' Kodak Fun Panoramic Camera. A film and a camera, all in one, and it works miracles. You won't need to focus, you don't need special lenses. Just aim, click

and... it's all yours. The total picture.

You take twelve panoramic pictures with one Kodak Fun Panoramic Camera. Then put the camera in for developing and printing.

Each print is 25 by 9 centimetres. Excellent depth of field. True Kodak Gold colours.

The Kodak Fun Panoramic Camera itself goes back to the factory, to be recycled. So that others too can capture one of those spectacular phooooooooooootoooooooooooooos.

HELSINKI

Nordic Arts Centre Museum, Suomenlinna. The works of living Nordic artists are featured here as part of regular exhibitions, in the handsome, rose-tinted Jetty Barracks and Galleria Augusta buildings at the Suomenlinna ferry landing. Ferries sail hourly from market square, Helsinki. Open: May–September daily 11am–7pm, October–April daily 10am–6pm. Admission: Free.

Museum of Finnish Architecture, Kasarmikatu 24. This museum has an excellent archive of architectural drawings, and changing exhibitions focusing on aspects of some of the better- and lesser-known Finnish architectural movements (including National Romantic, neoclassic, Jugend, Functionalist, and Modern). Open: Tuesday–Sunday 10am–4pm, Wednesday late closing 7pm. Archives open: Tuesday–Friday only, no late closing on Wednesday in summer. Admission: Free.

Museum of Applied Arts, Korkeavuorenkatu 23. This handsome museum houses a changing collection of renowned and lesser-known Finnish industrial and crafts design, like the Aalto furniture and Lapponia jewellery, as well as new works by international designers. Coffee room with art magazines. Open: Tuesday–Friday 11am–5pm, weekends 11am–4pm. Admission: charge.

Seurasaari Open-Air Museum, Seurasaarentie, Meilahti. Set on an island 2 miles from central Helsinki, Seurasaari is a celebration of folk-homes and traditions; most of the Karelian-style lodges and outbuildings were shipped here from eastern Finland. There is also a beautifully-preserved 17th-century gabled church. A small animal farm is open in summer, and on many evenings there are folk dance, music and drama performances. Take bus 24 from the Swedish Theatre to the final stop and cross the wooden bridge. Access at all times, but facilities (cafés) open summer daily 11am–5pm (11am–7pm Wednesday), May and September weekdays 9am–3pm, weekends 11am–5pm. Daytime admission: charge, but free most evenings. (Free during winter.)

Tamminiemi, President Urho Kekkonen Museum, Seurasaarentie 15. Facing Seurasaari, this early 20th-century Jugend style manor was home to the longest reigning postwar Finnish president, Urho Kekkonen. His splendid memorabilia include furniture and gifts from around the world; on view with guided tour only. (Tel: [9]0-480 684 to check English tour times or arrange group visits.) Open: May–early September daily 11am–4pm and 6–8pm Wednesday; mid-September–April daily 11am–3pm and 6–8pm Wednesday. Admission: charge.

Cygnaeus Gallery, Kalliolinnantie 8. This miniature gallery houses a mainly 19th-century collection of Finnish painting and sculpture in the tiny, exquisite wooden summer home of the poet Cygnaeus which overlooks Helsinki harbour. Open: Wednesday–Sunday 11am–4pm and 6–8pm Wednesday. Admission: charge

Mannerheim Museum, Kalliolinnantie 14. The medals, memorabilia, and domestic trappings of the life of the illustrious Finnish war hero and president, Carl Gustaf Mannerheim. Open: Friday and Saturday 11am–3pm, Sunday 11am–4pm. Admission: charge.

Gallen-Kallela Museum, Tarvaspää, Espoo. Studio and home of Akseli Gallen-Kallela, who painted, among other things, stunning interpretations of characters from the Finnish epic, *The Kalevala*, and dozens of art deco posters and advertisements. Tarvaspää is by the sea, in Espoo. Take tram 4 to Munkkiniemi, then walk one mile (signposted). Handsome café. Open: summer Monday–Thursday 10am–8pm, Friday–Sunday 10am–5pm; 1 September–15 May Tuesday–Saturday 10am–4pm, Sunday 10am–5pm. Admission: charge.

TURKU

Waino Aaltonen, Itäinen Rantakatu 38. Tel: (9)21-355 690. Many sculptures and paintings by Aaltonen, as well as painting, sculpture and graphic art by modern Finnish artists.

Greek Orthodox Cathedral, Kauppatori (Market Square). Tel: (9)21-311 890. Designed by C.L. Engel and dedicated to the 4th-century Roman martyr, the Empress Alexandra. A beautiful ornate cathedral.

Luostarinmäki Handicrafts Museum, Varitiovouori 4. Tel: (9)21-337150. A large collection of 19th-century artisans' buildings in a beautiful setting. Excellent café.

Maritime and Astrological Museum, on the Old Observatory Hill at Vartiovuori. Tel: (9)21-337 140. Ship models and paintings in a building designed by C.L. Engel.

Sibelius Museum, Piispankatu 17. Tel: (9)21-654 5494. Scores and other memorabilia of Finland's greatest composer and of other Finnish musical greats.

Sigyn and Suomen Joutsen (Swan of Findland) Ships, on the east bank of the River Aura. Tel: Sigyn (9)21-654 116. The barque *Sigyn* was built in Gothenburg, Sweden in 1887, and *Suomen Joutsen* in 1902 at St Nazaire in France.

Turku Castle (Turunlinna). Tel: (9)21-303 300. One of Turku's gems. Finland's history from the 13th to the 17th centuries, beautifully restored rooms with stained-glass windows. Also Turku Historical Museum, with Turku's beginnings, royal reminders, furniture, paintings, china, etc. from different eras.

Turku Cathedral, Cathedral Hill. Tel: (9)21-335 409. The most important medieval church building in Finland with interesting chapels and the Cathedral Museum showing church models and religious artefacts.

TAMPERE

Finnish Ice Hockey Museum, at the Indoor Ice Rink. The story of ice hockey in Finland. Open: during league matches and by arrangement.

Haihara Doll Museum, Haihara Manor, Kaukajärvi. Tel: (9)31-630 350. Has a huge doll collection, as well as wonderful costume and cultural history exhibitions.

Häme Museum, Näsilinna. Tel: (9)31-124 185. Ethnographic and cultural collection showing past of Tampere and old Häme province, with rooms in period styles.

Lenin Museum, Hämeenpuisto 28. Tel: (9)31-143 134. Full of Lenin relics, particularly of his connections with Finland, plus the history of the Russian Revolution.

Moominvalley Exhibition, Hämeenpuisto 20 (City Library Building). Tel: (9)31-121 244. The fantasy world created by Tove Jansson for her famous children's books brought to life in drawings and tableaux.

Sara Hildén Art Museum, Särkänniemi. Tel: (9)31-143 134. Changing exhibitions, largely of post-war Finnish and international artists, including Henry Moore et al; also graphics.

Workers' Museum of Amuri, Makasininkatu 12. Tel: (9)31-220 535. A restored row of buildings, 25 homes, two shops and a bakery, which show the way of life of Tampere workers during the early years of the 20th century.

MUSIC & OPERA

Most larger cities have a steady itinerary of concerts throughout the year, but music festivals abound in Finland in summer, and many of these are held in stunning countryside settings. The most famous of these are all held in July: the Savonlinna Opera Festival, at Olavinlinna Castle in Savonlinna, eastern Finland, the Kuhmo Chamber Music Festival, also in Eastern Finland, and the Kaustinen Folk Festival, in Western Finland. These festivals feature both domestic and international performers. Also in late summer are the Helsinki Juhlaviikot (festival weeks) featuring broad-ranging programmes with artists from Finland and abroad, set at different venues around the city; information from Helsinki Festival Office, Unioninkatu 28, 00100 Helsinki, tel: (9)0-659 688. Also, try the weekday evening series of concerts at the unique Temppeliaukio (church-in-the-rock) in Töölö, Helsinki.

During the rest of the year, main events are at Finlandia Concert Hall, many by the Radio Symphony Orchestra and the Helsinki Philharmonic Orchestra. Finnish opera has a great following, and much of it features domestic composers and performers. The national opera (and ballet) company's new hall opens in 1992.

TURKU

Turku is a lively musical city, with concerts given by the Turku City Orchestra, a series of concerts in the Sibelius Museum, and others in venues such as the Cathedral and the Castle. The Turku Musical Festival is one of the oldest in Finland and ranges from medieval music to first performances. Held in mid-August, it attracts visiting composers and international musicians. Also Ruisrock on the island of Ruissalo, Finland's oldest rock festival. Information on both: Foundation for the Turku Music Festivals, Uudenmaankatu 1 20500 Turku, tel: (9)21-511 162.

TAMPERE

Tampere has always had its share of music. Since 1975, the city has held an international choir festival each year and the Tampere Biennial, started in 1986, is a festival of new Finnish music, arranged in cooperation with the Association of Finnish Composers. For information contact: Tampere Biennial, Box 87, 33211 Tampere, tel: (9)31-196 136.

Since the opening of the new Tampere Hall, interest has soared. The main auditorium is one of the great concert halls of the world and the acoustics are acknowledged to be better than those of Helsinki's Finlandia Hall. The small auditorium is planned for chamber music, and the Hall is also a conference venue. As well, Tampere has long held concerts in its Cathedral and other churches and halls, and there is an annual Jazz Happening. For information contact: Tampere Jazz Happening, Box 71, 33101 Tampere, tel: (9)31-196 136.

THEATRE

The Finnish National Theatre and Svenska Teatern in Helsinki both enjoy long traditions of performance in, respectively, Finnish and Swedish. Unfortunately, there is no foreign-language theatre here to speak of but you may be interested in touring the theatre buildings themselves, or possibly even going to a play you know well enough to overcome the language barrier.

The many listings guides in Helsinki will list theatre events; equivalent guides in Turku and Tampere also carry listings.

TURKU

Plays performed are of a high standard but rarely in languages other than Finnish or Swedish. In winter, there are the Turku City Theatre on the bank of the River Aura and the Swedish Theatre on the corner of the Market Place. It is the oldest theatre in Finland still in use.

TAMPERE

Tampere rivals Helsinki for year-round theatre events but, again, the difficulty is language. One exception is the **Pyynikki Outdoor Summer Theatre** – the first revolving outdoor theatre – where you can see plays from mid-June to mid-August, with synopses in English. Worthwhile if you want to enjoy the setting at the edge of the lake, Pyhäjärvi. Booking is necessary, tel: (9)31-122 963. The Tampere Theatre Festival in August includes many international companies who produce plays in their own languages. Information from Tampere International Theatre Festival, Keskustori 4, 33100 Tampere, tel: (9)31-228 536.

CINEMA

Finns do not dub their films, and you can enjoy as good a selection of movies here as in any other European city of moderate size. **Nordia** (Yrjönkatu 36, tel: [9]0-1311 9250) in Helsinki shows a mix of commercial successes and slightly artier films while the Suomen Elokuva-arkisto at the **Orion** (Eerikinkatu 15–17, tel: [9]0-694 6558) has endless stocks of older films, both Finnish and foreign. At Eerikinkatu 11, tel: (9)0-604 873 is **Andorra**, owned by the Kaurismäki director brothers who have recently come to fame (Aki) for such films as *I Hired a Contract Killer*.

Film showings are usually 6 and 8.30pm. The kiosk outside the east entrance to the railway station has comprehensive listings, as do the newspapers; listings also available at the Tourist Board. Tickets are about 30 marks, and seats are reserved at the time you buy them. Box offices usually open 30 to 45 minutes before show time but at some cinemas may be purchased even earlier. Some cinemas showing recently released films are **Bio-Bio**, Mannerheimintie 5, tel: (9)0-1311 9215; **Forum**, Mannerheimintie 16, tel: (9)0-1311 9235; and **Maxim**, Kluuvikatu 1, tel: (9)0-1311 9245.

TURKU & TAMPERE

The same lack of dubbing from films shown all over Finland means that, as in Helsinki, it is possible to see films in their original languages.

NIGHTLIFE

Nightlife can be a difficult thing to get the hang of in Finland. In Helsinki, you will see hordes of revellers bar-crawling their way across town into the wee hours, but most are old acquaintances just getting drunk together. There are several clubs which attract the best music acts, for example the university-owned Tavastia. Occasionally a good jazz or rock act will make it to Helsinki but it is certainly not on the itinerary of most major performers.

Official drinking age is 18 and over but some clubs may have a minimum age limit of 21. Entrance fees can be anything from free to outrageous (50 marks, no live music). Nightclubs can cost as much as 65 marks to get in. Dance floors are hard to find, too. More easily found is the casual camaraderie of the few places that attract a sprinkling of foreigners, such as the pubs: Angleterre, O'Malley's, and Vanhan (mainly students), all listed below.

Angleterre, Fredrikinkatu 47. Tel: (9)0-647 371. Finland's answer to the British pub – attracts its fair share of Brits and other internationals; reasonable beer prices.

Botta, Museokatu 10. Tel: (9)0-446 940. Sunday nights are (usually) jam night and Tuesday is strictly Latin. Live DJ on Wednesday, and disco (younger crowd) Friday and Saturday. Occasional gay nights, for information contact gay switchboard, SETA tel: (9)0-769 642.

Café Socis, Kaivokatu 12. Tel: (9)0-170441. A relaxed dome-shaped bar with Victorian decor; through the lobby of the old-world Seurahuone hotel. Adjacent café is open late.

Gambrini, Iso Roobertinkatu 3. Tel: (9)0-644 391. Mellow café-bar from which to observe the passing pedestrian traffic of Iso Roobertinkatu, known as Roba. Every once in a while, it holds gay (men/women) evenings.

Kuu, Töölönkatu 27. Tel: (9)0-443 308. An intimate, older, very small bar with local jazz groups every second Monday. Light meals.

Liberatore, at Kaivohuone, Kaivopuisto. Tel: (9)0-177 881. The live music bar section of the refined, park restaurant Kaivohuone in the embassy district. Live soul and funk Sunday nights, live DJ Saturday, music of one sort or another Wednesday–Sunday.

O'Malleys, Yrjönkatu 28. Tel: (9)0-611 331. Irish, mellow, small, and usually crowded tavern. Some impromptu music.

Orfeus, Eerikinkatu 2. Tel: (9)0-640 378. A small,

easygoing streetside bar that has good to very good live music (usually rock, folk, blues) and a summer terrace. Light meals.

Parisitar, Fabianinkatu 29. Tel: (9)0-626 940. Brasserie by day, lively café-bar by night with live music Wednesday (no charge) and Sunday.

Robert, Iso Roobertinkatu 28. Tel: (9)0-616 4321. Large bar, dancing upstairs, and a streetside café are the diverse parts of this popular nightspot. Mini casino area, too.

Tavastia, Urho Kekkosenkatu 4–6. Tel: (9)0-694 8322. This university-owned club attracts some of Helsinki's best live music. Rocking atmosphere; downstairs is a usually packed, self-service bar, waiter service upstairs.

Vanhan Kellari, Vanha Yliopisto, Mannerheimintie 3. Tel: (9)0-174 357. University students' union-owned, Vanhan, which is set in a neoclassic building, flows with the traffic of devoted beer drinkers the year round. Occasional live music.

TURKU & TAMPERE

In these cities and smaller towns, nightlife tends to centre on the big hotels, which have a selection of restaurants, bars and some night spots. Turku Castle also sometimes holds special banquets and events.

During festival times, bars and late night cafés scarcely seem to close, and renowned musicians of all persuasions perform during these festivals. It is rare, however, for individual rock or jazz musicians to include Finland (except perhaps the capital, as above) on a major tour.

SHOPPING

WHAT TO BUY

If people know anything at all about Finnish design, they usually think of the smooth contemporary lines associated with Finnish architecture imposed on jewellery, woodwork, clothing, glassware, and sculpture. To see the best of the design, you might want to go first to the Applied Arts Museum in Helsinki.

Lapponia and Kaleva Koru jewellery are expressly Finnish, the first being a mainly contemporary collection and the second a collection based on designs from the Finnish epic poem *Kalevala*, rendered in silver, gold, and also in more affordable brass.

Aarikka puts out some of the finer woodwork

products, including cutting boards, Christmas decorations, baby toys, and some wooden jewellery. Pentik is known for its ceramics as well as beautifully crafted leather clothing. Marimekko is the quintessential Finnish clothing designer, with items made of brightly-coloured fabrics for men, women, and children, as well as textiles for home use. The most impressive ceramicists' work is commissioned by Arabia, one of the older Finnish firms in existence. Their factory (about 20 minutes' tram ride from downtown) has a small museum upstairs, and first and second quality goods on sale downstairs. All the names mentioned in this section can be found both in their own named stores and department stores in most Finnish towns of any size. Main shop on Pohjoisesplanadi, Helsinki.

SHOPPING AREAS

Apart from mainstream department stores and boutique shopping in Helsinki, there are several market squares that sell both fresh food and a range of other consumer goods of greatly varying quality, from second hand clothes and records to designer jewellery, Lapp mittens, and fur hats. **Kauppatori** is the main Helsinki market, followed by **Hietälah-dentori** and **Hakaniemietori**, all near the centre. Note that markets have extended hours in summer and are open until about 8pm, they close briefly from about 2–3pm.

The king of department stores in Finland is **Stockmann's**; it is the place for Finns to go when they want to hunt down some elusive item, some exotic gift. To the outsider it will probably seem merely a large, pleasant place to shop, but to Finns it is something of an institution; branches in Tampere, Turku, and Tapiola (Espoo). Stockmann's also owns the **Akateeminen Kirjakauppa** next door, Finland's best known (but pricey) bookstore.

Otherwise, the Esplanade is probably the hub of shopping delights in Helsinki. Another good department store to look out for throughout Finland is Sokos, with food hall. You'll find relatively few foreign retail outlets in Finland. The Finns seem particularly good at keeping competition from their Scandinavian neighbours to a minimum... there is no IKEA, no Hennes & Mauritz (H&M), or Nordiska Kristallmagasinet (NK). There is, however, **Body Shop** and **Benetton**.

TURKU

Turku has its own **Stockmann's** department store at Yliopistonkatu 22. Also on Yliopistonkatu are (no. 25) **Pentik**, famous for ceramics, and (27B) **Aarikka**, for handmade wooden crafts and decorations.

For crafts, look into **Sylvi Salonen**, specialising in linens and decorative crafts at Yliopistonkatu 29, or **Neoviska**, Juhana Herttuan Puisto 10 for handmade *ryiiy* (rya) rugs for wall-hanging, and other textiles.

THE KODAK GOLD GUIDE TO BETTER PICTURES.

Good photography is not difficult. Use these practical hints and Kodak Gold II Film: then notice the improvement.

Move in close. Get close enough to capture only the important elements.

Frame your Pictures. Look out for natural frames such as archways or tree branches to add an interesting foreground. Frames help create a sensation of depth and direct attention into the picture.

One centre of interest. Ensure you have one focus of interest and avoid distracting features that can confuse the viewer.

Use leading lines. Leading lines direct attention to your subject i.e. — a stream, a fence, a pathway; or the less obvious such as light beams or shadows.

Maintain activity. Pictures are more appealing if the subject is involved in some natural action.

Keep within the flash range. Ensure subject is within flash range for your camera (generally 4 metres). With groups make sure everyone is the same distance from the camera to receive the same amount of light.

Check the light direction. People tend to squint in bright direct light. Light from the side creates highlights and shadows that reveal texture and help to show the shapes of the subject. If shooting into direct sunlight fill-in flash can be effective to light the subject from the front.

CHOOSING YOUR KODAK GOLD II FILM.

Choosing the correct speed of colour print film for the type of photographs you will be taking is essential to achieve the best colourful results.

Basically the more intricate your needs in terms of capturing speed or low-light situations the higher speed film you require.

Kodak Gold II 100. Use in bright outdoor light or indoors with electronic flash. Fine grain, ideal for enlargements and close-ups. Ideal for beaches, snow scenes and posed shots.

Kodak Gold II 200. A multipurpose film for general lighting conditions and slow to moderate action. Recommended for automatic 35mm cameras. Ideal for walks, bike rides and parties.

Kodak Gold II 400. Provides the best colour accuracy as well as the richest, most saturated colours of any 400 speed film. Outstanding flash-taking capabilities for low-light and fast-action situations; excellent exposure latitude. Ideal for outdoor or well-lit indoor sports, stage shows or sunsets.

INSIGHT GUIDES

You'll find the colorset number on the spine of each Insight Guide.

Check locally for market days at the lovely main market (the market reopens late in summer from 4pm–8pm) and indoor 19th-century **Market Hallat** Eerikinkatu and Linnankatu. The **Hansa Shopping Centre** is also to be found here.

TAMPERE

Tampere has most of the medium-sized department stores found in Helsinki and Turku, as well as a host of smaller boutiques. A good collection is at **Kehräsaari Boutique Centre**, Laukontori 1, Keräsaari, in a converted textile mill. Visit also the **Verkaranta Arts and Crafts Centre** at Verkatehtaankatu 2, for a good selection of handicrafts and toys. The main **Tampere Market Hall** is at Hämeenkatu 19, opens Monday–Saturday, with 2pm closing on Saturdays, and the newer **Koskikeskus Shopping Centre** at Hatanpään Valtatie 1, near Hotel Ilves.

SHOPPING HOURS

Normal shopping hours are 9am–5pm, despite the fact that there is a higher percentage of working women here than anywhere else in Europe – in other words, almost everyone has to shop in the few hours, usually 9am–1pm or 9am–2pm, that shops are open on Saturdays. There are no Sunday opening hours for shops. (Banks are open weekdays only.)

Some larger department stores and malls such as the Forum shopping mall in Helsinki, are open until 8pm on weeknights. Also in Helsinki, the Asematunneli (station tunnel) underground and adjacent to the main railway station has shops open until 10pm.

TAX-FREE SHOPPING

When a non-resident spends more than 200 marks in a single place, he or she is eligible for a return of sales tax amounting to about 11–15 percent. (The tax is actually 17 percent but it is not possible to get it all back). Only shops with the Tax-Free emblem give back tax. They will issue you with a cheque which can be cashed at your departure airport or harbour. The amount can usually be paid back in major European currencies or US dollars at your request. Tax-free cheques can also be redeemed at the major land border crossings to Sweden, Norway and Russia. Goods should be presented sealed. For more information, call Finland Tax Free Shopping, tel: (9)0-693 2433.

SPORTS

PARTICIPANT

Finland is known as a sportive nation, a reputation which it lives up to in every Olympics Games by producing a disproportionately high number of medal winners at both summer and winter games. The devotion to training is constant; it is not unusual on a hot summer's day to see squadrons of muscular youths out on roller-skis to make sure they do not lose their touch for the coming winter.

Finns are famous as cross-country runners and skiers, as well as ski jumpers. You'll find facilities for the practice of any of these sports excellent; in most major urban areas there are maps of the non-auto paths set aside for such pastimes. Ask for the *Ulkoilukartta* (outdoor map) from tourist boards.

One can ski cross-country anywhere in Finland, but Lapland is a favourite spot for this very Nordic sport, as well as for downhill skiing (try to avoid school holiday weeks). Unlike Norway and even Sweden, Finland has very little in the way of mountains, except in the far north, where the Lappish hills, the highest over 4,000 ft (1,400 metres), are called *tunturi*.

There are many participant cross-country ski events as well; information from Suomen Latu (Finnish Ski Track Association), Fabianinkatu 7, 00130 Helsinki, tel: (9)0-170 101.

Bicycling and boating are also big in Finland. The countryside is ideal for cyclists, dead flat on the west coast leading to gently rolling hill areas; for suggested cycle routes, contact the Finnish Youth Hostel Association, Yrjönkatu 38B, 00100 Helsinki, tel: (9)0-694 0377. As for boating, it exists in all forms, and most harbours have guest marinas where one can dock for reasonable overnight fees.

Canoeing, orienteering, golf, hunting, fishing, and tennis are a few of the other popular sports here; as well, there are many enthusiasts of indoor sports like badminton and squash. Basically, if there's a sport you love, no matter how popular or obscure, you will probably find co-enthusiasts in Finland. For information on any sport in Finland, contact the Suomen Valtakunnan Urheiluliitto (The National Sports Association), Radiokatu 20, 00240 Helsinki (Ilmala), tel: (9)0-1581, fax: (9)0-147 304.

There is a near endless list of spectator sports for Finland but a shortlist of the most popular must include ski-jumping, regatta sailing, and hockey.

Lahti, about 65 miles north of Helsinki, is the place to watch ski-jumping. Matti Nykänen, the most famous of the Finnish jumpers, lives and occasionally practises here.

One of the biggest sailing events of the year is the Hanko regatta, which takes place in early July off Finland's south coast. Kotka also sponsors a yearly Tall Ships event. The biggest inland sailing regatta is on Lake Päijänne, also in July. Details from the Finnish Yachting Association, Radiokatu 20, 00240 Helsinki, tel: (9)0-1581. Before mid-June is the Finlandia Canoeing Relay, held in the Päijänne lakes region. It lasts five days and covers 350 miles (545 km), with day and night action. You can get accommodation help and further information by contacting Kymen Matkailu, Varuskuntkatu 11, 45100 Kouvola, tel: (9)51-21 763.

For winter spectator sports, the Finlandia Ski Race in mid-February is one of the top events. This 47-mile (75-km) event attracts the best of the Finnish skiers; ample spectator opportunities; for information, contact Finlandia Ski Race Office, Urheilukeskus, 15110 Lahti, tel: (9)18-49 811.

As is the case with participant sports all general sport information queries can be directed to the Suomen Valtakunnan Urheiluliitto (The National Sports Association), Radiokatu 20, 00240 Helsinki (Ilmala), tel: (9)0-1581, fax: (9)0-147 304.

SPECIAL INFORMATION

DOING BUSINESS

Doing business here probably does not differ tremendously from doing business elsewhere in Europe, with two exceptions.

Firstly, everything is done earlier. Lunch is earlier (as early as 11am, with 1pm the outside limit), and many offices operate from 8am–4pm as opposed to 9am–5pm; in summer, offices close early, usually at around 3pm.

Secondly, there is a marked lack of bombast. Finns tend not to dress anything up, but rather present things as they are, warts and all. In other words, they are terribly honest, and do not go in much for exaggeration of any kind, whether it relates to a person or a business deal. Hence, their way of selling things might seem a bit subdued but that is the way they operate here.

For business entertaining, you are as likely to be invited on a ski outing or sailboat ride as on a night out on the town. These days, Finns tend not to drink at lunch, but after hours drinking is still *de rigueur*, and as people on business accounts are about the only ones who can afford long spells of drinking here, if you get an invitation, enjoy it while you can.

It is ill-advised to be late at business meetings; Finns tend to be very punctual and courteous, though quite formal. Handshakes are good for meeting business as well as casual acquaintances; most people here have business cards, and many have mobile phones, which they are delighted to use, so do not be put off by the fact that office hours seem short; there is almost always a cellular phone link to the person in question.

Finally, try to avoid business in July and early August. The Finnish summer is short and sacred and you'll find some offices nearly deserted of staff at these times. (Conversely, this is a good time for tourists, to whom hotels offer bargains in order to compensate for the lost business trade.) Other blackout periods are the spring skiing break in late February (Southern Finland) or early March (Northern Finland) plus two weeks at Christmas, and nearly a week at Easter.

CHILDREN

Overall, Finland is a family- and child-orientated society, and hence one that is generally safe for children. Public conveniences usually include changing areas and most restaurants can provide high chairs. One does not have to fear, as in Britain, that children are not allowed in certain hotels; that is virtually unheard of here. In Helsinki, the Tourist Board can provide a list of qualified child minders.

The two-week Helsinki Festival in late August schedules many children's events. Suomenlinna fortress island in Helsinki also makes a good excursion with children; its doll and toy museum is sure to be a family pleaser. Also in the capital is the Korkeasaari Zoo (undergoing improvements), accessible by metro east to Kulosaari (cross under the track and follow signs; a 20-minute walk) or by boat from the east end of the market square throughout the summer. Another Helsinki island excursion suitable for families is Seurasaari, described in the Museum section above (children-oriented activities on Midsummer Eve). Linnanmäki Amusement Park just north of central Helsinki is the place to go for a roller coaster ride, and cotton candy.

Outside Helsinki, the main amusement park in southern Finland is Lystiland Children's Fun Park, just north of Karjaa town centre. It features a miniature train tour on an enchanted forest trail.

Heading away from Helsinki, there are several good spots in the lakelands for travellers with

For the fastest weekend refunds anywhere in the world.

Ensure your holiday is worry free even if
your travellers cheques are lost or stolen by buying
American Express Travellers Cheques from;

Lloyds Bank	Leeds Permanent Building Society*
Royal Bank of Scotland	Woolwich Building Society*
Abbey National*	National & Provincial Building Society
Bank of Ireland	Britannia Building Society*
Halifax Building Society*	American Express Travel Offices.

As well as many regional building societies and travel agents.

*Investors only.

Not all travellers cheques are the same.

Travellers Cheques

BREAK THE LANGUAGE BARRIER!

If you travel internationally, for business or pleasure - or if you are learning a foreign language - TI's electronic language -products can make communication a lot easier.

The **PS-5800** is a versatile 3-language dictionary with 30,000 entry words in each language. Available in English/German/French or English/Italian/French, it includes, travel sentences, business words, memory space to build and store your own vocabulary, currency and metric conversions, and more.

The **PS-5400** is a powerful 5-language translator fea-

turing up to 5,000 words and 1,000 structured sentences in English, German, French, Italian, and Spanish. Travel-related sentences, conveniently grouped by category, facilitate conversation in the language of your choice. To keep you on time and on top, there's also world time, alarm reminders, calculator, and metric conversions.

The **PS-5800** and **PS-5400**. Two pocket-sized ways to break the language barrier!

For more information, fax your request to:
Texas Instruments France, (33) 39 22 21 01

children. At Messilä Vacation Centre in Hollola near Lahti, there are all manner of supervised activities for children including horse and pony riding. In wintertime, there are skiing activities (Alpine and Nordic) for children and adults. A bit north from Hollola, toward Hartola, is the fascinating little Musta and Valkea Ratsu Dollhouse and Puppet Theatre on road 52 (signposted), address 19230 Onkiniemi, tel: (9)18-186 959.

In Outokumpu north of Savonlinna is The Land of the Mountain Troll, an amusement park and mineral and mining exhibition (information on tel: [9]73-54 795) and Mikkeli has the Visulahti Tourist Centre, including a dinosaur theme amusement park and waxworks. A little further from Mikkeli is an arboretum which includes a small menagerie. Contact Mikkeli Tourism, tel: (9)55-151 444.

When in the Åland islands, you might want to check out the amusement park by the west harbour (the former Dinosaur Park, with a few dinosaurs still remaining), the Pommern ship museum (at the west harbour), and Lilla Holmen bird park on the east harbour. Here you will see peacocks, ducks, and beautiful angora rabbits.

DISABLED TRAVELLERS

For disabled people, travelling should not pose tremendous problems in Finland. Most newer buildings have access for disabled people, both in terms of ramps and lifts. As well, the Finland Hotel guide indicates by symbol which hotels have access and facilities for handicapped people. With careful planning transportation should also go smoothly; when ordering a taxi, specify your needs (wheelchair is "pyörätuoli"). Public transport may be a bit more problematic, although some city buses "kneel". If you have queries related to disabled travellers in Finland, phone Mr Pekka Jarvansalo of Rullaten, tel: (9)-322 069 or write to him at Vartiokyläntie 9, 00950 Helsinki.

One travel agency in Helsinki arranges a major tour, on request, for disabled travellers. The 7-day historical/architectural/cultural "Triangle Tour" of the three major cities (Helsinki, Tampere, Turku) can be organised through Area Travel, Kaisaniemenkatu 13, 00100 Helsinki, tel: (9)0-18 551.

LANGUAGE

Good morning	*Hyvää huomenta*
Good day	*Hyvää päivää*
Good evening	*Hyvää iltaa*
Today	*Tänään*
Tomorrow	*Huomenna*
Yesterday	*Eilen*
Hello	*Päivää* or *terve*
How do you do	*Kuinka voit*
Goodbye	*Näkemiin* or *hei hei*
Yes	*Kyllä, joo*
No	*Ei*
Thank you	*Kiitos*
How much does this cost?	*Paljonko tämä maksaa?*
It costs...	*Se maksaa...*
How do I get to...?	*Miten pääsen...?*
Where is...?	*Missä on...?*
Right	*Oikealla*
To the right	*Oikealle*
Left	*Vasemalla*
To the left	*Vasemalle*
Straight on	*Suoraanpäin*
Breakfast	*Aamiainen*
Lunch	*Lounas*
Dinner	*Illalinen*
To eat	*Syödä*
To drink	*Juoda*
I would like to order	*Haluaisin tilata*
Could I have the bill?	*Saisko laskun?*
Could I have the key?	*Saisko avaimen?*
What time is it?	*Paljonko kello on?*
It is (the time is)	*Kello on*
Could I have your name?	*Saisko nimesi?*
My name is...	*Nimeni on...*
Do you have English newspapers?	*Onko englanninkielisia sanomalehtia?*
Do you speak English?	*Puhutko englantia?*
I only speak English	*Puhun vain englantia*
Can I help you?	*Voinko auttaa sinua?*
I do not understand	*En ymmärrä*
I do not know	*En tiedä*
It has disappeared	*Se on hävinnyt*
Toilet	*Vessa*
Gentleman	*Miehet* or *Herrat*
Ladies	*Naiset* or *Damer*
Vacant	*Vapaa*
Engaged	*Varattu*
Entrance	*Sisäänkäynti*

Exit	Uloskäynti	1	yksi
No entry	Sisäänpääsy kieletty	2	kaksi
Open	Avoinna, Auki	3	kolme
Closed	Suljettu, Kiini	4	neljä
Push	Työnnä	5	viisi
Pull	Vedä	6	kuusi
Chemist	Apteekki	7	seitsemän
Hospital	Sairaala	8	kahdeksan
Doctor	Lääkäri	9	yhdeksän
Police station	Poliisin laitos	10	kymmenen
Parking	Paikoitus	11	yksitoista
Department Store	Tavaratalo	12	kaksitoista
No smoking	Tupakointi kieletty	13	kolmetoista
Phrase book	Turistien sanakirja	14	neljätoista
Dictionary	Sanakirja	15	viisitoista
		16	kuusitoista
Car	Auto	17	seitsemäntoista
Bus, Coach	Bussi, Linja-auto	18	kahdeksantoista
Train	Juna	19	yhdeksäntoista
Aircraft	Lentokone	20	kaksikymmentä
		21	kaksikymmentäyski
Clothes	Vaateet	22	kaksikymmentäkaski
Overcoat	Päällystakki	30	kolmekymmentä
Jacket	Takki	40	neljäkymmentä
Suit	Puku	50	viisikymmentä
Shoes	Kengät	60	kuusikymmentä
Skirt	Hame	70	seitsemänkymmentä
Blouse	Pusero	80	kahdeksankymmentä
Jersey	Puuvilla or villa pusero	90	yhdeksänkymmentä
	(cotton or wool jersey)	100	sata
		200	kaksisataa
Handicraft	Käsityö	1.000	tuhat
Cheers	Kippis, skål		
To rent	Vuokrata		
For sale	Myytävänä		
Free, no charge	Ilmainen		
Room to rent	Vuokrattavana huone		
Cottage	Mökki		

Grocery store	Ruoka kauppa
Shop	Kauppa
Food	Ruoka
To buy	Ostaa
Liquor store	Alko
Sauna	Sauna (pronounced sow-na)
Wash	Pestää
Launderette	Pesula
Dry cleaning	Kemiallinen pesu
Dirty	Likainen
Clean	Puhdas
Stain	Tahra
Money	Raha

Monday	Maanantai
Tuesday	Tiistai
Wednesday	Keskiviikko
Thursday	Torstai
Friday	Perjantai
Saturday	Launantai
Sunday	Suununtai

USEFUL ADDRESSES

Finnish Tourist Board, Tourist Information, Unioninkatu 26, SF-00131 Helsinki, Finland.
Finish Tourist Board (North), Maakuntakatu 10, PB 8154, SF-96101 Rovaniemi, Finland.

TOURIST OFFICES ABROAD

Great Britain: Finnish Tourist Board UK Office, 66–68 Haymarket, London SW1Y 4RF, England.
USA: Finnish Tourist Board, 655 Third Avenue, 18th floor, New York, NY 10017.
Sweden: Finska Turistbyrån, Kungsgatan 4A, S-11143, Stockholm.
Norway: Finlands Turistkontor, Lille Grensen 7, N-0159, Oslo.
Denmark: Finlands Turistbureau, Vester

Farimagsgade 3, DK-1606, Copenhagen-V.
Germany: Finnisches Fremdenverkehrsamt, Georgplatz 1, W-2000, Hamburg 1; Finnisches Fremdenverkehrsamt, Rosenheimerstr 69, W-8000, Munich 80.
Switzerland: Finnische Zentrale fur Tourismus, Schweizergasse 6, CH-8001, Zurich.
France: Office National de Tourisme de Finlande, 13 Rue Auber, F-75009, Paris.
The Netherlands: Fins Nationaal Verkeersbureau Voor de Benelux, Stadhouderskade 69, NL-1072 AD, Amsterdam.
Spain: Oficina Nacional Finlandesa de Turismo, Fuencarral 139.6 A, E-28101, Madrid.

TOURIST INFORMATION

Finland has dozens of tourist information offices, usually marked with an I for information at most locations. There are over 50 main tourist offices, and summer tourist offices spring up along harbours and lakes where need dictates.

In Helsinki, book hotels through the Hotel Booking Centre at Asema-aukio 3, 00100 Helsinki, tel: (9)0-171 133, fax: (9)0-175 524. Helsinki City Tourist Office is at Pohjoisesplanadi 19, 00100 Helsinki, tel: (9)0-169 3757 or (9)0-174 088. All-Finland information from Finnish Tourist Board address listed above. Any of these offices can help you arrange for travel within Finland and make suggestions for which agents to use for onward travel from Finland.

Some useful publications in Helsinki include *Helsinki This Week, The Helsinki Guide,* and the various brochures and listings put out by the Tourist Board to keep you up to date on events and tours for the current season.

In the rest of the country, use local tourist offices. A full listing can be obtained at the main Helsinki and Rovaniemi offices, but here are two more in major locations

Turku City Tourist Office, Käsityöläiskatu 3, 20100 Turku, tel: (9)21-336 366. Tampere City Tourist Office, Verkatehtaankatu 2, PB 87, 33211 Tampere, tel: (9)31-126 652.

ART/PHOTO CREDITS

INDEX

L

M

N

O

P

T

INSIGHT GUIDES

FINLAND

Finland is a land for all seasons. In winter, there are great reindeer round-ups in Lapland and terrific skiing. In summer, the sea and the lakes fill with sails and swimmers. In spring, the whole country seems to turn green in just a week, and the autumn is full of reds and browns as leaves swirl across the city squares.

Although Finland is Europe's fifth largest country, it has a population of just over five million. As a result the Finnish character is a paradoxical mix, sometimes looking parochially inwards, sometimes eagerly embracing the world outside.

The expert writers and photographers behind *Insight Guide: Finland* have assembled a lavishly illustrated and compellingly topical guide, explaining what makes the people tick and what makes the country worth seeing. It takes you through a turbulent history, introduces you to the culture and provides a comprehensive guide to what's worth doing and what's not. With full-colour maps, plus tips on travel, accommodation and restaurants, it is both a practical guide and an inspiring companion.

Forests

Sails

Summers

Snow

Fun

Frocks

Far Away

Pastimes

Places

ISBN 0-395-66793-3

90000>

9 780395 667934

6-20285   FPT   0119459

Finland $19.95